W9-AFO-800

The Scarecrow Author Bibliographies

1. John Steinbeck (Tetsumaro Hayashi). 1973.
2. Joseph Conrad (Theodore G. Ehrsam). 1969.
3. Arthur Miller (Tetsumaro Hayashi). 2d ed. 1976.
4. Katherine Anne Porter (Waldrip & Bauer). 1969.
5. Philip Freneau (Philip M. Marsh). 1970.
6. Robert Greene (Tetsumaro Hayashi). 1971.
7. Benjamin Disraeli (R. W. Stewart). 1972.
8. John Berryman (Richard W. Kelly). 1972.
9. William Dean Howells (Vito J. Brenni). 1973.
10. Jean Anouilh (Kathleen W. Kelly). 1973.
11. E. M. Forster (Alfred Borrello). 1973.
12. The Marquis de Sade (E. Pierre Chanover). 1973.
13. Alain Robbe-Grillet (Dale W. Frazier). 1973.
14. Northrop Frye (Robert D. Denham). 1974.
15. Federico Garcia Lorca (Laurenti & Siracusa). 1974.
16. Ben Jonson (Brock & Welsh). 1974.
17. Four French Dramatists: Eugène Brieux, François de Curel, Emile Fabre, Paul Hervieu (Edmund F. Santa Vicca). 1974.
18. Ralph Waldo Ellison (Jacqueline Covo). 1974.
19. Philip Roth (Bernard F. Rodgers, Jr.). 1974.
20. Norman Mailer (Laura Adams). 1974.
21. Sir John Betjeman (Margaret Stapleton). 1974.
22. Elie Wiesel (Molly Abramowitz). 1974.
23. Paul Laurence Dunbar (Eugene W. Metcalf, Jr.). 1975.
24. Henry James (Beatrice Ricks). 1975.
25. Robert Frost (Lentricchia & Lentricchia). 1976.
26. Sherwood Anderson (Douglas G. Rogers). 1976.
27. Iris Murdoch and Muriel Spark (Tominaga & Schneidermeyer). 1976.
28. John Ruskin (Kirk H. Beetz). 1976.
29. Georges Simenon (Trudee Young). 1976.
30. George Gordon, Lord Byron (Oscar José Santucho). 1976.
31. John Barth (Richard Vine). 1977.
32. John Hawkes (Carol A. Hryciw). 1977.
33. William Everson (Bartlett & Campo). 1977.
34. May Sarton (Lenora Blouin). 1978.
35. Wilkie Collins (Kirk H. Beetz). 1978.
36. Sylvia Plath (Lane & Stevens). 1978.
37. E. B. White (A. J. Anderson). 1978.
38. Henry Miller (Lawrence J. Shifreen). 1979.
39. Ralph Waldo Emerson (Jeanetta Boswell). 1979.
40. James Dickey (Jim Elledge). 1979.
41. Henry Fielding (H. George Hahn). 1979.
42. Paul Goodman (Tom Nicely). 1979.
43. Christopher Marlowe (Kenneth Friedenreich). 1979.
44. Leo Tolstoy (Egan & Egan). 1979.
45. T. S. Eliot (Beatrice Ricks). 1980.
46. Allen Ginsberg (Michelle P. Kraus). 1980.
47. Anthony Burgess (Jeutonne P. Brewer). 1980.
48. Tennessee Williams (Drewey Wayne Gunn). 1980.

Tennessee Williams:
A Bibliography

by

Drewey Wayne Gunn

Scarecrow Author Bibliographies, No. 48

The Scarecrow Press, Inc.
Metuchen, N.J., & London
1980

Library of Congress Cataloging in Publication Data

Gunn, Drewey Wayne, 1939-
Tennessee Williams, a bibliography.

(Scarecrow author bibliographies ; no. 48)
Includes index.
1. Williams, Tennessee, 1911- --Bibliography.
Z8976.424.G85 [PS3545.I5365] 016.812'54
ISBN 0-8108-1310-6 80-12714

Manufactured in the United States of America

For J. M. M. (C 23)

ACKNOWLEDGMENTS

It is a pleasure to record all the people who have helped me on this project; I hope I have forgotten no one. My colleagues Donna Vogt and Earl Herrick have patiently listened to my musing about various problems for too long now. Paul Goode and Margaret Hancock of the Texas A&I University library and Ellen S. Dunlap of the Humanities Research Center at the University of Texas have diligently chased down materials I have needed. Antonio Martinez of the Corpus Christi Public Library and George Gause of Pan American University library were also helpful. I also used the facilities of the Kingsville Public Library; the libraries at Rice University, the University of Houston, the University of California, and Trinity University; and the American Library in Paris as well as the Bibliothèque Nationale. Norma Beth Drake searched out references for me at Texas Tech University, and Nicole Boireau did the same at the Université de Metz.

Many of the anthologies listed in Section B were located by my browsing through the offices of my colleagues Katherine Kantz, Howard German, George Cook, Blake Richard, and Randall Buchanan. Sharon George provided information she had accumulated. Others who located items for me were Al Tellinghuisen of the A&I music department, Allen B. Page, Joel and Loyd Self, Winston Leyland, Dorothy Shapiro of the International Herald Tribune, Odette Tavolara of Editions Robert Laffont, Hon Ying Tang, May Campbell, Karen Kirk-Sørensen, Ruslana Antonowicz, Gunther Mende, David Deacon, Pam Hill, Ronnie Ormond, and Ed Hammonds. Joan M. Ling of the English Theatre Guild and William S. Gray answered questions I had posed them. My parents and Jacques Murat located papers I had left stored in their homes.

Above all, I must thank Hildegard Schmalenbeck, Julia Smith,

Roland R. Hinojosa, George M. Harper, and C. Hugh Holman, without whom this book would never have been compiled.

I shudder to think of all the mistakes that have undoubtedly crept into it and all the omissions that may exist. I take heart that certainly a second edition will one day be called for as Williams, critics, directors, and reviewers continue to add bibliographical items. I hope readers will follow the example of Gerald Weales, a perfect gentleman and scholar: when he discovered I had claimed in 1978 to be the first to note a fact he had documented in 1965 (that there are two editions of Streetcar published by New Directions), he took the time to drop me a postcard to set the record straight. I promise likewise to record any additions or corrections others may bring to my attention.

Drewey Wayne Gunn
Kingsville, Texas
March 1, 1979

CONTENTS

HOW TO USE THIS BIBLIOGRAPHY

Because of the abundance of materials presented here, I felt that a division of primary and secondary works only would ultimately be less useful than grouping materials by various principles so that users can more easily find what they are looking for. But since this presentation is somewhat unorthodox, the reader should glance at the table of contents and below before thumbing through the book. The entire work is cross-referenced throughout.

1. The person interested in a PARTICULAR PLAY or OTHER WORK by Williams should turn first to Part 2.

2. The person interested only in the PRODUCTION RECORD should go immediately to Section K. But Section F will also be useful.

3. The critic interested in pure BIBLIOGRAPHICAL DATA, contents of COLLECTIONS, and PUBLICATION CHRONOLOGY should turn to Part 1.

4. The ordinary student doing a term paper will use Section P (CRITICISM) most heavily, but he should also look to Part 2 for the particular works he is interested in, to Part 4 for REVIEWS of plays and screenplays, and to the Index. If he is interested in BIOGRAPHICAL DATA, he should turn at once to Part 5.

5. The graduate student and the critic, of course, will want to examine the entire body of materials presented here.

CHRONOLOGY

1911	26 March: Thomas Lanier Williams born in Columbus, Mississippi, second child, first son of Cornelius Coffin and Edwina Dakin Williams (older sister, Rose; brother Dakin born several years later). Childhood spent in various towns in Mississippi, often with maternal grandparents, Rev. and Mrs. Walter E. Dakin.
1918	Family moved to St. Louis, Missouri.
c. 1922	Began friendship with Hazel Kramer.
1927	"Can a Good Wife Be a Good Sport?" published in *Smart Set*.
1928	"The Vengeance of Nitocris" published in *Weird Tales*. First trip to Europe.
1929	Graduated from University City (Mo.) High School.
1929-31	Enrolled in University of Missouri; joined Alpha Tau Omega fraternity; won prize for short play "Beauty Is the Word."
1931-34	Worked for St. Louis shoe company. Friendship with Clark Mills McBurney; wrote many poems and short stories.
1934	"After a Visit" published in *Voices* and *Literary Digest*. Nervous breakdown; joined grandparents in Memphis, Tennessee.
1935	"Cairo, Shanghai, Bombay" produced in Memphis.
1936-37	Enrolled in Washington University, St. Louis.
1936	"The Magic Tower" produced in Webster Groves, Mo.; "Headlines" produced in St. Louis.
1937	Enrolled in University of Iowa; wrote *Spring Storm*. *Candles to the Sun* and *The Fugitive Kind* produced in St. Louis. Rose suffered prefrontal lobotomy.
1938	Received bachelor's degree from Iowa. Wrote *Not About Nightingales*.

1939 "The Field of Blue Children" published in Story, first work to appear under name Tennessee Williams. Audrey Wood became agent. Won Group Theatre award for series of short plays; Rockefeller grant.

1939-44 Itinerant writer and worker at odd jobs in New York, Massachusetts, Louisiana, Missouri, New Mexico, California, Mexico, Georgia, and Florida; became friends or acquaintances with Paul and Jane Bowles, "Kip," Donald Windham, Paul Bigelow, Jordan Massee, Christopher Isherwood, Marion Black Vaccaro, Oliver Evans, Gilbert Maxwell, Tony Smith, Jackson Pollock, Hans Hofmann, Tallulah Bankhead, Margo Jones, and William Inge.

1940 Battle of Angels produced in Boston (pub. 1945).

1943 You Touched Me produced in Cleveland and Pasadena (pub. 1947).

1944 Death of maternal grandmother. Five Young American Poets published; The Glass Menagerie produced in Chicago (pub. 1945).

1945 Glass won New York Drama Critics' Circle, Sidney Howard, and Donaldson awards. 27 Wagons Full of Cotton published (rev. 1953). Return to Mexico.

1946 Became friends with Francisco Rodriguez and Carson McCullers.

1947 Stairs to the Roof produced in Pasadena; Summer and Smoke produced in Dallas (pub. 1948); A Streetcar Named Desire produced in New York (pub. 1947), collaboration begun between Williams and Elia Kazan. Met Frank Phillip Merlo.

1948 Streetcar won Pulitzer, Drama Critics' Circle, and Donaldson awards. One Arm and Other Stories and American Blues published. Second trip to Europe; became friends with Gore Vidal, Maria Britneva, Truman Capote, Luchino Visconti, Anna Magnani. Thereafter always spent part of each year abroad; in the States alternated between homes in Key West, New Orleans, and New York.

1950 The Roman Spring of Mrs. Stone published; film The Glass Menagerie released; The Rose Tattoo opened in Chicago (pub. 1951).

1951 Tattoo won Tony award. I Rise in Flame, Cried

Phoenix published (produced in New York 1959); film A Streetcar Named Desire released (pub. 1971).

1952 Streetcar won New York Film Critics' Circle award. [Ballet version (choreography by Bettis) produced in Montreal and New York.] Elected to National Institute of Arts and Letters. Became acquainted with José Quintero.

1953 Camino Real produced in New York (pub. 1953). Directed Windham's The Starless Air in Houston.

1954 Hard Candy published; Visconti's Senso released.

1955 Opera "Lord Byron's Love Letter" produced in New Orleans (pub. 1955); Cat on a Hot Tin Roof produced in New York (pub. 1955), won Pulitzer, Drama Critics' Circle, and Donaldson awards; film The Rose Tattoo released. Death of maternal grandfather.

1956 In the Winter of Cities published (rev. 1964); Sweet Bird of Youth produced in Miami (pub. 1959); film Baby Doll released (pub. 1956).

1957 Orpheus Descending produced in New York (pub. 1958). Began psychoanalysis. Death of father.

1958 Garden District produced in New York (Suddenly Last Summer pub. 1958); three short plays televised; Period of Adjustment produced in Miami (pub. 1960). [Film of Cat (Screenplay by Poe and Brooks) released.]

1959 The Night of the Iguana produced in Spoleto (pub. 1962); film Suddenly Last Summer released. First trip to Far East.

1960 Film The Fugitive Kind released. Time magazine cover story. Death of Diana Barrymore.

1961 Four short plays televised. [Films of Roman Spring (screenplay by Lambert) and Smoke (screenplay by Poe and Brooks) released.]

1962 Iguana won New York Drama Critics' Circle award; The Milk Train Doesn't Stop Here Anymore produced in Spoleto (pub. 1964). [Films of Sweet Bird (screenplay by Brooks) and Period (screenplay by Lennart) released.]

1963 Donated papers to University of Texas. Death of Merlo.

1964 Grand published; The Eccentricities of a Nightingale produced in summer stock (pub. 1964). [Film of Iguana (screenplay by Veilar) released.]

1965 Iguana won London Critics' Poll for Best Foreign Play. Brandeis University Creative Arts award.

1966 Slapstick Tragedy produced in New York (pub. 1965); Glass and early version of Camino televised; The Knightly Quest published. [Film This Property Is Condemned (screenplay by Coppola, Coe, Sommers) released.]

1967 The Two-Character Play produced in London (pub. 1969). Death of McCullers.

1968 The Seven Descents of Myrtle produced in New York (Kingdom of Earth pub. 1968); film Boom! released. Death of Bankhead.

1969 In the Bar of a Tokyo Hotel produced in New York (pub. 1969); Dragon Country published. [Film Last of the Mobile Hot-Shots (screenplay by Vidal) released.] Doctor of Humanities, University of Missouri; Gold Medal for Drama from American Academy of Arts and Letters. Converted briefly to Roman Catholicism. Committed to a St. Louis mental ward for three months.

1970 Two short plays televised.

1971 Out Cry produced in Chicago (pub. 1977). Break with Wood; Bill Barnes became agent. [Opera version of Smoke (libretto by Wilson) produced in St. Paul.]

1972 Small Craft Warnings produced in New York (pub. 1972); Smoke televised in Britain. National Theatre Conference Annual Award; Doctor of Humanities, University of Hartford.

1973 Special on "Tennessee William's South" (script by Rasky) televised in Canada; Glass televised; revised Cat produced in West Springfield (pub. 1975). Medal of the Cathedral Church of St. John the Divine. Deaths of Magnani, Jane Bowles, and Inge.

1974 The Latter Days of a Celebrated Soubrette produced in New York; Eight Mortal Ladies Possessed published; "The Migrants" (script by Wilson based on an idea by Williams) televised. Entertainment Hall of Fame award.

1975 Moise and the World of Reason and Memoirs published; The Red Devil Battery Sign produced in Boston. Medal of Honor for Literature from National Arts Club. Elected to three-year term on governing council of Dramatists Guild.

1976 Letters to Donald Windham published; This Is (An Entertainment) produced in San Francisco; Eccentricities and Cat televised. President of jury at Cannes Film Festival.

1977 Vieux Carré produced in New York; Androgyne, Mon Amour published. Tennessee Williams Fine Arts Center of Florida Keys Community College dedicated at Key West.

1978 Tiger Tail produced in Atlanta; Creve Coeur produced in Charleston; Where I Live and The World of Tennessee Williams published.

1979 Mugged in Key West. Chosen as speaker at University of Pennsylvania commencement exercises.

PART 1

WILLIAMS'S PUBLICATIONS

Introduction

In 1968-1969 Whit Burnett (for a new edition of his anthology This Is My Best), polled authors, teachers, bookstore managers, readers of Atlantic and Harper's, and other such diverse groups interested in literature to find out who they considered to be America's most distinguished living authors. Tennessee Williams received the highest number of mentions. He outstripped such near contenders as John Steinbeck and Archibald MacLeish and was far ahead of such critical favorites as Saul Bellow and Robert Lowell.

The academic and critical world reacted with some shock. Williams's reputation was at an all-time low. Although he was awarded the gold medal for drama by the American Academy and the National Institute of Arts and Letters in 1969, he had seen his last four plays fail. Williams himself had written of his "decline of creative energy" (Knightly Quest, p. 179). On June 10, 1969, Life magazine decided to announce the death of his talent in a full-page advertisement on page 96 of the New York Times, as that magazine tried to ward off its own impending demise. (Some readers, including Frank D. Gilroy, reacted angrily: see the New York Times, 22 June 1969, sec. 2, p. 11.)

Critics had begun regularly to write Williams off as a failed writer. It was almost as if his accomplishment during those remarkable eighteen years (1944-1961) was not enough. His plays, especially The Glass Menagerie, were regularly included in drama anthologies, but not a one of the textbooks designed for college surveys of American literature included a work of his, although Eugene O'Neill and by then Edward Albee were side by side with Faulkner and Eliot, Hemingway and "the other" Williams, Bellow and O'Connor.

Even now only the Norton Anthology of American Literature (4th edition), so far as I know, ranks Williams as a major writer. But, although the situation is confused, the critical climate does seem to have changed slightly in the seventies. The success of a new play in 1972, followed by his Memoirs in 1975, helped. In 1977 three books and an increased number of critical articles about him appeared. Still, Williams's work has not been the subject of a top-notch analysis, and many are still skittish about accepting him for what he is: America's foremost dramatist, living or dead. When I sent in an earlier version of Section F to the Educational Theatre Journal for consideration, although the editor was glad to have the bibliography, he reacted somewhat nervously to my ranking Williams higher than O'Neill; and when the Journal published the checklist, it simply omitted that part of my introduction.

Yet, Williams has never gone unrecognized. He has won several major awards, including four New York Drama Critics' Circle Awards, two Pulitzer Prizes, the Brandeis University Creative Arts Award, and the Centennial Medal of the Cathedral Church of St. John the Divine. Two American universities (Missouri and Hartford) have awarded him honorary doctorates. Ten of his plays have been included in the Burns Mantle Best Plays series; seven were chosen by John Gassner for his Best American Plays series; and seven have been anthologized in the Margaret Mayorga Best One-Act Plays series. Also, although not enough attention has been paid Williams's fiction, three of his short stories have been selected by Martha Foley for her Best American Short Stories series.

Above all, Williams has been published, read, and his plays produced. Signi Falk observed astutely: "The popularity of Tennessee Williams can be illustrated by the fact that in many libraries works that are listed in the card catalogue can no longer be located on the shelves" (Tennessee Williams, 2nd ed., p. 169). Williams's production record is detailed in Section K.

The Glass Menagerie, of course, is the most popular of Williams's plays--so much so that one can sympathize with the playwright's momentary attempt to ban it from production. It has been reprinted so far in at least forty-two different anthologies. Curiously enough, no one has ever assembled a collection of essays about the play, although two have been published on A Streetcar Named Desire. That play, however, has been anthologized only eight times. The majority of these anthologies are for college audiences; probably many American editors are still wary about Williams's concern with sexuality. (Miller has always seemed safer since he is concerned with "ideas," and college teachers long praised Williams's contemporary as if both playwrights did not have a place in the modern American theater. Directors have always had a more balanced attitude.) These two plays are by general agreement Williams's masterpieces.

He has also given us a large number of other plays of great interest: Cat on a Hot Tin Roof (generally considered Williams's third best play, but present in only three anthologies, perhaps because of the problem of two third acts as well as its flirtation with homosexuality); The Rose Tattoo (anthologized five times); Camino Real (likewise five); Summer and Smoke (three); The Night of the Iguana (three); and Suddenly Last Summer (which appears in only one anthology but which a coterie of admirers considers Williams's masterpiece). Among his shorter plays the most popular are "27 Wagons Full of Cotton" (which has been produced professionally several times and which appears in six different anthologies), "Something Unspoken," and "Lord Byron's Love Letter."

Anyone who has produced such a body of work doesn't need to apologize for the somewhat flabby nature of some of his recent work. But Williams represents another instance of the American artist's being snared by commercial success. Since audiences are not willing to follow him into the new and exciting territories of "The Gnädiges Fräulein," The Two-Character Play, and The Red Devil Battery Sign and since his most recent successes have been those plays in which he mined the materials and the atmosphere of his earliest works, Williams has apparently been constantly torn between following a new dramatic direction and trying for a popular and critical success. Thus we have a playwright who for the past seventeen years (1962-1978) has alternated between writing plays that are marginally worth considering with some of his more exciting theater.

What we are seeing also, perhaps, is his increasing inability to reconcile the two aspects of his genius. There have always been two Williams: one is sensitive, lyrical, and pensive; the other is boisterous, vulgar, and somewhat pretentious. The best work--in fiction, drama, and even poetry--has occurred when these two fused; the flawed, when Williams allowed one or the other to dominate. But if we would stop demanding that a writer always turn out masterpieces and would start enjoying even the work he has written with his left hand (and, in Williams's case, if we could get rid of some of our sexual hang-ups), we should discover that even the worst of his writings can be fun.

The following pages list his writings for the first time in detail. This bibliography, however, is designed for the student of Williams, not the book collector. In assembling the information, I have worked with standard catalogues, some prior bibliographies (see Section O), and the Williams holdings assembled by Andreas Brown--to whom all students of Williams owe an immeasurable debt--at the Humanities Research Center at the University of Texas in Austin. Since I have arranged the works in chronological order in each section (Williams poses too many problems to follow the traditional method of listing publications), anyone interested in a specific play or story should turn first to Part 2. Although there should be few if any omissions in the list of books and pamphlets and the list of recordings, the other three sections in this Part are undoubtedly incomplete. I should welcome further information.

A. BOOKS AND PAMPHLETS†

1. *Battle of Angels. Pharos, 1 / 2 (Spring 1945), 1-123. Play, 5-109, "The History of a Play (With Parentheses)," 110-121; "A Note on 'Battle of Angels'" by Margaret Webster, 122-123.

   Published in Murray, Utah, as a little magazine and distributed by New Directions, this was the sole issue and was apparently designed merely to get the play into print.

2. *The Glass Menagerie: A Play. New York: Random House, 1945. xii, 124 p. ils. "The Characters," vii; "Production Notes," ix-xii; play, 1-124.

   Reviews: Book Week, 9 September 1945, p. 7; Booklist, 42 (September 1945), 11; Christian Science Monitor, 29 September 1945, p. 16; Library Journal, 70 (15 September 1945), 821: George Freedley; New York Herald Tribune Weekly Book Review, 16 September 1945, p. 22: W. P. Eaton; New York Times, 9 September 1945, sec. 2, p. 1: Lewis Nichols; New York Times Book Review, 2 September 1945, p. 8: James McBride.

3. *27 Wagons Full of Cotton and Other One-Act Plays. Norfolk, Conn.: New Directions, 1945. [vi], 207 p. On spine: Tennessee Williams' One-Act Plays. "27 Wagons Full of Cotton: A Mississippi Delta Comedy" (B 8), 1-28; "The Purification" (B 6), 29-62; "The Lady of Larkspur Lotion" (B 3), 63-72; "The Last of My Solid Gold Watches" (B 5), 73-85; "Portrait of a Madonna," 87-104; "Auto-Da-Fé: A Tragedy in One Act," 105-120; "Lord Byron's Love Letter," 121-132; "The Strangest Kind of Romance: A Lyric Play in Four Scenes," 133-158; "The Long Goodbye," 159-179; "Hello from Bertha," 181-193; "This Property Is Condemned" (B 2), 195-207.

   Reviews: Book Week, 3 February 1946, p. 3: Leo Kennedy; Library Journal, 71 (15 March 1946), 407: George Freedley; Nation, 162 (2 March 1946), 267: Joseph Wood Krutch; New York Herald Tribune Weekly Book Review, 19 May 1946, p. 24: W. P. Eaton; New York Times Book Review, 24 February 1946, p. 8: Denham Sutcliffe; Theatre Arts, 30 (September 1946), 557.

4-7. *Blue Mountain Ballads. Words by Tennessee Williams; Music by Paul Bowles. Heavenly Grass; Lonesome Man; Cabin;

†Arranged chronologically.
*Denotes the first publication of a work or a major revision.

Sugar in the Cane. New York: G. Schirmer, 1946. 4 p. each.

Sharing a common title page, each song was published separately.

8. *You Touched Me! A Romantic Comedy in Three Acts by Tennessee Williams and Donald Windham, Suggested by a short story of the same name by D. H. Lawrence. New York: Samuel French, 1947. 116 p. Play, 3-114; "Story of the Play," 116.

9. 27 Wagons Full of Cotton and Other One-Act Plays (Falcon Press Book). London: Grey Walls Press, 1947. Same as A 3.

10. *Three. Music by Paul Bowles; Poem by Tennessee Williams. New York: Hargail Music Press, 1947. 4 p.

11. *A Streetcar Named Desire. New York: New Directions, 1947. 171 p. Play, 9-171.

Reviews: Booklist, 44 (15 February 1948), 214; Library Journal, 73 (1 March 1948), 399: George Freedley; New York Herald Tribune Weekly Book Review, 29 February 1948, p. 14: W. P. Eaton; New York Times Book Review, 1 February 1948, p. 17: C. V. Terry.

12. *One Arm and Other Stories. [New York:] New Directions, 1948. [iv], 210 p. "One Arm," 5-29; "The Malediction" (C 31), 31-57; "The Poet," 59-69; "Chronicle of a Demise," 71-80; "Desire and the Black Masseur" (B 16), 81-94; "Portrait of a Girl in Glass," 95-112; "The Important Thing" (C 33), 113-134; "The Angel in the Alcove," 135-149; "The Field of Blue Children" (C 29 rev.), 151-166; "The Night of the Iguana," 167-196; "The Yellow Bird" (C 38), 198-210.

Limited editions (50 and 1500 copies).

13. *American Blues: Five Short Plays [...]: Acting Edition. New York: Dramatists Play Service, 1948. 77 p. "Publisher's Note," 3; "Moony's Kid Don't Cry" (B 1), 5-14; "The Dark Room," 15-21; "The Case of the Crushed Petunias: A Lyrical Fantasy," 22-32; "The Long Stay Cut Short, or The Unsatisfactory Supper" (B 10), 33-42; "Ten Blocks on the Camino Real: A Fantasy," 43-77.

Review: Library Journal, 74 (15 January 1949), 129: George Freedley.

14. *The Glass Menagerie [...]: Play in Two Acts. New York: Dramatists Play Service, 1948. viii, 64 p. "Staging the Play: Practical Suggestions by the Publisher," v-vi; "Author's Production Notes," vii-viii; play (A 2 rev.), 1-60.

15. The Glass Menagerie: A Play in Two Acts. London: John Lehmann, 1948. xvi, 95 p. "Introduction by Tennessee

Williams: The Catastrophe of Success" (C 41), v-x; rest of contents same as A 2.

16. *Summer and Smoke. New York: New Directions, 1948. xii, 130 p. ils. "Author's Production Notes," vii-x; play, xi-130.
Reviews: Booklist, 45 (15 March 1949), 239; Library Journal, 74 (15 January 1949), 129: George Freedley; New Republic, 119 (15 November 1948), 28: Harold Clurman; New York Times Book Review, 16 January 1949, p. 20: Lewis Funke.

17. 27 Wagons Full of Cotton and Other One-Act Plays. London: John Lehmann, 1949. 192 p. Contents same as A 3.

18. A Streetcar Named Desire: A Play. London: John Lehmann, 1949. 112 p. Contents same as A 11.
Apparently distribution was later turned over to Secker & Warburg.

19. The Glass Menagerie: A Play (New Classics). New York: New Directions, 1949. xx, 124 p. ils. Same as A 2, plus "The Catastrophe of Success" (C 41), xiii-xix.

20. *Summer and Smoke: Acting Version: Play in Two Parts. New York: Dramatists Play Service, 1950. 82 p. il. "Author's Note on the Setting," 4-5; "Author's Description of Set Interiors," 6; play (A 16 rev.), 7-79.

21. *The Roman Spring of Mrs. Stone. New York: New Directions, 1950. [viii], 148 p. Novel, 1-148.
Limited edition (500 copies) and trade edition.
Reviews: Atlantic, 186 (November 1950), 101: Charles J. Rolo; Booklist, 47 (1 October 1950), 62; Commonweal, 53 (3 November 1950), 99: George Miles; Kirkus, 18 (15 July 1950), 395; Library Journal, 75 (1 September 1950), 1409: George Freedley; New York Herald Tribune Book Review, 22 October 1950, p. 14: Alfred Hayes; New York Times, 29 September 1950: Orville Prescott; New York Times Book Review, 1 October 1950, p. 4: Charles J. Rolo; New Yorker, 26 (25 November 1950), 149; Newsweek, 36 (9 October 1950), 94; Saturday Review, 33 (30 September 1950), 18: Hollis Alpert; Theatre Arts, 34 (November 1950), 2; Time, 56 (30 October 1950), 109.

22. The Roman Spring of Mrs. Stone. London: John Lehmann, 1950. 126 p. Contents same as A 21.
Review: Manchester Guardian, 15 December 1950, p. 5: Norman Shrapnel.

23. *A Streetcar Named Desire. New York: New Directions, n. d. 166 p. Play (A 11 rev.), 9-166.
"Seventh printing," published in or sometime before 1951.

24. *The Rose Tattoo. [Edited by Paul Bigelow.] New York: New Directions, 1951. xvi, 144 p. il. "The Timeless World of a Play" (C 63), vi-xi; "Author's Production Notes," xiii-xiv; play, 1-144.
Reviews: Booklist, 47 (1 June 1951), 342. Library Journal, 76 (15 May 1951), 868: George Freedley.

25. *I Rise in Flame, Cried the Phoenix: A Play about D. H. Lawrence [...] with a Note by Freida Lawrence. Norfolk, Conn.: James Laughlin, 1951. 42 p. "A Preface by the Author," 5-6; "A Note by Freida Lawrence," 7-8; play, 9-42.
Limited editions (10 and 300 copies).

26. A Streetcar Named Desire [...] with an Introduction by the Author (Signet Book). New York: New American Library, 1951. 142 p. ils. "On a Streetcar Named Success" (C 39), 7-10; play (A 23), 13-142.

27. Summer and Smoke: A Play. London: John Lehmann, 1952. 95 p. Contents same as A 16.
Apparently distribution was later turned over to Secker & Warburg.

28. The Roman Spring of Mrs. Stone (Signet Book). New York: New American Library, 1952. 141 p. Contents same as A 21.

29. Facts about Me. N. p.: n. d. Biography (D 1).
Probably published about 1952.

30. *A Streetcar Named Desire: Acting Edition: Play in Three Acts. New York: Dramatists Play Service, 1953. 107 p. il. Play (A 23 rev.), 5-103.

31. *Camino Real. Norfolk, Conn.: New Directions, 1953. xvi, 161 p. il. "Foreword" (C 69), viii-xi; "Afterword," xii-xiii; "Editor's Note," xiv; play (A 13 rev.), 1-161.
Review: Theatre Arts, 37 (October 1953), 26-27, 96: William Hawkins.

32. *27 Wagons Full of Cotton and Other One-Act Plays. Norfolk, Conn.: New Directions, 1953. xii, 238 p. Same as A 3, plus "Something Wild..." (C 53), vii-xii; "Talk to Me Like the Rain and Let Me Listen...," 209-218; "Something Unspoken," 219-238.

33. The Glass Menagerie. Edited by Shoichi Saeki. Tokyo: Eihosha, 1953. 144 p.

34. *Hard Candy: A Book of Stories. [New York:] New Directions, 1954. 220 p. "Three Players of a Summer Game" (C 68), 7-44; "Two on a Party," 45-78; "The Resemblance between

a Violin Case and a Coffin" (C 56), 79-100; "Hard Candy," 101-121; "Rubio y Morena (B 20), 123-144; "The Mattress by the Tomato Patch" (C 74), 145-161; "The Coming of Something to the Widow Holly" (B 42), 163-177; "The Vine" (C 71), 179-200; "The Mysteries of the Joy Rio," 201-220.
Limited edition.

35. *The Kingdom of Earth, with Hard Candy: A Book of Stories. [New York:] New Directions, 1954. 242 p. Same as A 33, plus "The Kingdom of Earth," 223-242.
Limited edition (100 copies), not for sale.

36. One Arm and Other Stories. [New York:] New Directions, 1954. [iv], 211 p. Same as A 12, except "The Yellow Bird" (D 1), 198-211.
Trade edition.
Reviews: Chicago Review, 9 (Summer 1955), 86-94: Robert Roth. New Republic, 132 (24 January 1955), 26-27: Paul Engle. New York Times, 5 June 1955, p. 36. New York Times Book Review, 2 January 1955, p. 5: James Kelly. Saturday Review, 38 (8 January 1955), 11-12: William H. Peden.

37. The Rose Tattoo. London: Secker & Warburg, 1954. xvi, 144 p. Same as A 24.

38. *Cat on a Hot Tin Roof. New York: New Directions, 1955. xiv, 197 p. il. "Person-to-Person" (C 75), vi-x; "Notes for the Designer," xiii-xiv; play, 1-150; "Note of Explanation," 151-152; "Act Three as Played in New York Production," 153-197.

39. *Lord Byron's Love Letter: Opera in One Act by Raffaello de Banfield; Libretto by Tennessee Williams. New York: Ricordi, 1955. 16 p. Opera (A 3 rev.).

40. The Rose Tattoo (Signet Book). New York: New American Library, 1955. 128 p. Contents same as A 24.

41. *I Rise in Flame, Cried the Phoenix: Acting Edition: A Play in One Act about D. H. Lawrence. New York: Dramatists Play Service, n. d. 18 p. [Note], 3; play (A 25 rev.), 5-18.
Copyright 1951; almost surely published later but before 1958.

42. *In the Winter of Cities: Poems. [Edited with help of William S. Gray.] Norfolk, Conn.: New Directions, 1956. 117 p. PART I: In Jack-O'-Lantern's Weather: "In Jack-O'-Lantern's Weather" (B 7 rev.), 11-14; "Testa dell'Effebo" (B 29), 15; "Cried the Fox" (B 7), 16; "The Eyes" (B 20), 17-18; "Faint as Leaf Shadow" (B 29), 19; "The Siege" (B 7), 20; "The Soft City" (B 20 rev.), 21-22; "A Wreath

for Alexandra Molostova," 23-24; "The Beanstalk Country" (B 7), 25; "Old Men with Sticks" (B 29 rev.), 26; "Orpheus Descending" (C 65), 27-28; "Pulse" (B 7), 29-30; "Lament for the Moths" (B 7), 31; "The Angels of Fructification" (B 7 rev.), 32-34; "The Interior of the Pocket" (B 34), 35-36; "Those Who Ignore the Appropriate Time of Their Going," 37-41. PART II: The Summer Belvedere: The Summer Belvedere" (B 7), 45-48; "Cortege" (B 7), 49-52; "Everyman" (C 32), 53; "Part of a Hero" (C 82), 54-55; "Descent" (C 65), 56; "Shadow Boxes" (B 7), 57; "Intimations" (B 7 rev.), 58-59; "The Dangerous Painters" (B 7), 60-66. PART III: The Jockeys at Hialeah: "The Jockeys at Hialeah" (B 11 rev.), 69-73; "Recuerdo" (B 11), 74-76; "The Legend" (B 7), 77-79; "Life Story," 80-81; "The Man in the Dining Car" (B 7), 82-83; "The Death Embrace" (B 7), 84-87; "The Christus of Guadalajara" (C 50), 88-90; "Carrousel Tune" (C 65), 91; "Iron Is the Winter" (B 7), 92. PART IV: Hoofprints of a Little Horse: "Which Is My Little Boy?" (C 57), 95; "Lady, Anemone" (B 11), 96; "Heavenly Grass" (A 4), 97; "Lonesome Man" (A 5), 98; "Cabin" (A 6), 99; "Sugar in the Cane" (A 7), 100; "Kitchen Door Blues (C 30), 101; "Gold Tooth Blues" (D 1), 102; "Her Head on the Pillow" (B 29), 103; "Across the Space" (C 65), 104-105; "My Little One" (D 1), 106; "The Island Is Memorable to Us" (B 29), 107; "San Sebastiano de Sodoma" (B 29), 108; "Tuesday's Child" (C 48), 109; "Towns Become Jewels" (B 7), 110; "Mornings on Bourbon Street" (B 7), 111-112; "The Last Wine" (B 7), 113; "The Road" (B 7), 114-115; "Little Horse" (D 1), 116; "Death Is High" (B 29), 117. (Also see C 54, C 55.)

Limited edition (100 copies) and trade edition.

Reviews: Booklist, 52 (15 July 1956), 478. Christian Science Monitor, 28 June 1956, p. 11: Rod Nordell. Library Journal, 81 (1 October 1956), 2262: G. D. McDonald. New Mexico Quarterly, 26 (Autumn 1956), 302-304: E. W. Tedlock. New York Times Book Review, 8 July 1956, p. 10: Dudley Fitts. Poetry, 90 (July 1957), 256-258: John Woods. Theatre Arts, 40 (August 1956), 10. Time, 67 (25 June 1956), 94. Voices, 162 (January-April 1957), 45-46: George Scarbrough. Yale Review, 46 (Winter 1957), 297: Donald Hall.

43. Four Plays [...]: The Glass Menagerie; A Streetcar Named Desire; Summer and Smoke; Camino Real. London: Secker & Warburg, 1956. vii, 320 p. Contents same as A 2, A 11 & A 18, A 16 & A 27, and A 31.

Review: Spectator, 197 (14 December 1956), 879: Anthony Hartby.

44. Cat on a Hot Tin Roof. London: Secker & Warburg, 1956. xiv, 197 p. il. Same as A 38.

Review: Times Literary Supplement, 10 February 1956.

45. *Baby Doll: The Script for the Film [...] Incorporating the Two One-Act Plays Which Suggested It: 27 Wagons Full of Cotton; The Long Stay Cut Short, or The Unsatisfactory Supper. New York: New Directions, 1956. 208 p. "Publisher's Note," 5; script, 7-140; "27 Wagons Full of Cotton" (A 3), 143-190; "The Long Stay Cut Short, or The Unsatisfactory Supper" (A 13), 191-208.

Review: Mainstream, 9 (November 1956), 50-51: Helen Davis.

46. The Script for the Film Baby Doll (Signet Book). New York: New American Library, 1956. 128 p. ils. Contents: script from A 45.

47. Baby Doll: The Script for the Film. London: Secker & Warburg, 1957. 140 p. ils. Same as A 45 pp. 1-140.

48. Baby Doll: The Script for the Film. Harmondsworth, Middlesex: Penguin Books, 1957. 123 p. ils. Contents same as A 47.

49. Cat on a Hot Tin Roof. Harmondsworth, Middlesex: Penguin Books, 1957. 132 p. Contents same as A 38 & A 44, plus "Editorial Note" by E. Martin Browne, 15.

50. The Roman Spring of Mrs. Stone. London: Secker & Warburg, 1957. 126 p. Contents same as A 21 & A 22.

51. A Streetcar Named Desire. London: Secker & Warburg, 1957. 96 p. Contents same as A 11, A 15, and A 43 pp. 65-154.

52. Summer and Smoke. London: Secker & Warburg, 1957. 80 p. Contents same as A 16, A 27, and A 43 pp. 155-228.

53. Camino Real. London: Secker & Warburg, 1958. 96 p. Contents same as A 31 and A 43 pp. 229-320.

54. *Orpheus Descending, with Battle of Angels: Two Plays. New Directions, 1958. x, 238 p. "The Past, the Present and the Perhaps" (C 87), v-x; Orpheus Descending (A 1 rev.), 1-118; Battle of Angels (A 1), 119-238.

Reviews: Booklist, 54 (15 June 1958), 581. Library Journal, 83 (1 April 1958), 1108: George Freedley.

55. *Suddenly Last Summer. New York: New Directions, 1958. 88 p. il. Play, 13-88.

56. Suddenly Last Summer. New York: Dramatists Play Service, 1958. 44 p. Contents same as A 55.

57. *Cat on a Hot Tin Roof [...]: A Play in Three Acts. New York: Dramatists Play Service, 1958. 85 p. il. Play (A 38 rev.), 5-81.

58. Cat on a Hot Tin Roof (Signet Book). New York: New American Library, 1958. 158 p. ils. Contents same as A 38.

59. Orpheus Descending: A Play. London: Secker & Warburg, 1958. 96 p. Contents same as A 54 pp. i-118.
Review: Times Literary Supplement, 14 November 1958, p. 652.

60. The Rose Tattoo; Camino Real. Introduced and Edited by E. Martin Browne (Penguin Plays). Harmondsworth, Middlesex: Penguin Books, 1958. 233 p. Contents same as A 37 and A 53, plus "Introduction" by E. Martin Browne, 7-8; and "Camino Real: An Appreciation" by John Whiting, 117-118.

61. A Streetcar Named Desire; The Glass Menagerie. Introduced and Edited by E. Martin Browne (Penguin Plays). Harmondsworth, Middlesex: Penguin Books, 1959. 207 p. Contents same as A 51 and A 2, plus "Introduction" by E. Martin Browne, 7-8.

62. Garden District: Two Plays [...]: Something Unspoken; Suddenly Last Summer. London: Secker & Warburg, 1959. 72 p. "Something Unspoken" (A 32), 7-25; Suddenly Last Summer (A 55), 27-72.

63. *Orpheus Descending [...]: A Play in Three Acts. New York: Dramatists Play Service, 1959. 83 p. Play (A 54 rev.), 5-78.

64. Hard Candy: A Book of Stories. [New York:] New Directions, 1959. 220 p. Same as A 34.
Trade edition.
Review: New York Times Book Review, 7 August 1959, p. 2: J. Donald Adams.

65. *Sweet Bird of Youth. New York: New Directions, 1959. xiv, 114 p. il. "Foreword" (C 95), vii-xi; play (C 101 rev.), 1-114, including "Synopsis of Scenes," 2.
Reviews: Library Journal, 85 (15 January 1960), 299: George Freedley. Theatre Arts, 44 (February 1960), 91.

66. The Glass Menagerie [...]: Play in Two Acts. New York: Dramatists Play Service, n. d. 72 p. Same as A 14, with revised pagination.
Published before 1962.

67. Suddenly Last Summer (Signet Book). New York: New American Library, 1960. 93 p. ils. Contents same as A 55.

68. The Fugitive Kind (Original Play Title: Orpheus Descending) (Signet Book). New York: New American Library, 1960. 144 p. ils. Contents same as A 54.

69. Three Players of a Summer Game and Other Stories. London: Secker & Warburg, 1960. 223 p. "Three Players of a Summer Game" (A 34), 7-38; "The Important Thing" (A 12), 39-55; "One Arm" (A 12), 56-74; "Portrait of a Girl in Glass" (A 12), 75-87; "The Coming of Something to the Widow Holly" (A 34), 88-99; "Two on a Party" (A 34), 100-127; "The Yellow Bird" (A 36), 128-137; "The Field of Blue Children" (A 12), 138-149; "The Malediction" (A 12), 150-170; "The Angel in the Alcove" (A 12), 171-181; "The Resemblance between a Violin Case and a Coffin" (A 34), 182-199; "The Night of the Iguana" (A 12), 200-223.

70. *Period of Adjustment: High Point over a Cavern: A Serious Comedy. New York: New Directions, 1960. [viii], 120 p. Play (C 101 rev.), 1-120.

71. Sweet Bird of Youth: A Play. London: Secker & Warburg, 1961. 93 p. Contents same as A 65.
Review: Times Literary Supplement, 13 January 1961, p. 23.

72. Period of Adjustment: High Point over a Cavern: A Serious Comedy. London: Secker & Warburg, 1961. 95 p. Contents same as A 70.

73. *Period of Adjustment, or High Point Is Built on a Cavern: A Serious Comedy. New York: Dramatists Play Service, 1961. 78 p. il. Play (A 70 rev.), 5-71.

74. Summer and Smoke (Signet Book). New York: New American Library, 1961. 127 p. ils. Contents same as A 16.

75. The Roman Spring of Mrs. Stone (Signet Book). New York: New American Library, 1961. 128 p. ils. Contents same as A 21 & A 28.

76. Orpheus Descending; Something Unspoken; Suddenly Last Summer (Penguin Plays). Harmondsworth, Middlesex: Penguin Books, 1961. 188 p. Contents same as A 58 and A 62.

77. *The Night of the Iguana. New York: New Directions, 1962. 128 p. il. [Note on setting], 5; play (C 107 rev.), 7-127; "Nazi Marching Song," 128.
Reviews: Booklist, 58 (15 May 1962), 638. Bookmark, 21 (June 1962), 258.

78. Sweet Bird of Youth [...] with a Foreword by the Author (Signet Book). New York: New American Library, 1962; Toronto: New American Library of Canada, 1962. 124 p. ils. Contents same as A 65.

79. Sweet Bird of Youth; A Streetcar Named Desire; The Glass

Menagerie. Edited by E. Martin Browne (Penguin Plays). Harmondsworth, Middlesex: Penguin Books, 1962. 313 p. On spine: Sweet Bird of Youth and Other Plays. A 61, plus new play (contents same as A 71).

80. Five Plays [. . .]: Cat on a Hot Tin Roof; The Rose Tattoo; Garden District; Something Unspoken, Suddenly Last Summer; Orpheus Descending. London: Secker & Warburg, 1962. xvi, 374 p. Contents same as A 44, A 37, A 62, and A 59.
Review: Spectator, 206 (30 March 1962), 418: John Whiting.

81. After a Visit [by] Thomas Lanier Williams. N. p.: Roger Roppe, 1962. Poem (C 19).
Limited (5 copies), hand-set edition.

82. One Arm and Other Stories. Edited by Motoo Takigawa and Tadamasa Shima. Tokyo: Eihosha, 1962. 120 p.

83. Period of Adjustment: High Point over a Cavern: A Serious Comedy (Signet Book). New York: New American Library, 1962; Toronto: New American Library of Canada, 1962. 127 p. ils. Contents same as A 70.

84. *Sweet Bird of Youth. New York: Dramatists Play Service, 1962. 72 p. Play (A 65 rev.), 5-60; "Alternate Ending," 60-61.

85. The Night of the Iguana: A Play. London: Secker & Warburg, 1963. 107 p. Contents same as A 77.

86. *The Night of the Iguana. New York: Dramatists Play Service, 1963. 93 p. il. [Note on setting], 4; play (A 77 rev.), 5-78; "Nazi Marching Song," 80.

87. Period of Adjustment / Summer and Smoke (Four Square Books). London: New English Library, 1963. [255] p. A 83 and A 74 bound together.

88. The Glass Menagerie. Edited by Heinz Nyszkiewicz. Frankfurt: Hirschgraben, 1963. 64 p.

89. The Glass Menagerie, Complete and Unabridged. Edited by Heinz Pähler. Paderborn: Ferdinand Schöningh, 1963. 98 p.

90. *The Milk Train Doesn't Stop Here Anymore. New York: New Directions, 1964. [viii], 118 p. "Author's Notes," 1-2; play (B 104 rev.), 3-118.

91. The Milk Train Doesn't Stop Here Anymore. New York: Dramatists Play Service, 1964. 90 p. Contents same as A 90.

92. The Milk Train Doesn't Stop Here Anymore: A Play. London: Secker & Warburg, 1964. 94 p. Contents same as A 90, plus few additional lines.

93. *Grand. New York: House of Books, 1964. Unpaged. Memoir. Limited edition (300 copies).

94. Three Plays of Tennessee Williams: The Rose Tattoo; Camino Real; Sweet Bird of Youth. New York: New Directions, 1964. 452 p. Same as A 24, A 31, and A 65.

95. *The Eccentricities of a Nightingale and Summer and Smoke: Two Plays. New York: New Directions, 1964; Toronto: McClelland & Stewart, 1964. [ii], 248 p. "Author's Note," 4; The Eccentricities of a Nightingale (A 16 rev.), 5-107; plus A 16.

96. *In the Winter of Cities: Poems (New Directions Paperbook). Norfolk, Conn.: New Directions, 1964. 129 p. Same as A 42 with additions and consequent shifts in pagination: pp. 1-41, same; "Photographs and Pearls," 42-43; "The Comforter and the Betrayer," 44-45; pp. 43-117 become pp. 47-121; "Old Men Are Fond," 122-123; "Covenant," 124; "Shadow Wood," 125; "A Separate Poem," 126-129.
Review: Prairie Schooner, 39 (Fall 1965), 273-276: Oliver Evans.

97. The Night of the Iguana (Signet Book). New York: New American Library, 1964. 127 p. ils. Contents same as A 77.

98. The Night of the Iguana (Penguin Play). Harmondsworth, Middlesex: Penguin Books, 1964. 117 p. Contents same as A 85.

99. A Streetcar Named Desire (Foreign Language Series). Tokyo: Hoko-Shobo, 1964. 163 p.

100. Summer and Smoke (Contemporary Library). Tokyo: Nan-un-Do, 1964. 148 p.

101. Three Players of a Summer Game and Other Stories. Harmondsworth, Middlesex: Penguin Books, 1965. 193 p. Contents same as A 69.

102. Camino Real: A Play. New York: Dramatists Play Service, [1965]. 96 p. Contents same as A 31.

103. The Rose Tattoo [...]: Play in Three Acts. New York: Dramatists Play Service, [1965]. 88 p. il. Contents same as A 24.

104. A Perfect Analysis Given by a Parrot [...]: Comedy in One

Act. New York: Dramatists Play Service, n. d. 18 p. il. Play (C 93), 3-16.
Copyright 1958; published mid-1960s.

105. *The Knightly Quest: A Novella and Four Short Stories. New York: New Directions, 1966. [viii], 103 p. "The Knightly Quest," vii-101; "Mama's Old Stucco House" (C 112), 103-121; "Man Bring This Up Road" (C 97), 123-143; "The Kingdom of Earth" (A 35), 145-165; "'Grand'" (A 93), 167-183.
Reviews: Best Sellers, 26 (1 March 1967), 440: J. J. Quinn. Critic, 25 (June 1967), 90. Library Journal, 92 (15 April 1967), 1647: Ervin J. Gaines. New York Times Book Review, 2 April 1967, p. 4: John Wakeman. Newsweek, 69 (27 February 1967), 92: Paul D. Zimmerman. Saturday Review, 50 (25 February 1967), 53: Brooks Atkinson.

106. The Glass Menagerie: A Play (New Classic / New Directions Paperbook). New York: New Directions, 1966; Toronto: McClelland & Stewart, 1966. xii, 124 p. Same as A 19.

107. 27 Wagons Full of Cotton and Other One-Act Plays (New Directions Paperbook). New York: New Directions, 1966; Toronto: McClelland & Stewart, 1966. xii, 238 p. Same as A 32.

108. The Glass Menagerie: A Play Embossed in One Volume. Louisville, Ky.: American Printing House for the Blind, 1966.

109. A Streetcar Named Desire. Louisville, Ky.: American Printing House for the Blind, 1966.

110. The Night of the Iguana. Louisville, Ky.: American Printing House for the Blind, 1966.

111. *The Gnädiges Fräulein [...]: A Play in One Act. New York: Dramatists Play Service, 1967. 37 p. il. "Production Notes," 4; play (C 116 rev.), 5-35.

112. *The Mutilated [...]: A Play in One Act. New York: Dramatists Play Service, 1967. 48 p. il. "Production Notes," 4; play (C 116 rev.), 5-42; "Variations," 43-46.

113. One Arm and Other Stories (New Directions Paperbook). New York: New Directions, 1967; Toronto: McClelland & Stewart, 1967. [iv], 211 p. Same as A 36.

114. Hard Candy: A Book of Stories (New Directions Paperbook). New York: New Directions, 1967; Toronto: McClelland & Stewart, 1967. 220 p. Same as A 34 and A 63.

115. Hard Candy and Other Stories. Edited by Motoo Takigawa and Tadamasa Shima (Modern English Series). Tokyo: Kinseido, 1967.

116. Suddenly Last Summer (Modern English Series). Tokyo: Kinseido, 1967. 112 p.

117. The Glass Menagerie [...] with an Introduction by E. R. Wood (Hereford Plays). London: Heinemann Educational, 1968. xxiv, 76 p.

118. *Kingdom of Earth (The Seven Descents of Myrtle). New York: New Directions, 1968. [vi], 111 p. On spine: The Kingdom of Earth. Play (C 121 expanded), 1-111.
Reviews: Choice, 6 (July 1969), 667. Library Journal, 94 (15 February 1969), 775: A. C. Willers.

119. The Knightly Quest: A Novella and Twelve Short Stories. London: Secker & Warburg, 1968. 253 p. "The Knightly Quest" (A 105), 9-90; "The Poet" (A 12), 91-98; "Chronicle of a Demise" (A 12), 99-105; "Desire and the Black Masseur" (A 12), 106-115; "Hard Candy" (A 34), 116-131; "Rubio y Morena" (A 34), 132-149; "The Mattress by the Tomato Patch" (A 34), 150-162; "The Vine" (A 34), 163-180; "The Mysteries of the Joy Rio" (A 34), 181-196; "Mama's Old Stucco House" (A 105), 197-210; "Man Bring This Up Road" (A 105), 211-226; "The Kingdom of Earth" (A 105), 227-241; "Grand" (A 105), 242-253.

120. Baby Doll: The Script for the Film; Something Unspoken; Suddenly Last Summer (Penguin Plays). Harmondsworth, Middlesex: Penguin Books, 1968. 159 p. On spine: Three Plays. Contents same as A 48, half of A 76.

121. The Night of the Iguana; Orpheus Descending (Penguin Plays). Harmondsworth, Middlesex: Penguin Books, 1968. 224 p. On spine: Two Plays. Contents same as A 98, plus rest of A 76.

122. The Milk Train Doesn't Stop Here Anymore; Cat on a Hot Tin Roof (Penguin Plays). Harmondsworth, Middlesex: Penguin Books, 1969. 224 p. Contents same as A 92, plus A 49.

123. *Kingdom of Earth (The Seven Descents of Myrtle) [...]: A Play in Seven Scenes. New York: Dramatists Play Service, 1969. 87 p. il. "A Note on the Song Excerpts Included in the Play," 3-4; play (A 118 rev.), 7-81.

124. *In the Bar of a Tokyo Hotel. New York: Dramatists Play Service, 1969. 45 p. il. Play, 5-40.

125. The Roman Spring of Mrs. Stone (New Directions Paperbook).

New York: New Directions, 1969; Toronto: McClelland & Stewart, 1969. [viii], 148 p. Same as A 21.

126. *The Two-Character Play. New York: New Directions, 1969. [iv], 96 p. Play, 1-96.
Limited edition (350 copies).

127. *Dragon Country: A Book of Plays. New York: New Directions, 1969; Toronto: McClelland & Stewart, 1969 (copyright 1970). [vi], 278 p. In the Bar of a Tokyo Hotel (A 124), 1-53; "I Rise in Flame, Cried the Phoenix: A Play in One Act about D. H. Lawrence" (A 41), 55-75; "The Mutilated" (A 112 rev.), 77-130; "I Can't Imagine Tomorrow" (C 118 rev.), 131-150; "Confessional," 151-196; "The Frosted Glass Coffin," 197-214; "The Gnadiges Fraulein" (A 111), 215-262; "A Perfect Analysis Given by a Parrot" (A 104), 263-278.

128. Dragon Country: A Book of Plays (New Directions Paperbook). New York: New Directions, 1969; Toronto: McClelland & Stewart, 1969. [vi], 278 p. Same as A 126.

129. The Glass Menagerie (New Classic / New Directions Paperbook). New York: New Directions, 1970; Toronto: McClelland & Stewart, 1970. 115 p. Contents same as A 19 & A 106 with few changes in stage directions.

130. Camino Real (New Directions Paperbook). New York: New Directions, 1970; Toronto: McClelland & Stewart, 1970. xiv, 161 p. Same as A 31.

131. The Theatre of Tennessee Williams. Volume I: Battle of Angels; The Glass Menagerie; A Streetcar Named Desire. New York: New Directions, 1971; Toronto: McClelland & Stewart, 1971. [viii], 419 p. Same as A 54 pp. 119-238, A 129, and A 23 with different breaks in pages.

132. The Theatre of Tennessee Williams. Volume II: The Eccentricities of a Nightingale; Summer and Smoke; The Rose Tattoo; Camino Real. New York: New Directions, 1971; Toronto: McClelland & Stewart, 1971. [viii], 591 p. Same as A 95, A 24, and A 31 & A 130.

133. The Theatre of Tennessee Williams. Volume III: Cat on a Hot Tin Roof; Orpheus Descending; Suddenly Last Summer. New York: New Directions, 1971; Toronto: McClelland & Stewart, 1971. [viii], 376 p. il. Same as A 38, A 54 pp. v-118, and A 55.

134. The Theatre of Tennessee Williams. Volume IV: Sweet Bird of Youth; Period of Adjustment; The Night of the Iguana. New York: New Directions, 1972; Toronto: McClelland & Stewart, 1972. [viii], 376 p. ils. Same as A 65, A 70, and A 77.

135. *Summer and Smoke: Opera in Two Acts. Music by Lee Hoiby; Libretto by Lanford Wilson. New York: Belwin-Mills, 1972. 66 p.

136. *Small Craft Warnings. New York: New Directions, 1972; Toronto: McClelland & Stewart, 1972. [vi], 87 p. il. "Too Personal?" 3-6; play (A 127 rev.), 7-73; "Notes after the Second Invited Audience (And a Troubled Sleep)," 74-79; "Small Craft Warnings: Genesis and Evolution" [letters], 80-87.
Reviews: Choice, 9 (February 1973), 1594. Library Journal, 97 (1 September 1972), 2748: B. L. Wimble.

137. Small Craft Warnings (New Directions Paperbook). New York: New Directions, 1972; Toronto: McClelland & Stewart, 1972. [vi], 87 p. il. Same as A 136.

138. Small Craft Warnings. London: Secker & Warburg, 1973. vi, 86 p. Same as A 136.

139. *Out Cry. New York: New Directions, 1973. [viii], 86 p. ils. Contents same as A 140.

140. Out Cry. New York: New Directions, 1973; Toronto: McClelland & Stewart, 1973. [vi], 72 p. ils. "A Dispensable Foreword," 3; "Synopsis of Scenes," 6; play (A 126 rev.), 7-72.
Reviews: Choice, 11 (June 1974), 604. Virginia Quarterly Review, 50 (Winter 1974), xvi.

141. Out Cry (New Directions Paperbook). New York: New Directions, 1973; Toronto: McClelland & Stewart, 1973. [vi], 72 p. ils. Same as A 140.

142. *Eight Mortal Ladies Possessed: A Book of Stories. New York: New Directions, 1974; Toronto: McClelland & Stewart, 1974. [viii], 100 p. "Happy August the Tenth" (C 135, C 138), 1-18; "The Inventory of Fontana Bella" (C 142), 19-29; "Miss Coynte of Greene" (C 147), 31-56; "Sabbatha and Solitude" (C 148), 57-78; "Completed," 79-90; "Oriflamme" (C 149), 91-100.
Reviews: Choice, 11 (January 1975), 1636. Commonweal, 102 (11 April 1975), 55: Robert Phillips. Library Journal, 99 (1 April 1974), 1060: Rowe Portis. New York Times Book Review, 6 October 1974, p. 14: Edmund White. Saturday Review / World, 2 (21 September 1974), 24: Ned Rorem. Sewanee Review, 82 (Fall 1974), 712-729: William Peden. Southern Literary Journal, 8 (Fall 1975), 165-169: Jacob H. Adler.

143. Eight Mortal Ladies Possessed: A Book of Stories (New Directions Paperbook). New York: New Directions, 1974; Toronto: McClelland & Stewart, 1974. [viii], 100 p. Same as A 142.

144. Eight Mortal Ladies Possessed: A Book of Stories. London: Secker & Warburg, 1974. [viii], 100 p. Same as A 142.
Reviews: London Magazine, 15 (June-July 1975), 68-74: Ned Rorem. New Statesman, 90 (4 July 1975), 29: Paul Bailey. Sunday Times, 29 June 1975, p. 31. Times Literary Supplement, 1 August 1975, p. 865: Gabriele Annan.

145. *Battle of Angels. New York: Dramatists Play Service, 1975. 76 p. il. Play (A 1 rev.), 5-73.

146. *Cat on a Hot Tin Roof. New York: New Directions, 1975; Toronto: McClelland & Stewart, 1975. 173 p. "Notes for the Designer," 15-16; play (A 38 rev.), 17-173.

147. Cat on a Hot Tin Roof (New Directions Paperbook). New York: New Directions, 1975; Toronto: McClelland & Stewart, 1975. 173 p. Same as A 146.

148. Sweet Bird of Youth (New Directions Paperbook). New York: New Directions, 1975; Toronto: McClelland & Stewart, 1975. xiv, 114 p. Same as A 65.

149. *Moise and the World of Reason. New York: Simon & Schuster, 1975. 190 p. Novel, 11-190.
Limited edition (350 copies) and trade edition.
Reviews: Best Sellers, 35 (August 1975), 114: R. J. Thompson. Library Journal, 100 (15 June 1975), 1243: John Agar. New Republic, 172 (24 May 1975), 24: Foster Hirsch. New York Times, 15 May 1975, p. 41: Christopher Lehmann-Haupt. New York Times Book Review, 13 July 1975, p. 26: Karyl Roosevelt. Virginia Quarterly Review, 51 (Autumn 1975), cxliv.

150. *Memoirs. Garden City, N.Y.: Doubleday, 1975. xxii, 264 p. ils. "Foreword," xv-xix; autobiography (C 137 expanded), 1-252.
Limited edition (400 copies); trade edition; Book-of-the-Month Club Selection.
Reviews: America, 134 (10 January 1976), 10: Catherine Hughes; Reprint: Stanton, Tennessee Williams, pp. 171-173. Best Sellers, 35 (March 1976), 378: Frank Wilson. Choice, 12 (February 1976), 1578. Gay Sunshine, 29-30 (Summer-Fall 1976), 11: Andrew Dvasin. Library Journal, 100 (1 November 1975), 2045: Gary Carey. National Review, 28 (16 April 1976), 405: D. K. Mano. New Republic, 173 (27 December 1975), 31: Gerald Weales. New York Review of Books, 23 (5 February 1976), 13: Gore Vidal; reprint: Matters of Fact and Fiction, pp. 129-147. New York Times, 7 November 1975, pp. 42-44: Jack Richardson. Saturday Review / World, 3 (1 November 1975), 29: Stanley Kauffmann. Time, 106 (1 December 1975), 83: T. E. Kalem. Times, 22

November 1975, p. 10. Virginia Quarterly Review, 52 (Spring 1976), 42. Yale Review, 65 (Summer 1976), 587: M. G. Cooke. Yale Theatre, 8 (Fall 1976), 78-82: M. Lassell.

151. *The Theatre of Tennessee Williams. Volume V: The Milk Train Doesn't Stop Here Anymore; Kingdom of Earth (The Seven Descents of Myrtle); Small Craft Warnings; The Two-Character Play. New York: New Directions, 1976; Toronto: McClelland & Stewart, 1976. [viii], 370 p. ils. Same as A 90 and A 136, plus Kingdom of Earth (A 118 rev.), 121-214; The Two-Character Play (A 126 & 139 rev.), 301-370.

152. Summer and Smoke: Opera in Two Acts: Vocal Score. Music by Lee Hoiby; Libretto by Lanford Wilson, Based on the Play by Tennessee Williams. New York: Belwin-Mills, 1976. 332 p.

153. Moise and the World of Reason. London: W. H. Allen, 1976. 190 p. Same as A 149.
Reviews: Sunday Times, 7 March 1976, p. 41. Times Literary Supplement, 12 March 1976, p. 283. Response: 18 March 1976, p. 13.

154. *Memoirs. London: W. H. Allen, 1976. xvi, 268p. Same as A 150, plus four new pages of text.
Reviews: New Statesman, 92 (12 November 1976), 683: Russell Davis. Sunday Times, 12 December 1976, p. 40. Times, 18 November, 1976, p. 11. Times Literary Supplement, 17 December 1976, p. 1576.

155. Cat on a Hot Tin Roof; The Milk Train Doesn't Stop Here Anymore; The Night of the Iguana (Penguin Plays). Harmondsworth, Middlesex: Penguin Books, 1976. 329 p. Same as A 122, plus part of A 121.

156. The Rose Tattoo; Camino Real; Orpheus Descending (Penguin Plays). Harmondsworth, Middlesex: Penguin Books, 1976. 347 p. Same as A 60, plus rest of A 121.

157. *Tennessee Williams' Letters to Donald Windham 1940-65. Edited and with Comments by Donald Windham. Verona, Italy: Sandy M. Campbell, 1976. xii, 333 p. ils. "Introduction" by Donald Windham, v-xi; letters, 1-317; "Appendix," 219-323.
Limited editions (26 and 500 copies).
Review: Time, 109 (7 February 1977), 94: Gerald Clarke.

158. Four Plays: Summer and Smoke; Orpheus Descending; Suddenly Last Summer; Period of Adjustment (Signet Modern Classic). New York: New American Library, 1976. [496] p. Same as A 74, A 68, A 67, and A 83.

159. Three by Tennessee: Sweet Bird of Youth; The Rose Tattoo; The Night of the Iguana (Signet Modern Classic). New York: New American Library, 1976. [508] p. Same as A 78, A 40, and A 97.

160. Memoirs. New York: Bantam Books, 1976. xiv, 334 p. ils. Contents same as A 150.

161. Moise and the World of Reason. New York: Bantam Books, 1976. [viii], 214 p. Contents same as A 149.

162. The Roman Spring of Mrs. Stone. New York: Bantam Books, 1976. 128 p. Same as A 75.

163. *Androgyne, Mon Amour: Poems. New York: New Directions, 1977; Toronto: McClelland & Stewart, 1977. 92 p. "Old Men Go Mad at Night," 9-11; "'Winter Smoke Is Blue and Bitter,'" 12; "Dark Arm, Hanging over the Edge of Infinity" (B 7 rev.), 13-14; "Events Proceed," 15; "Androgyne, Mon Amour" (C 156), 16-18; "Speech from the Stairs" (B 7), 19; "Young Men Waking at Daybreak" (C 123), 20-21; "Apparition," 22; "Counsel" (B 20 rev.), 23-28; "One Hand in Space" (B 7), 29-30; "Impressions through a Pennsy Window," 31-32; "The Couple," 33-39; "Evening," 40-42; "The Brain's Dissection," 43-44; "Crepe-de-Chine" (C 128), 45-46; "Les Etoiles d'un Cirque," 47-49; "The Wine-Drinkers" (B 7 rev.), 50; "A Daybreak Thought for Maria," 51; "A Liturgy of Roses" (C 35 rev.), 52-55; "Miss Puma, Miss Who?" (C 144), 56-57; "A Mendicant Order," 58-59; "Cinder Hill: A Narrative Poem," 60-63; "You and I," 64; "Stones Are Thrown," 65-66; "The Harp of Wales" (C 49), 67; "The Diving Bell," 68-69; "His Manner of Returning," 70-73; "Night Visit," 74-76; "One and Two" (B 7), 77-78; "Two Poems from The Two-Character Play" ["Fear is a monster vast as night"; "Old beaux and faded ladies play"] (A 125), 79; "The Lady with No One at All," 80-82; "Wolf's Hour," 83-85; "The Ice-Blue Wind" (B 7 rev.), 86-87; "Turning Out the Bedside Lamp," 88; "Tangier: The Speechless Summer" (C 133), 89-92. Reproduction of painting on dust-jacket.
Limited (200 copies) and trade editions.
Reviews: Best Sellers, 37 (July 1977), 122: M. T. Siconolfi. Choice, 14 (November 1977), 1218. Library Journal, 102 (15 April 1977), 929: Margaret Gibson. New Republic, 176 (4 June 1977), 32: Gerald Weales. Virginia Quarterly Review, 53 (Autumn 1977), 146.

164. Memoirs (Star Book). London: W. H. Allen, 1977. xvi, 268 p. ils. Same as A 154.

165. The Roman Spring of Mrs. Stone. Frogmore, St. Albans, Hereshire: Panther Books, 1977. 111 p. Contents same as A 22.

166. *The Eccentricities of a Nightingale. New York: Dramatists Play Service, 1977. 57 p. "Author's Note (Written Prior to Broadway Production)," 5; play (A 95 rev.), 7-55.

167. Tennessee Williams' Letters to Donald Windham 1940-1965. Edited and with Comments by Donald Windham. New York: Holt, Rinehart & Winston, 1977. xii, 333 p. ils. Same as A 157.

Reviews: Best Seller, 37 (March 1978), 394. Choice, 15 (March 1978), 75. Library Journal, 102 (15 October 1977), 2164: Larry Earl Bone. National Review, 30 (1 September 1978), 1094: Selden Rodman. New Republic, 178 (4 February 1978), 38: W. A. H. Kinnucan. New York Times Book Review, 20 November 1977, p. 9: Robert Brustein. Saturday Review, 5 (15 October 1977), 35.

168. *Where I Live: Selected Essays. Edited by Christine R. Day and Bob Woods with an Introduction by Christine R. Day. New York: New Directions, 1978; Toronto: McClelland & Stewart, 1978. xvi, 171 p. "Introduction: Personal Lyricism" by Christine R. Day, vii-xiv; "Preface to My Poems" (B 7), 1-6; "Something Wild..." (A 32), 7-14; "On a Streetcar Named Success" (A 19), 15-22; "Questions without Answers" (C 45), 23-27; "A Writer's Quest for a Parnassus" (C 58), 28-34; "The Human Psyche--Alone" (C 61), 35-39; "Introduction to Carson McCullers's Reflections in a Golden Eye" (B 26), 40-48; "The Timeless World of a Play" (A 24), 49-54; "The Meaning of The Rose Tattoo" (C 64), 55-57; "Facts about Me" (D 1), 58-62; "Foreword to Camino Real" (A 31), 63-67; "Afterword to Camino Real" (A 31), 68-69; "Critic Says 'Evasion,' Writer Says 'Mystery'" (C 77), 70-74; "Person-to-Person" (A 38), 75-80; "The Past, the Present, and the Perhaps" (A 54), 81-87; "The World I Live In" (C88), 88-92; "Author and Director: A Delicate Situation" (C 90), 93-99; "If the Writing Is Honest" (C 91, B 62), 100-104; "Foreword to Sweet Bird of Youth" (A 65), 105-110; "Reflections on a Revival of a Controversial Fantasy" (C 98), 111-113; "Tennessee Williams Presents His POV" (C 99), 114-120; "Prelude to a Comedy" (C 100), 121-126; "Five Fiery Ladies" (C 102), 127-132; "Biography of Carson McCullers" (C 104), 133-136; "A Summer of Discovery" (C 106), 137-147; "T. Williams's View of T. Bankhead" (C 111), 148-154; "Too Personal?" (A 135), 155-159; "Homage to Key West" (C 139), 160-164; "The Pleasures of the Table," 165-167; "The Misunderstandings and Fears of an Artist's Revolt," 168-171.

Reviews: Booklist, 75 (1 November 1978), 451. Kirkus, 46 (15 October 1978), 1180. Publishers Weekly, 214 (16 October 1978), 112. Saturday Review, 5 (December 1978), 54.

169. Where I Live: Selected Essays. Edited by Christine R. Day and Bob Woods with an Introduction by Christine R. Day (New Directions Paperbook). New York: New Directions, 1978; Toronto: McClelland & Stewart, 1978. xvi, 171 p. Same as A 168.

170. Vieux Carré. New York: New Directions, 1979; Toronto: George J. McLeod, 1979. iv, 116 p. [Note on setting], 4; play, 5-116.

171. Vieux Carré (New Directions Paperbook). New York: New Directions, 1979; Toronto: George J. McLeod, 1979. iv, 116 p. Same as A 170.

B. WORKS IN ANTHOLOGIES AND BOOKS BY OTHER AUTHORS†

1. Mayorga, Margaret, ed. The Best One-Act Plays of 1940. New York: Dodd, Mead, 1941. *Moony's Kid Don't Cry," 29-44.

2. Kozlinko, William, ed. American Scenes. New York: John Day, 1941. *Landscape with Figures: Two Mississippi Plays: [Autobiographical note]; I. "At Liberty"; "This Property Is Condemned," 173-193.

3. Mayorga, Margaret, ed. The Best One-Act Plays of 1941. New York: Dodd, Mead, 1942. *"The Lady of Larkspur Lotion," 121-132.

4. Smith, Betty, ed. 25 Non-Royalty One-Act Plays for All-Girl Casts. New York: Greenberg, 1942. "At Liberty" (B 2).

5. Mayorga, Margaret, ed. The Best One-Act Plays of 1942. New York: Dodd, Mead, 1942. *"The Last of My Solid Gold Watches," 1-15.

6. New Directions 1944 (#8). New York: New Directions, 1944. *"Dos Ranchos, or The Purification," 230-256.

7. Five Young American Poets, Third Series, 1944. Norfolk, Conn.: New Directions, 1944. *The Summer Belvedere: "Preface to My Poems--Frivolous Version," 122-124; "Preface to My Poems--Serious Version," 124-126; "The Summer Belvedere," 127-130; "The Beanstalk Country," 130; "Mornings on Bourbon Street," 131-132; "Lament for the Moths," 132-133; "Dark Arm, Hanging over the Edge of Infinity," 133-135; "The Road," 135-136; Morgenlied," 136-137; "The Angels of Fructication," 137-139; "The Legend," 139-141; "One and Two," 141-142; "Towns Become Jewels," 142-143; "The Last Wine," 143; "The Man in the Dining Car," 144-145; "The Wine Drinkers," 146; "The Marvelous Children," 147-149; "Cried the Fox," 149; "Pulse," 150; "Speech from the Stairs," 151; "The Dangerous Painters," 152-157; "Iron Is the Winter," 157; "The Ice Blue Wind," 158-159; "Intimations," 159-160;

†Arranged chronologically.
*Denotes the first publication of a work or a major revision.

"The Siege," 161; "Shadow Boxes," 162; "Cortege," 163-166; "The Death Embrace," 166-169; "One Hand in Space," 169-170.

Sometimes listed as Williams's "first book," it also contained work by Eve Merriam, John Frederick Nims, Jean Garrigue, and Alejandro Carrion.

Review: New York Times Book Review, 17 June 1945, p. 10.

8. Mayorga, Margaret, ed. The Best One-Act Plays of 1944. New York: Dodd, Mead, 1945. *"27 Wagons Full of Cotton," 155-183.

9. Mantle, Burns, ed. The Best Plays of 1944-45 and the Year Book of the Drama in America. New York: Dodd, Mead, 1945. The Glass Menagerie: A Drama in Seven Scenes [A 2 excerpts], 140-175.

10. Mayorga, Margaret, ed. The Best One-Act Plays of 1945. New York: Dodd, Mead, 1945. *"The Unsatisfactory Supper," 235-249.

11. New Directions in Prose and Poetry #9. New York: New Directions, 1946. *Three Poems: "Camino Real"; "Recuerdo"; "Lady, Anemone," 77-83.

12. Wednesday Club Verse: An Anthology of Honor Poems from the Annual and Special Poetry Contests of the Wednesday Club of St. Louis. St. Louis: 1946. *Sonnets for the Spring: I. "Singer of Darkness" (C 21); II. "The Radiant Guest"; III. "A Branch for Birds," 53-54.

13. Gassner, John, ed. Best Plays of the Modern American Theatre, Second Series. New York: Crown, 1947. The Glass Menagerie (A 2), 1-38.

14. Spearhead: 10 Years' Experimental Writing in America. New York: New Directions, 1947. "27 Wagons Full of Cotton" (A 3).

15. Chapman, John, ed. The Burns Mantle Best Plays of 1947-48 [...]. New York: Dodd, Mead, 1948. A Streetcar Named Desire; A Play in Eleven Scenes [A 11 excerpts], 32-62.

16. New Directions in Prose and Poetry #10. New York: New Directions, 1948. *"Desire and the Black Masseur," 239-246.

17. Women: A Collaboration of Artists and Writers. New York: 1948. "An Appreciation" [Laurette Taylor] (C 37).

18. Burnett, Whit, and Hallie Burnett, eds. Story: The Fiction

of the Forties. New York: E. P. Dutton, 1949. "The Important Thing" (C 33), 38-51.

19. Hatcher, Harlan, ed. Modern American Drama, New Edition. New York: Harcourt, Brace, 1949. The Glass Menagerie (A 2), 233-274.

20. New Directions in Prose and Poetry #11. New York: New Directions, 1949. *"Rubio y Morena" (C 46), 459-471. Three Poems: "The Soft City"; "Counsel"; "The Eyes," 472-478.

21. Cubeta, Paul M., ed. Modern Drama for Analysis. New York: William Sloane, 1950. The Glass Menagerie (A 2).

22. Evans, Oliver. Young Man with a Screwdriver. Lincoln: University of Nebraska Press, 1950. *"Foreword," 1-3.
Review: New York Times Book Review, 4 June 1950, p. 28: Milton Crane.

23. Gallaway, Marian. Constructing a Play. New York: Prentice-Hall, 1950. *"Foreword," vii-xi.

24. Gassner, John, ed. A Treasury of the Theatre (from Henrik Ibsen to Arthur Miller). New York: Simon & Schuster, 1950. The Glass Menagerie (A 2), 1039-1059.

25. Lehmann, John, ed. Penguin New Writing #40. Harmondsworth, Middlesex: Penguin Books, 1950. "The Resemblance between a Violin Case and a Coffin" (C 56), 13-28.

26. McCullers, Carson. Reflections in a Golden Eye (New Classics). New York: New Directions, 1950. *"Introduction: This Book," ix-xxi.

27. Wall, Vincent, and James Patton McCormick, eds. Seven Plays of the Modern Theatre. New York: American Book Company, 1950. The Glass Menagerie (A 2).

28. Windham, Donald. The Dog Star. Garden City, N. Y.: Doubleday, 1950. *[Blurb on dust-jacket.]

29. New Directions in Prose and Poetry #12. New York: New Directions, 1950. *Eight Poems: "This Island Is Memorable to Us"; "Testa dell'Effebo" (C 44); "Old Men with Sticks"; "Her Head on the Pillow"; "Faint as Leaf Shadow"; "The Goths"; "Death Is High"; "San Sebastino de Sodoma," 393-397.

30. Six Modern American Plays. New York: Modern Library, 1950. The Glass Menagerie (A 2), 271-340.

31. Chapman, John, ed. The Best Plays of 1940-1951 [. . .]. New York: Dodd, Mead, 1951. The Rose Tattoo: A Play in Three Acts [A 24 excerpts], 210-236.

32. Clark, Barrett H., and William H. Davenport, eds. Nine Modern Plays. New York: Appleton-Century-Crofts, 1951. The Glass Menagerie (A 2).

33. Foley, Martha, ed. The Best American Short Stories 1951. Boston: Houghton, Mifflin, 1951. "The Resemblance between a Violin Case and a Coffin" (C 56), 338-350. Review: Saturday Review, 34 (18 August 1951), 17: William Peden.

34. New Directions in Prose and Poetry #13. New York: New Directions, 1951. *"The Interior of the Pocket," 530-531.

35. Gassner, John ed. Best American Plays, Third Series, 1945-1951. New York: Crown, 1952. A Streetcar Named Desire (A 23), 49-93; Summer and Smoke (A 16), 665-701.

36. New World Writing #1 (Mentor Book). New York: New American Library, 1952. "I Rise in Flame, Cried the Phoenix: A Play about D. H. Lawrence" (A 25), 46-47.

37. Warnock, Robert, ed. Representative Modern Plays: American. Chicago: Scott, Foresman, 1952. The Glass Menagerie (A 2), 580-653.

38. Foley, Martha, ed. The Best American Short Stories 1953. Boston: Houghton, Mifflin, 1953. "Three Players of a Summer Game" (C 68), 363-383.

39. Hatcher, Harlan H. , ed. A Modern Repertory. New York: Harcourt, Brace, 1953. Summer and Smoke (A 16).

40. Tucker, S. Marion, and Alan S. Downer, eds. Twenty-Five Modern Plays, Third Edition. New York: Harper, 1953. A Streetcar Named Desire (A 23).

41. Waite, Harlow O. , and Benjamin B. Atkinson, eds. Literature for Our Time. New York: Henry Holt, 1953. The Glass Menagerie (A 2).

42. New Directions in Prose and Poetry #14. New York: New Directions 1953. *"The Coming of Something to the Widow Holly," 194-201.

43. Maxwell, Gilbert. Go Looking: Poems, 1933-1953. Boston: Bruce Humphries, 1954. *"Some Words Before," [5-6].

44. Sper, Felix, ed. Living American Plays. New York: Globe Books, 1954. The Glass Menagerie (A 2).

45. Chapman, John, ed. Theatre '55. New York: Random House, 1955. Cat on a Hot Tin Roof [A 38 excerpts], 69-93.

46. Cooper, Charles W., ed. Preface to Drama. New York: Ronald Press, 1955. The Glass Menagerie (A 2).

47. Cowley, Malcolm, ed. Best Tales of the Deep South. New York: Lion Library, 1955. "The Yellow Bird" (A 36), 128-135.

48. Gaver, Jack, ed. Critics' Choice: New York Drama Critics' Circle Prize Plays, 1935-1955. New York: Hawthorn Books, 1955. The Glass Menagerie (A 2), 290-326; A Streetcar Named Desire (A 23), 366-408; Cat on a Hot Tin Roof (A 38), 643-657.

49. Havighurst, Walter, et al., eds. Selection: A Reader for College Writing. New York: Dryden Press, 1955. The Glass Menagerie (A 2), 607-638.

50. Knickerbocker, Kenneth L., and H. Willard Reninger, eds. Interpreting Literature. New York: Henry Holt, 1955. The Glass Menagerie (A 2).

51. Kronenberger, Louis, ed. The Best Plays of 1954-1955 [...]. New York: Dodd, Mead, 1955. Cat on a Hot Tin Roof: A Drama in Three Acts [A 38 excerpts], 288-312.

52. Kunitz, Stanley J., ed. Twentieth Century Authors, First Supplement: A Biographical Dictionary of Modern Literature. New York: H. W. Wilson, 1955. ["Facts About Me"] (D 1), 1087-1088.

53. Mayorga, Margaret, ed. The Best Short Plays of 1955-1956. Boston: Beacon Press, 1956. "Something Unspoken" (A 32), 83-110.

54. Watson, E. Bradlee, and Benfield Pressey, eds. Contemporary Drama: Eleven Plays--American, English, European. New York: Charles Scribner's Sons, 1956. The Glass Menagerie (A 2), 137-169.

55. Six Great Modern Plays. New York: Dell, 1956. The Glass Menagerie (A 2), 435-512.

56. Kronenberger, Louis, ed. The Best Plays of 1956-1957 [...]. New York: Dodd, Mead, 1957. Orpheus Descending: A Play in Three Acts [A 54 excerpts], 248-268.

57. Mayorga, Margaret, ed. The Best Short Plays. 20th Anniversary Edition. Boston: Beacon Press, 1957. "27 Wagons Full of Cotton" (B 8), 381-404.

58. Vidal, Gore. Visit to a Small Planet. Boston: Little, Brown, 1957. *[Blurb on dust-jacket.].

59. Six Poems. New York: New Directions, 1957. "My Little One" (A 42), 6.

60. Cerf, Bennett, and Van H. Cartmell, eds. 24 Favorite One-Act Plays. New York: Doubleday, 1958. "27 Wagons Full of Cotton" (A 32), 95-116.

61. Gassner, John, ed. Best American Plays, Fourth Series, 1951-1957. New York: Crown, 1958. Cat on a Hot Tin Roof (A 38), 37-90; The Rose Tattoo (A 24), 91-132.

62. Inge, William. The Dark at the Top of the Stairs. New York: Random House, 1958. "Introduction" (C 91), vii-vix.

63. Oppenheimer, George, ed. The Passionate Playgoer: A Personal Scrapbook. New York: Viking Press, 1958. "The Writing Is Honest" (C 91), 246-249.

64. Kronenberger, Louis, ed. The Best Plays of 1958-1959 [...]. New York: Dodd, Mead, 1959. Sweet Bird of Youth: A Play in Three Acts [A 65 excerpts], 209-231.

65. Collection of Contemporary American Literature #13. Tokyo: 1959. Summer and Smoke (A 16), 235-313.

66. Words and Music: Comments by Famous Authors about the World's Greatest Artists. Camden, N. J.: RCA Victor, n. d. *"'As if a rose might somehow be a throat' Writes Tennessee Williams about Licia Albanese," 5.

67. Abels, Cyrilly, and Margarita G. Smith, eds. 40 Best Stories from Mademoiselle 1935-1960. New York: Harper & Brothers, 1960. "The Vine" (C 71), 296-308.

68. Downer, Alan S., ed. American Drama. New York: Thomas Y. Crowell, 1960. The Glass Menagerie (A 14, A 66).

69. Grebanier, Bernard D. N., and Seymour Reiter, eds. Introduction to Imaginative Literature. New York: Thomas Y. Crowell, 1960. The Rose Tattoo (A 24).

70. Herlihy, James. All Fall Down. New York: E. P. Dutton, 1960. *[Blurb on dust-jacket.].

71. Inge, William. The Dark at the Top of the Stairs. New York: Bantam Books, 1960. "Introduction" (B 62).

72. McCullers, Carson. Reflections in a Golden Eye. New York: Bantam Books, 1960. "Introduction: This Book" (B 26), vii-xvi.

73. McNamee, Maurice B., et al., eds. Literary Types and Themes. New York: Rinehart, 1960. The Glass Menagerie (A 2).

74. Markel, Lester, ed. Background and Foregrounds: An Anthology of Articles from the New York Times Magazine. Great Neck, N.Y.: Channel Press, 1960. "Tennessee Williams Presents His POV" (C 99), 301-305.

75. Steinberg, M. W., ed. Aspects of Modern Drama. New York: Holt, Rinehart & Winston, 1960. The Glass Menagerie (A 2), 559-615.

76. Summers, Hollis Spurgeon, and Edgar Whan, eds. Literature: An Introduction. New York: McGraw-Hill, 1960. "Something Unspoken" (A 32).

77. Barnett, Sylvan, et al., eds. An Introduction to Literature: Fiction, Poetry, Drama, Fourth Edition. Boston: Little, Brown, 1961. The Glass Menagerie (A 2), 694-748.

78. Cerf, Bennett, ed. Six American Plays for Today. New York: Modern Library, 1961. Camino Real (A 31), 1-114; "Introduction" to Dark at the Top of the Stairs (B 62), 117-120.

79. Engle, Paul, ed. Midland: Twenty-Five Years of Fiction and Poetry Selected from the Writing Workshop of the State University of Iowa. New York: Random House, 1961. "Little Horse" (A 42), 573.

80. Funke, Lewis, and John E. Booth, eds. Actors Talk about Acting. New York: Avon Books, 1961. *[Blurb on front cover.]

81. Gold, Herbert, and David C. Stevenson, eds. Stories of Modern America. New York: St. Martins Press, 1961. "Three Players of a Summer Game" (A 64).

82. Goodman, Randolph, ed. Drama on Stage. New York: Holt, Rinehart & Winston, 1961. A Streetcar Named Desire (A 23); "The World I Live In" (C 88), 274-377.

83. Hamalian, Leo, and Edmond L. Volpe, eds. Pulitzer Prize Reader. New York: Popular Library, 1961. "27 Wagons Full of Cotton" (A 32).

84. Hurrell, John D., ed. Two Modern American Tragedies: Reviews and Criticism of Death of a Salesman and A Streetcar Named Desire. New York: Charles Scribner's Sons, 1961. "The Timeless World of a Play" (A 24), 49-52.

85. Kronenberger, Louis, ed. The Best Plays of 1960-1961 [...]. New York: Dodd, Mead, 1961. Period of Adjustment: A Play in Three Acts [A 70 excerpts], 115-132.

86. Miller, Jordan Y., ed. American Dramatic Literature: Ten Modern Plays in Historical Perspective. New York: McGraw-Hill, 1961. Camino Real (A 31), 139-91.

87. Moon, Samuel, ed. One Act: Short Plays of the Modern Theatre (Evergreen). New York: Grove Press, 1961. "27 Wagons Full of Cotton" (A 32).

88. Nelson, Benjamin. Tennessee Williams: The Man and His Work. New York: Ivan Obolensky, 1961. *"Tenor Sax Taking the Breaks," 46-48; "I think the strange, the crazed, the queer," 196-197; excerpts from letters to Audrey Wood, Paul Bigelow, Jordan Massee, 43-44, 50, 76-77, 89, 155, 288.

89. Reinert, Otto, ed. Modern Drama: Nine Plays. Boston: Little, Brown, 1961. The Glass Menagerie (A 2), 387-449.

90. Ulanov, Barry, ed. Makers of the Modern Theatre. New York: McGraw-Hill, 1961. Camino Real (A 31).

91. Block, Haskell M., and Robert G. Shedd, eds. Masters of Modern Drama. New York: Random House, 1962. The Glass Menagerie (A 2), 989-1017.

92. Burnett, Whit, ed. Firsts of the Famous. New York: Ballantine Books, 1962. "The Field of Blue Children" (B 29), 224-234.

93. Clayes, Stanley A., and David G. Spencer, eds. Contemporary Drama. New York: Charles Scribner's Sons, 1962. The Rose Tattoo (A 24).

94. Fitzjohn, Donald, ed. English One-Act Plays of Today. New York / London: Oxford University Press, 1962. "Lord Byron's Love Letter" (A 32).

95. Hewes, Henry, ed. The Best Plays of 1961-1962 [...]. New York: Dodd, Mead, 1962. The Night of the Iguana: A Play in Two Acts [A 77 excerpts], 170-187.

96. Strasberg, Lee, ed. Famous American Plays of the 1940's (Laurel Drama Series). New York: Dell, 1962. Camino Real (A 31), 127-227.

97. Yates, Richard. Eleven Kinds of Loneliness: Short Stories. Boston: Little, Brown, 1962. *[Blurb on dust-jacket.]

98. Yates, Richard. Revolutionary Road. New York: Bantam Books, 1962. [Blurb on cover.]

99. Vogue's Gallery. London: Condé Nast, 1962. "Man Bring This Up Road" (C 97), 172-184.

100. Bonazza, Blaxe O., and Emil Roy, eds. Studies in Drama, Form A. New York: Harper & Row, 1963. The Glass Menagerie (A 2), 279-333.

101. Cerf, Bennett, and Van H. Cartmell, eds. 24 Favorite One-Act Plays. New York: Dolphin Books, 1963. "27 Wagons Full of Cotton" (B 60), 119-146.

102. Gassner, John, ed. Best American Plays, Fifth Series, 1957-1963. New York: Crown, 1963. The Night of the Iguana (A 77), 55-104; Orpheus Descending (A 54), 509-551.

103. Gassner, John, and Morris Sweetkind, eds. Introducing the Drama. New York: Holt, Rinehart & Winston, 1963. The Glass Menagerie (A 2).

104. Hewes, Henry, ed. The Best Plays of 1962-1963 [...]. New York: Dodd, Mead, 1963. *The Milk Train Doesn't Stop Here Anymore: A Play in Two Acts [excerpts], 151-169.

105. Howes, Barbara, ed. Twenty-Three Modern Stories. New York: Vintage Books, 1963. "The Field of Blue Children" (A 36), 92-102.

106. Rehder, Jessie C., ed. The Story at Work: An Anthology. New York: Odyssey Press, 1963. "The Yellow Bird" (A 36), 327-335.

107. Weiss, Morton Jerome, ed. Ten Short Plays. New York: Dell, 1963. "The Case of the Crushed Petunias: A Lyrical Fantasy" (A 13), 31-53.

108. Williams, Edwina Dakin, as told to Lucy Freeman. Remember Me to Tom. New York: G. P. Putnam's Sons, 1963. *"I walk the path that," 40; "Look Both Ways Before Crossing Streets," 40-41; "Nature's Thanksgiving," 43; "Old Things," 43-44; "After a Visit" (C 19), 45-46; "Can a Good Wife Be a Good Sport?" (C 2), 47-48; "Sonnets for the Spring (A Sequence)" (B 12), 76-77; "Dear Silent Ghost...," 251; excerpts from story, 65-67; autobiography, 19, 26, 202; notes, 132-138, 140-141; letters and telegrams to family, 45, 52-53, 64, 71, 79-83, 89-96, 101-103, 109-112, 114-117, 119, 125-129, 141, 152-153, 158, 187, 195-196, 219, 224-230, 233-234, 242-247.

109. Windham, Donald. Emblems of Conduct. New York: Charles Scribner's Sons, 1963. *[Blurb on dust-jacket.]

110. Brown, Leonard, ed. A Quarto of Modern Literature, Fifth Edition. New York: Charles Scribner's Sons, 1964. The Glass Menagerie (A 2), 345-373.

111. Burnett, Whit, and Hallie Burnett, eds. The Modern Short Story in the Making. New York: Hawthorne Books, 1964. "The Important Thing" (A 36), 125-139.

112. Carruth, Hayden, and John Laughlin, eds. A New Directions Reader. New York: New Directions, 1964. "The Coming of Something to the Widow Holly" (A 64), 164-173.

113. Corrigan, Robert W., ed. The Modern Theatre. New York: Macmillan, 1964. The Glass Menagerie (A 2).

114. Corrigan, Robert W., and James L. Rosenberg, eds. The Art of the Theatre: A Critical Anthology of Drama. San Francisco: Chandler, 1964. The Rose Tattoo, "The Timeless World of a Play" (A 24), 475-568.

115. Gassner, John, and Ralph G. Allen, eds. Theatre and Drama in the Making. Boston: Houghton, Mifflin, 1964. "Portrait of a Girl in Glass" (A 36), 840-848.

116. Ogawa, Kazua, and Tatsumi Funatsu, eds. The Best American One-Act Plays. Tokyo: Kaibunsha, 1964. "Lord Byron's Love Letter" (A 32), 1-16.

117. Weiss, Samuel A., ed. Drama in the Modern World: Plays and Essays. Boston: D. C. Heath, 1964. The Glass Menagerie (A 2); "The Timeless World of a Play" (A 24).

118. Bloomfield, Morton W., and Robert C. Elliot, eds. Great Plays: Sophocles to Brecht. New York: Henry Holt, 1965. The Glass Menagerie (A 2).

119. Bowles, Jane, Two Serious Ladies. London: Peter Owen, 1965. *[Blurb on dust-jacket.]

120. Foley, Martha, ed. Fifty Best American Short Stories 1915-1965. Boston: Houghton, Mifflin, 1965. "Three Players of a Summer Game" (B 38), 466-487.

121. Frenz, Horst, ed. American Playwrights on Drama. New York: Hill & Wang, 1965. "On a Streetcar Named Success" (A 26), 63-67; "The Timeless World of a Play" (A 24), 84-88.

121a. Steffensen, James L., Jr., ed. Great Scenes from the World Theatre, Volume 1. New York: Avon, 1965. The Glass Menagerie [A 2 excerpts], 59-73, 91-93, 181-182, 308-313; Summer and Smoke [A 16 excerpt], 314-327; A Streetcar Named Desire [A 23 excerpts], 328-335, 518-527.

122. Bowles, Jane. The Collected Works of Jane Bowles. New York: Noonday, 1966. [Blurb on dust-jacket.]

123. Cohn, Ruby, and Bernard F. Dukore, eds. Twentieth Century Drama: England, Ireland, the United States. New York: Random House, 1966. The Glass Menagerie (A 2), 331-402.

124. McDowell, Roddy. Double Exposure. New York: Delacourte Press, 1966. *"Gore Vidal."

125. Cerf, Bennett, ed. Plays of Our Times. New York: Random House, 1967. A Streetcar Named Desire (A 23), 145-235.

126. Barnett, Sylvan, et al., eds. Tragedy and Comedy: An Anthology of Drama. Boston: Little, Brown, 1967. A Streetcar Named Desire (A 23), 281-368.

127. 20th Century Art Songs for Medium Voice and Piano: A Collection of Contemporary Songs for Recital and Study. New York: G. Schirmer, 1967. "Cabin" (A 6), 20-21.

128. Goldstone, Richard, ed. Contexts of the Drama. New York: McGraw-Hill, 1968. Summer and Smoke (A 16), 603-664.

129. Hollander, John, ed. American Short Stories since 1945 (Perennial Classics). New York: Harper, 1968. "The Mattress by the Tomato Patch" (A 64).

130. Rohrberger, Mary, et al., eds. An Introduction to Literature. New York: Random House, 1968. The Glass Menagerie (A 2), 886-948.

131. Sanders, Thomas E., ed. The Discovery of Drama. Glenview, Ill.: Scott, Foresman, 1968. Camino Real (A 31), 526-602.

132. Singer, Kurt, ed. Famous Short Stories, Volume 1. Minneapolis: T. S. Denison, 1968. "The Vengeance of Nitocris" (C 3).

132a. Sweetkind, Morris, ed. Ten Great One Act Plays (Bantam World Drama). New York: Bantam, 1968. "Something Unspoken" (A 32), 123-141.

133. Barnes, Clive, ed. 50 Best Plays of the American Theatre, Volume 3. New York: Crown, 1969. The Glass Menagerie (A 2), 137-174; A Streetcar Named Desire (A 23), 339-383.

134. Goldstone, Richard H., and Abraham H. Lass, eds. The Mentor Book of Short Plays. New York: New American Library, 1969. "Lord Byron's Love Letter" (A 32).

135. Lief, Leonard, and James F. Light, eds. The Modern Age: Literature. New York: Holt, Rinehart & Winston, 1969. Suddenly Last Summer (A 55).

136. Steen, Mike. A Look at Tennessee Williams. New York: Hawthorn Books, 1969. *Letters to Jessica Tandy, 179, 181.

137. Burnett, Whit, ed. America's 85 Greatest Living Authors Present: This Is My Best in the Third Quarter of the Century. Garden City, N.Y.: Doubleday, 1970. The Departure of Lord Byron: Letter to Whit Burnett, 649; Camino Real, Block 8 (A 31), 650-655.

138. Dean, Leonard F., ed. Twelve Great Plays. New York: Harcourt, Brace & World, 1970. The Glass Menagerie (A 2), 681-737.

139. Goodstone, Roy, ed. The Pulps: Fifty Years of American Pop Culture. New York: Chelsea House, 1970. "The Vengeance of Nitocris" (C 3), 167-172.

140. Olfson, Lewy, ed. 50 Great Scenes for Student Actors (Bantam World Drama). New York: Bantam Books, 1970. Orpheus Descending (A 54 excerpts). 39-44.

141. Perrine, Laurence, ed. Literature: Structure, Sound and Sense. New York: Harcourt, Brace & World, 1970. The Glass Menagerie (A 2), 1279-1332.

142. Richards, Stanley, ed. Best Plays of the Sixties. Garden City, N.Y.: Doubleday, 1970. The Night of the Iguana (A 77).

143. Shroyer, Frederick B., and Louis G. Gardemal, eds. Types of Drama. Glenville, Ill.: Scott, Foresman, 1970. The Glass Menagerie (A 2), 511-599.

144. Cox, R. David, and Shirley S. Cox, eds. Themes in the One-Act Play. New York: McGraw-Hill, 1971. "Something Unspoken" (A 32), 167-179.

145. Garrett, George P., et al, eds. Film Scripts One. New York: Appleton-Century-Crofts, 1971. *A Streetcar Named Desire, 330-484.

146. Richards, Stanley, ed. The Best Short Plays 1971 (Margaret Mayorga Series). Philadelphia: Chilton Books, 1971. "I Can't Imagine Tomorrow" (A 126), 75-95.

147. Smith, Margarita G., ed. The Mortgaged Heart [by] Carson McCullers. Boston: Houghton, Mifflin, 1971. *"Praise to Assenting Angels" [excerpts], xii-xiii, xvii-xix.

148. Guernsey, Otis L., Jr., ed. *The Best Plays of 1971-1972 [...].* New York: Dodd, Mead, 1972. *Small Craft Warnings: A Play in Two Acts* [A 135 excerpts], 276-290.

149. Cohen, Lorraine, ed. *Scenes for Young Actors* (Discus Book). New York: Avon Books, 1973. *Summer and Smoke* [A 16 excerpts], 17-22, 349-353.

150. Foley, Martha, ed. *The Best American Short Stories 1973 [...].* Boston: Houghton, Mifflin, 1973. "Happy August 10th" (C 137), 276-288.

151. Perrine, Laurence, ed. *Dimensions of Drama.* New York: Harcourt, Brace, Jovanovich, 1973. *The Glass Menagerie* (B 141), 425-478.

152. Richards, Stanley, ed. *Best Short Plays of the World Theatre 1968-1973.* New York: Crown, 1973. "Confessional" (A 126), 1-21.

153. Simonson, Harold P., ed. *Quartet: A Book of Stories, Plays, Poems, and Critical Essays*, Second Edition. New York: Harper & Row, 1973. *The Glass Menagerie* (A 2), 457-513.

154. Young, Ian, ed. *The Male Muse: A Gay Anthology.* Trumansburg, N.Y.: Crossing Press, 1973. "The Interior of the Pocket" (A 42), 107-108.

155. *Esquire: The Best of Forty Years.* New York: David McKay, 1973. "A Perfect Analysis Given by a Parrot: A Play in One Act" (C 145), 269-272.

156. Bradley, Sculley, et al., eds. *The American Tradition in Literature*, Fourth Edition (Norton Anthology). New York: Grosset & Dunlap, 1974. *The Glass Menagerie* (A 2), 1090-1146.

157. Carr, Virginia Spencer. *The Lonely Hunter: A Biography of Carson McCullers.* Garden City, N.Y.: Doubleday, 1975. *"Some Words Before," xvii-xix.

157a. Pickering, Jerry V., ed. *A Treasury of Drama, Classical through Modern.* St. Paul, Minn.: West, 1975. *The Glass Menagerie* (A 2), 417-485.

158. Bowles, Jane. *Feminine Wiles.* Santa Barbara: Black Sparow, 1976. "Foreword," 7-8.

159. Dukore, Bernard, ed. *17 Plays: Sophocles to Baraka.* New York: Thomas Y. Crowell, 1976. *The Night of the Iguana* (A 77), 698-771.

160. Miller, Jordan Y., ed. The Heath Introduction to Drama [...]. Lexington, Mass.: D. C. Heath, 1976. The Glass Menagerie (A 2), 727-783.

161. Bain, Carl E., et al., eds. The Norton Introduction to Literature, Second Edition. New York: W. W. Norton, 1977. The Glass Menagerie (A 2), 1176-1234; "The Long Goodbye" (A 32), 1235-1247.

162. Kleinberg, Seymour, ed. The Other Persuasion: An Anthology of Short Fiction about Gay Men and Women. New York: Vintage Books, 1977. "Two on a Party" (A 64), 175-194.

163. Richards, Stanley, ed. The Tony Winners: A Collection of Ten Exceptional Plays, Winners of the Tony Award for the Most Distinguished Play of the Year. Garden City, N.Y.: Doubleday, 1977. The Rose Tattoo (A 24), 111-214.

164. Shaw, Patrick W., ed. Literature: A College Anthology. Boston: Houghton, Mifflin, 1977. The Glass Menagerie (A 2), 859-910.

165. 14 Great Plays. London: William Heinemann / Octopus Books, 1977. A Streetcar Named Desire (A 18), 547-625.

166. Abcarian, Richard, and Marvin Klotz, eds. Literature: The Human Experience, Second Edition. New York: St. Martin's Press, 1978. The Glass Menagerie (A 2), 211-264.

167. Beurdeley, Cecile, ed. L'Amour Bleu. New York: Rizzoli, 1978. Memoirs [excerpt], 291.

168. Forkner, Benjamin, and Patrick Samway, eds. Stories of the Modern South. New York: Bantam Books, 1978. "The Yellow Bird" (A 36), 408-415.

168a. Handman, Wynn, ed. Modern American Scenes for Student Actors (Bantam / American Place Theatre). New York: Bantam, 1978. A Streetcar Named Desire [A 23 excerpt], 141-151; Orpheus Descending [A 54 excerpt], 267-270.

169. Hine, Daryl, and Joseph Parisi, eds. The Poetry Anthology 1912-1977: Sixty-Five Years of America's Most Distinguished Verse Magazine. Boston: Houghton, Mifflin, 1978. "My Love Was Light" (C 28), 183.

170. Leavitt, Richard F., ed. The World of Tennessee Williams. New York: G. P. Putnam's Sons, 1978. *"Introduction," 9-10; "Of Roses," 21; "An Appreciation" (C 37), 57; "Little Horse" (A 42), 74; "Author's Note" [to Sweet Bird of Youth], 114; letters, postcards, and telegrams, 38, 40-41, 47, 49, 52, 67, 77 (B 136), 82, 85, 118, 146 (C 127),

151; painting, 64a.
Review: Library Journal, 103 (15 November 1978), 2330: Larry Earl Bone.

171. Richardson, Stanley, ed. Twenty One Act Plays: An Anthology for Amateur Performing Groups (Dolphin Books). Garden City, N.Y.: Doubleday, 1978. "Portrait of a Madonna" (A 32), 61-79.

172. Scholes, Robert, ed. Elements of Literature: Essay, Fiction, Poetry, Drama, Film. New York: Oxford University Press, 1978. Cat on a Hot Tin Roof (A 145), 1147-1229.

173. Allison, Alexander W., et al., eds. Masterpieces of the Drama, Fourth Edition. New York: Macmillan, 1979. The Glass Menagerie (A 2), 823-858.

174. Kennedy, X. J., ed. Literature: An Introduction to Fiction, Poetry, and Drama, Second Edition. Boston: Little, Brown, 1979. The Glass Menagerie (A 2).

C. WORKS IN PERIODICALS†

Published under some variant of the name Thomas Lanier Williams

1. *"Demon Smoke." Junior-Life Year Book. St. Louis: Ben Blewett Junior High School, 1925.

2. *"Can a Good Wife Be a Good Sport?" Smart Set, 80 (May 1927), 9, 13.

3. *"The Vengeance of Nitocris." Weird Tales, 12 (August 1928), 253-260, 280.

4. *"A Day at the Olympics." U. City Pep, 9 (30 October 1928), 5.

5. *"The Tomb of the Capuchins." U. City Pep, 9 (12 November 1928), 2, 5.

6. *"A Night in Venice." U. City Pep, 9 (20 December 1928), 2, 4.

7. *"A Trip to Monte Carlo." U. City Pep, 9 (16 January 1929), 2.

8. *"The Ruins of Pompeii." U. City Pep, 9 (5 February 1929), 2.

9. *"A Tour of the Battle-fields of France." U. City Pep, 9 (19 February 1929), 2.

10. *"A Festival Night in Paris." U. City Pep, 9 (5 March 1929), 2.

11. *"The Amalfi Drive and Sorrento." U. City Pep, 9 (19 March 1929), 2.

12. *"The First Day Out." U. City Pep, 9 (16 April 1929), 2.

13. *"A Lady's Beaded Bag." Columns, 1 (May 1930), 11-12.

14. *Letter to the Editor: "Dictator of Fashion Comments in Style."

---

†Arranged chronologically.
*Denotes the first publication of a work or a major revision.

Link (Gamma Rho chapter of Alpha Tau Omega), August 1932.

15. *"October Song." Neophyte, 1 (Christmas-New Year 1932-1933), 36.

16. *"Under the April Rain." Inspiration, 2 (Spring 1933), page unnumbered.

17. *"Modus Vivendi." Counterpoint, 1 (July 1933), 11.

18. *"Ave Atque Vale." Alouette, 4 (October 1933), 201.

19. *"After a Visit"; "Cacti." Voices, 77 (August-September 1934), 40.

20. *"After a Visit" (C 19). Literary Digest, 118 (1 September 1934), 23.

21. *"Singer of Darkness." St. Louis Star Times, 26 March 1936.

22. *"Twenty-Seven Wagons Full of Cotton." Manuscript, 3 (August 1936), 25-28.

23. *Two Metaphysical Sonnets: "The Mind Does Not Forget"; "Le Coeur A Ses Raisons." Eliot (Washington University), 4 (December 1936), 19.

24. *"Lyric"; "Clover"; "Lament." College Verse, 6 (January 1937), 59-61.

25. *"Swimmer and Fish Group." College Verse, 6 (March 1937), 100-101.

26. *"Inheritors." College Verse, 6 (April 1937), 127-130.

27. *"Sacre de Printemps." College Verse, 6 (May 1937), 158-159.

28. *The Shuttle: "This Hour"; "My Love Was Light." Poetry, 50 (June 1937), 142-143.

Published under the name Tennessee Williams

29. *"The Field of Blue Children." Story, 15 (September-October 1939), 66-72.

30. *"The Kitchen Door Blues." Maryland Quarterly, 2 (1944), 58-59.

31. *"The Malediction." Town and Country, 100 (June 1945), 66-67, 114-119.

32. *"Everyman." Contemporary Poetry, 5 (Summer 1945), 4.

33. *"The Important Thing." Story, 27 (November-December 1945), 17-25.

34. *"Something about Him." Mademoiselle, 23 (June 1946), 168-169, 235-239.

35. *"A Liturgy of Roses." Chicago Review, 1 (Summer 1946), 163-166.

36. *"Which Is My Little Boy?" Experiment, 2 (Fall 1946), 161.

37. *"An Appreciation" [Laurette Taylor]. New York Times, 15 December 1946, sec. 2, p. 4.

38. *"The Yellow Bird." Town and Country, 101 (June 1947), 40-41, 102-107.

39. *"On a Streetcar Named Success." New York Times, 30 November 1947. sec. 2, pp. 1,3.

40. *"My Current Reading." Saturday Review of Literature, 31 (6 March 1948), 26.

41. *"The Catastrophe of Success" (C 39 rev.). Story, 32 (Spring 1948), 67-72.

42. *Letter to the Editor [reply to Sidney Carroll]. Esquire, 29 (May 1948), 46.

43. *"A Movie Called 'La Terra Trema'" [by Luchino Visconti]. '48 Magazine, June 1948.

44. *"Testa dell'Efebo" [sic]. Harper's Bazaar, 82 (August 1948), 172.

45. *"Questions without Answers." New York Times, 3 October 1948, sec. 2, pp. 1, 3.

46. *"Rubio y Morena." Partisan Review, 15 (December 1948), 1293-1306.

47. *"An Appreciation" [Hans Hofmann]. Derrière le Miroir, 16 (January 1949), 5.

48. *"Tuesday's Child." Partisan Review, 16 (April 1949), 367.

49. *"The Harp of Wales." Prairie Schooner, 23 (1949), 330.

50. *"The Christus of Guadalajara"; "The Stonecutter's Angels." Botteghe Obscura, 4 (1949), 335-339.

51. A Streetcar Named Desire (A 11). London Evening Standard, 24 October-November 1949.

52. *"An Allegory of Man and His Sahara" [review of Paul Bowles's The Sheltering Sky]. New York Times Book Review, 4 December 1949, pp. 7, 38.

53. *"Something Wild...." New York Star, about 1949.

54. *Poem(s). Panorama, date not verified.

55. *Poem(s). Semi-Colon, date not verified.

56. *"The Resemblance between a Violin Case and a Coffin." Flair, 1 (February 1950), 40-41, 126-128.

56a. *"What I Look For in a Film: A Symposium." Films in Review, 1 (March 1950), 1-2.

57. "Which Is My Little Boy?" (C 36). Mademoiselle, 31 (July 1950), 67.

58. *"A Writer's Quest for a Parnassus." New York Times Magazine, 13 August 1950, pp. 16, 35.

59. *Letter to the Editor [Oliver Evans, José García Villa]. Saturday Review of Literature, 33 (19 August 1950), 24.

60. The Glass Menagerie (A 2). New York Post Magazine, 1 October 1950, pp. 7-13.

61. *"The Human Psyche--Alone" [review of Paul Bowles's The Delicate Prey]. Saturday Review of Literature, 33 (23 December 1950), 19-20.

62. "The Glass Menagerie" [synopsis of film; not written by Williams]. Screen Hits Annual, 5 (1950), 46-50.

63. *"Concerning the Timeless World of a Play." New York Times, 14 January 1951, sec. 2, pp. 1, 3.

64. *["The Meaning of The Rose Tattoo."] Vogue, 117 (15 March 1951), 96.

65. *Seven Poems: "Orpheus Descending"; "Faint as Leaf Shadow" (B 29); "Across the Space"; Two Early Poems ["I confess I cannot guess"; "I am an exile here, some other land"]; "Descent"; "Carrousel Tune (from Camino Real)." Voices, 149 (September-December 1952), 5-11.

66. "This Property Is Condemned" (B 2, A 3). Perspectives USA, 1 (January 1952), 95-105.

67. "The Field of Blue Children" (C 29, A 12). Housewife, 14 (October 1952), 38, 83-86.

68. *"Three Players of a Summer Game." New Yorker, 28 (1 November 1952), 27-36.

69. *"On the 'Camino Real.'" New York Times, 15 March 1953, sec. 2, pp. 1, 3.

70. "The Long Stay Cut Short, or The Unsatisfactory Supper" (B 10, A 13). Perspectives USA, 8 (Summer 1954), 104-114.

71. *"The Vine." Mademoiselle, 39 (July 1954), 25-30, 93.

72. "Camino Real: Foreword... and Afterword" (A 31). Theatre Arts, 38 (August 1954), 34-35.

73. "The Complete Text of Camino Real" (A 31). Theatre Arts, (August 1954), 36-64.

74. *"The Mattress by the Tomato Patch." London Magazine, 1 (October 1954), 16-24.

75. *"Person-to-Person." New York Times, 20 March 1955, sec. 2, pp. 1, 3.

76. "Three Players of a Summer Game" (C 68, A 34). Perspectives USA, 11 (Spring 1955), 15-39.

77. *"Critic Says 'Evasion,' Writer Says 'Mystery.'" New York Herald Tribune, 17 April 1955.

78. "The Timeless World of a Play" (A 24). Theatre Arts, 39 (May 1955), 32-33, 96.

79. "The Complete Text of The Rose Tattoo" (A 24). Theatre Arts, 39 (May 1955), 34-64.

80. *Comment: "American Playwrights Self-Appraisals." Saturday Review, 38 (3 September 1955), 18-19.

81. *Letter to the Editor [reply to Arthur B. Waters]. Theatre Arts, 39 (October 1955), 3.

81a. *Comment on Film. Film en Roman de Kim, 6/7 (1956), 14.

82. *"Part of a Hero." London Magazine, 3 (February 1956), 16-17.

83. *Letter to the Editor: "A Tribute from Tennessee Williams to 'Heroic Tallulah Bankhead.'" New York Times, 4 March 1956, sec. 2, p. 3.
Review: Theatre Arts, 40 (June 1956), 11.

84. "The Field of Blue Children" (C 29, A 12). Dude, 1 (August 1956), 38-40, 66-67.

85. *"On Meeting a Young Writer" [Françoise Sagan]. Harper's Bazaar, 90 (August 1956), 124.

86. *Letter to the Editor [reply to Charles Thomas Samuels]. Syracuse Review, 2 (January 1957), 19.

87. *"Tennessee Williams on the Past, the Present and the Perhaps." New York Times, 17 March 1957, sec. 2, pp. 1, 3.

88. *"The World I Live In." London Observer, 7 April 1957, p. 14.

89. "The Complete Text of Cat on a Hot Tin Roof" (A 38). Theatre Arts, 41 (June 1957), 33-71.

90. *"Author and Director: A Delicate Situation." Playbill, 1 (30 September 1957), 9-13.

91. *"The Writing Is Honest" [preface to William Inge's The Dark at the Top of the Stairs]. New York Times, 16 March 1958, sec. 2, pp. 1, 3.

92. "Complete Text of Orpheus Descending" (A 54). Theatre Arts, 42 (September 1958), 26-55.

93. *"A Perfect Analysis Given by a Parrot: A Play in One Act." Esquire, 50 (October 1958), 131-134.

94. *"The Enemy: Time--The One-Act Play Which Became Sweet Bird of Youth." Theatre, 1 (March 1959), 14-17.

95. *"Williams' Wells of Violence." New York Times, 8 March 1959, sec. 2, pp. 1, 3.

96. *Sweet Bird of Youth. Esquire, 51 (April 1959), 114-155.

97. *"Man Bring This Up Road." Mademoiselle, 49 (July 1959), 56-61, 102.

98. *"Reflections on a Revival of a Controversal Fantasy" [Camino Real]. New York Times, 15 May 1960, sec. 2, pp. 1, 3.

99. *"Tennessee Williams Presents His POV" [reply to Marya Mannes]. New York Times Magazine, 12 June 1960, pp. 19, 78.
Response: 26 June 1960, p. 16; 7 August 1960, p. 2.

100. *"Prelude to a Comedy." New York Times, 6 November 1960, sec. 2, pp. 1, 3.

101. *Period of Adjustment (or High Point Is Built on a Cavern: A Serious Comedy). Esquire, 54 (December 1960), 210-276.

102. *"Five Fiery Ladies" [Anna Magnani, Vivien Leigh, Geraldine Page, Katharine Hepburn, Elizabeth Taylor]. Life, 50 (3 February 1961), 84-89.

103. *[Blurb on James Purdy's Color of Darkness]. Paris Review, 26 (Summer-Fall 1961), 176.

104. *"The Author" [Carson McCullers]. Saturday Review, 44 (23 September 1961), 14-15.

105. "The Roman Spring of Mrs. Stone: Script Extract" [written by Gavin Lambert]. Films and Filming, 8 (October 1961), 20-21, 38.

106. *"A Summer of Discovery." New York Herald Tribune, 24 December 1961.

107. *The Night of the Iguana. Esquire, 57 (February 1962), 47-62, 115-130.

108. *"The Agent as Catalyst" [Audrey Wood]. Esquire, 58 (December 1962), 216, 260.

109. *Letter to the Editor [Eugene O'Neill and Edward Albee; reply to quotation, Newsweek, 4 February 1963, p. 5]. Newsweek, 61 (18 February 1963), 6.

110. "The Vengeance of Nitocris" (C 3). Gamma, 1 (1963), 27-38.

111. *"T. Williams's View of T. Bankhead." New York Times, 29 December 1963, sec. 2, pp. 1, 3.

112. *"Mama's Old Stucco House." Esquire, 62 (January 1965), 87-90.

113. "Man Bring This Up Road: A Short Story" (C 97). International (London), 1 (Spring 1965), 61-65.

114. "Mama's Old Stucco House" (C 112). London Weekend Telegraph, 7 May 1965, pp. 49-54.

115. The Night of the Iguana (A 85). Plays and Players, 12 (May 1965, June 1965).

116. *Slapstick Tragedy: Two Plays: "Preface"; I. "The Mutilated"; II. "The Gnädiges Fräulein." Esquire, 64 (August 1965), 96-102, 130-134.

117. *"The Wolf and I." New York Times, 20 February 1966, sec. 2, pp. 1, 5.

118. *"I Can't Imagine Tomorrow: A Play in One Act." Esquire, 65 (March 1966), 76-79.

119. "Gore Vidal" (B 124). McCall's, 94 (October 1966), 107.

120. "'Grand'" (A 93). Esquire, 66 (November 1966), 136, 158.

121. *"Kingdom of Earth: A One-Act Play." Esquire, 67 (February 1967), 98-100, 132-134.

122. *"Concerning Eugene O'Neill." Center Theatre Group of Ahmanson's Theatre's Inaugural Season Program, 12 September 21 October 1967, p. 9.

123. *"Young Men Waking at Daybreak." Evergreen Review, 50 (December 1967), 29.

124. "I Rise in Flame, Cried the Phoenix: A Play about D. H. Lawrence" (A 25). Ramparts, 6 (January 1968), 14-19.

125. *"Happiness Is Relevant' to Mr. Williams." New York Times, 24 March 1968, sec. 2, pp. 1, 3.

126. *"'Tennessee, Never Talk to an Actress.'" New York Times, 4 May 1969, sec. 2, pp. 1, 16.

127. *"Tennessee Williams Talks about His Play 'In the Bar of a Tokyo Hotel'" [letter used in advertisement]. New York Times, 14 May 1969, p. 36.

128. *"Crepe de Chine." New Yorker, 45 (5 July 1969), 28.

129. *"A Recluse and His Guest." Playboy, 17 (January 1970), 101-102, 124, 244.

130. "Man Bring This Up Road" (C 97, A 113). Mayfair, 2 (June 1970), 24-25, 64-67.

131. *Letter to the Editor: "An Open Response to Tom Buckley." Atlantic, 227 (January 1971), 34-35.

132. *"What's Next on the Agenda, Mr. Williams?" Mediterranean Review, 1 (Winter 1971), 15-19.

133. *"Tangier: The Speechless Summer." Antaeus, 1 (Summer 1970), 43-45.

134. *"The Demolition Downtown: A One-Act Play." Esquire, 75 (June 1971), 124-127, 152.

135. *"Happy August the Tenth." Antaeus, 4 (Winter 1971), 22-33.

136. *"We Are Dissenters Now." Harper's Bazaar, 105 (January 1972), 40-41.

137. *"Survival Notes: A Journal." Esquire, 78 (September 1972), 130-134, 166-168.

138. "Happy August the 10th" (C 135). Esquire, 78 (December 1972), 256-260.

139. *Letter to the Editor [on Dr. Max Jacobson]. New York Times, 12 December 1972, p. 46.

140. *"Homage to Key West." Harper's Bazaar, 106 (January 1973), 50-51.

141. "Survival Notes: A Journal" (C 137). London Times Saturday Review, 20 January 1973, pp. 8-9.

142. *"The Inventory at Fontana Bella." Playboy, 20 (March 1973), 77-78, 172.

143. *"Let Me Hang It All Out." New York Times, 4 March 1973, sec. 2, pp. 1, 3.

144. *"To William Inge: An Homage." New York Times, 1 July 1973, sec. 2, pp. 1, 8.

145. *"Miss Puma, Miss Who?" Antaeus, 11 (Autumn 1973), 23-24.

146. "A Perfect Analysis Given by a Parrot: A Play in One Act" (C 93). Esquire, 80 (October 1973), 288-290, 486-488.

147. *"Miss Coynte of Greene." Playboy, 20 (December 1973), 184-188, 198, 237-240.

148. *"Sabbatha and Solitude." Playgirl, 1 (September 1973), 49-51, 122-124, 129.

149. *"Red Part of a Flag, or Oriflamme." Vogue, 163 (March 1974), 124, 158-159.

150. "Born Forty Years Too Soon" [A 150 excerpts]. Vogue, 165 (November 1975), 193-195, 232-238.

150a. "W. H. Auden: A Few Reminiscences." Harvard Advocate, 108 ii-iii (1975), 59.

151. *Statement to Clive Barnes: "The Arts in America." New York Times, 29 August 1976, sec. 2, p. 16.

152. *"'I Have Rewritten a Play for Artistic Purity'" [The Eccentricities of a Nightingale]. New York Times, 21 November 1976, sec. 2, pp. 1, 5.

153. *Letter to the Editor [reply to Andrew Dvosin]. Gay Sunshine, 31 (Winter 1977), 26.

154. *"Mother Yaws: A Story." Esquire, 87 (May 1977), 78-80, 154-155.

155. *"I Am Widely Regarded as the Ghost of a Writer.'" New York Times, 8 May 1977, sec. 2, pp. 3, 20.

156. *"Androgyne, Mon Amour." Ambit, 69 (1977), 2-3.

157. *"Candida: A College Essay." Shaw Review, 20 (May 1977), 60-62.

158. *Letter to the Editor: "Tennessee Williams--Donald Windham." New York Times Book Review, 15 January 1978, pp. 14, 18.

159. *"The Killer Chicken and the Closet Queen." Christopher Street, 3 (July 1978), 17-26.

160. "A Playwrights' [sic] Choice of 'Perfect' Plays." New York Times, 14 January 1979, sec. 2, p. 10.

[NOTE: Two short plays, "Life-Boat Drill" and "Stopped Rocking," as well as a screenplay, "One Arm," may have been published 1977-1978, but the author can find no record for any of them.]

D. RECORDINGS

1. Tennessee Williams Reading from The Glass Menagerie, The Yellow Bird, and Five Poems. Caedmon Records, 1952. 2 sides. On record: Tennessee Williams Reading from His Works (recorded in New York on June 6, 1952). "Facts About Me," on cover.

   *The Glass Menagerie, opening monologue and closing scenes (A 2); "Cried the Fox" (B 7); "The Eyes" (B 20); "The Summer Belvedere" (B 7); Some Poems Meant for Music: "Which Is My Little Boy?" (C 57); "Little Horse"; "Gold Tooth Blues"; "Kitchen Door Blues" (C 30); "Heavenly Grass" (A 4); "My Little One"; "The Yellow Bird" (A 12 rev.).

2. Songs by American Composers. Strand Records, 1962. Side 411 B. On record: Songs of American Composers.

   Blue Mountain Ballads (A 4-7), sung by Donald Gramn, accompanied by Richard Cumming.

3. The Glass Menagerie. Caedmon Records, 1964. 4 sides.

   Play (A 2, K 23). Notes by Tennessee Williams and William Inge in container; note by John Gassner on cover.

4. Tennessee Williams Reads Hart Crane. Caedmon Records, 1965. 2 sides. On record: The Poems of Hart Crane.

   *[Note on Hart Crane], on cover.

5. The Rose Tattoo. Caedmon Records, 1967. 6 sides.

   Play (A 24, K 53); "Facts About Me" (D-1); Robert W. Corrigan, "The World of Tennessee Williams," in container.

6. A Streetcar Named Desire. Caedmon Records, 1973. 6 sides.

   Play (A 23, K 61). Note by Marianne Mantell on cover.

7. Tennessee Williams' A Streetcar Named Desire. Mark 56, 1974. 2 sides.

   Reproduction of 4 April 1948 radio broadcast presenting New York Drama Critics' Circle Award to Williams, followed by scenes from the original production.

E. TRANSLATIONS

ARABIC

1. [The Glass Menagerie.] Trans. Al-Hute. Cairo: United Association of Publishers, n. d. 154 p.

2. [A Streetcar Named Desire.] Trans. Abdul-Azis Metri Abdul-Malek. Cairo: Cooperative Association for Printing and Publishing, n. d. 245 p.

3. [The Rose Tattoo.] Trans. Lila Al-Haft. Beirut: Library of Education, 1960. 104 p.

4. [Summer and Smoke.] Trans. Abdul-Qader Al-Qutt. Cairo: Library of Egypt, 1961. 187 p.

5. [Cat on a Hot Tin Roof.] Trans. Abdul-Haleen Bashlawee. Cairo: Library of Egypt, n. d. 162 p.

6. [The Night of the Iguana.] Trans. Fahmi Fawzi Farag. Cairo: Anglo-Egyptian Bookshop, 1961. 184 p.

BENGALI

7. Hridayer Rita [Summer and Smoke]. Trans. Shamsur Rahman. N. p.: n. d. 148 p.

8. [A Streetcar Named Desire.] Calcutta: Mitralaya, 1966. 160 p.

CHINESE

9. [The Glass Menagerie.] Hong Kong: World Today Press, 1966. 101 p.

10. [The Rose Tattoo.] N. p.: n. d. 125 p.

11. [Sweet Bird of Youth.] Trans. Chang Shih. Taipei: Buffalo Book Company, 1969.

12. [Theater: A Streetcar Named Desire, trans. Lin Ke Tuan; Orpheus Descending, trans. Liao Hwei-mei.] Taipei: 1970.

CZECH

13. Skleneny zverinec (The Glass Menagerie): Hra o dvou dílech (osmi obrazech). Trans. Ota Ornest. Prague: Dilia, 1960.

14. Sestup Orfeův [Orpheus Descending]. Prague: Orbis, 1962. 113 p.

15. Léto a dým [Summer and Smoke]. Trans. Hana Budínova. Prague: Orbis, 1964. 106 p.

16. Tetovaná ruze [The Rose Tattoo]. Trans. Hana Budínova. Prague: Orbis, 1964. 105 p.

17. Tři Hráči jedné letní hry [Cat on a Hot Tin Roof]. Svetová, 6 (1964), 106-118.

18. Rímska jar pani Stoneovej [The Roman Spring of Mrs. Stone]. Trans. J. Z. Novák. Revue Svetovej Literatury, 2 (August 1965), 68-104.

19. 7 X [one-act plays]. Prague: Orbis, 1966. 133 p.

20. Rímska jar pani Stoneovej [see E 18] (Edice Ilustrovanych Novel). Prague: Spisovatel, 1966. 133 p.

21. Sladké ptáce mládí [Sweet Bird of Youth]. Trans. Luba and Redolf Pellarovi. Prague: Delia, 1960.

DANISH

22. Den Tatoverende Rose [The Rose Tattoo]. Trans. Holger Bech. Copenhagen: Fremad, 1951. 95 p.

23. Mrs. Stones Romerske Porar [The Roman Spring of Mrs. Stone]. Trans. Aage Dons. Copenhagen: Fremad, 1951. 156 p.

24. "Tre Kroketspillere" ["Three Players of a Summer Game"]. Trans. Ole Storm. Modern Amerikanske Noveller. Copenhagen: Thaming & Appels, 1954.

25. Engleni Alkoven, og Ti Andre Noveller [One Arm]. Trans. Aage Dons. Copenhagen: Fremad, 1956. 177 p.

26. Mrs. Stones Romerske Porar [see E 23]. Copenhagen: Vintens Forlag, 1965. 149 p.

27. Glassmenageriet [The Glass Menagerie]. Trans. Knud Sønderby. Odense: Gyldendals Teater, 1966. 97 p.

DUTCH

28. De Romeinse Lente von Mrs. Stone [The Roman Spring of Mrs. Stone]. Trans. Max Schuchart. Amsterdam: Salamander, 1951. 195 p.

29. "Drie Spelers van een Zomerspel" ["Three Players of a Summer Game"]. Amerikaans Cultureel Perspectief. Ultrecht: W. De Haan, 1954. Pp. 45-72.

30. "Het Veld de Blauve Kinderen" ["The Field of Blue Children"]. Zo Begonnen Ze. Amsterdam: T. M. Meulenhoft, 1964. pp. 178-188.

31. Eeen Kwestie van Aanpassen of Voorstadje Boven een Grot [Period of Adjustment]. Baarn: Hollandia, n. d. 90 p.

FINNISH

32. Mrs. Stonen Rooman-Kevät [The Roman Spring of Mrs. Stone]. Trans. Jorma Partanen. Jyväskylä: K. J. Gummerus Osakeyhtiö, 1952. 1952 p.

FRENCH

33. Un tramway nommé Désir [A Streetcar Named Desire]. Trans. Paule de Beaumont; adapted by Jean Cocteau. Paris: Bordas, 1949. 218 p. il.

34. Le printemps romain de Mrs. Stone [The Roman Spring of Mrs. Stone]. Trans. Jean & Jacques Tournier. La Table Ronde, 44 (August 1951); 45 (September 1951).

35. Le printemps romain de Mrs. Stone [see E 34]. Paris: Plon, 1951. 196 p. (Limited and trade editions.)

36. La rose tatouée [The Rose Tattoo]. Trans. Paule de Beaumont. Les Oeuvres Libres, 87 (1953), 225-312.

37. La rose tatouée [see E 36]. France Illustration Supplément, 136 (August 1953), 1-32.

38. Eté et fumées [Summer and Smoke]. Trans. Paule de Beaumont. Paris Theatre, 8 (January 1954), 15-49.

39. "Un long séjour interrompu, ou Les suites d'un mauvais dîner" ["A Long Stay Cut Short"]. Profils, 8 (Summer 1954), 92-104.

40. "Les joueurs de l'été" ["Three Players of a Summer Game"]. Profils, 11 (Spring 1955), 58-82.

41. "Je renais dans les flammes, criat le phénix: Pièce sur D. H. Lawrence" ["I Rise in Flames, Cried the Phoenix"]. Trans. Benoît Braun. Les Oeuvres Libres, 122 (1956), 3-20.

42. La chatte sur un toit brulant [Cat on a Hot Tin Roof]. Trans. André Obey. Paris Theatre, 11 (1958), 19-50.

43. Théâtre [The Rose Tattoo (see E 36); The Glass Menagerie, trans. Marcel Duhamel; A Streetcar Named Desire, trans. Paule de Beaumont; Cat on a Hot Tin Roof (see E 42); Summer and Smoke (see E 38)]. Paris: Robert Laffont, 1958. 656 p.

44. La descente d'Orphée [Orpheus Descending]. Trans. Raymond Rouleau. Les Oeuvres Libres, 158 (1959), 155-244.

45. La descente d'Orphée [see E 44]. L'Avant Scène, 200 (1 July 1959), 8-33.

46. La descente d'Orphée [see E 44]. Paris: Avant-Scène, 1959. 46 p. il.

47. Le cri du phoenix: Un acte traduit par F. J. Temple avec des illus. orignales d'Arthur Secunda ["I Rise in Flame, Cried the Phoenix"]. Montpellier: Licorne, 1960. 38 p. ils. (Limited edition.)

48. La statue mutilée (One Arm): Nouvelles. Trans. Maurice Pons. Paris: Robert Laffont, 1960. 272 p.

49. Bosquet, Alain, ed. Trente-cinq jeunes poètes américains ["The Man in the Dining Car," "Life Story," in English and French; autobiographical note by Williams]. Paris: Gallimard, 1960. Pp. 250-251, 448.

50. Théâtre II [Orpheus Descending (E 44); Suddenly Last Summer, "Portrait of a Madonna," "This Property Is Condemned," trans. Jacques Guicharnaud; "Talk to Me Like the Rain," trans. Robert Postec; Baby Doll, "The Long Stay Cut Short," "27 Wagons Full of Cotton," trans. Jacques Guicharnaud]. Paris: Robert Laffont, 1962. 468 p.

51. Le printemps romain de Mrs. Stone (E 35). Lausanne: Guild du Livre, 1963.

52. Un tramway nommé Désir, suivi de La chatte sur un toit brûlant (E 43). Paris: Livre de Poche, 1963. 431 p.

53. Le printemps romain de Mrs. Stone: Roman (E 35). Paris: Livre de Poche, 1964. 190 p.

54. Dans l'hiver des villes: Poèmes ["The Eyes," "Faint as Leaf Shadow," "Orpheus Descending," "Pulse," "The Angels of

Fructification," "Those Who Ignore the Appropriate Time of Their Going," "The Summer Belvedere," "Cortege," "Part of a Hero," "Intimations," "Life Story" (E 49), "The Man in the Dining Car" (E 49), "The Death Embrace," in English and French]. Trans. Renaud de Jouvenel. Paris: Pierre Seghers, 1964. 87 p.

55. Sucre d'orge: Nouvelles [Hard Candy]. Trans. Bernard Willerval. Paris: Robert Laffont, 1964. 236 p.
Reviews: Langues Modernes, 58 (May-June 1964), 267-270: Pierre Dommergues. Pourquoi Pas, 2375 (5 June 1964), 137-139: Fernand Denis.

56. "Homme monté ça par chemin" ["Man Bring This Up Road"]. Trans. Henri Robillot. Revue de Poche, 5 (September 1965), 3-21.

57. La quête du chevalier: Nouvelles [The Knightly Quest]. Trans. Henriette de Sarbois. Paris: Robert Laffont, 1968. 232 p.

58. La statue mutilée (One Arm): Nouvelles [see E 48]. Paris: Livre de Poche, 1970.

59. Théâtre III [Sweet Bird of Youth, trans. Maurice Pons; The Night of the Iguana. trans, Marcel Aymé]. Paris: Robert Laffont, 1972. 293 p.

60. Théâtre IV [The Milk Train Doesn't Stop Here Anymore, trans. Michel Arnaud; Kingdom of Earth, trans. Matthieu Galey]. Paris: Robert Laffont, 1972. 293 p.

61. Baby Doll (Scénario) [see E 50]. Paris: Livre de Poche, 1972. 189 p.

62. Une femme nommé Moïse [Moise and the World of Reason]. Trans. Francis Ledoux. Paris: Robert Laffont, 1976. 198 p.

62a. La menagerie de verre (Glass Menagerie) [see E 43]. Paris: Librarie Théâtrale, 1977(?). 104 p.

63. Un tramway nommé Désir [see E 43]. Paris: Librarie Théâtrale, 1977. 166 p.

63a. Soudain l'été dernier: Pièce en 4 tableaux [see E 50]. Paris Librairie Théâtrale, 1977(?). 79 p.

63b. Propriété condamnée: Pièce en un acte [see E 50]. Paris: Librairie Théâtrale, 1977(?). 23 p.

63c. La rose tatouée (Rose Tattoo): Pièce en trois actes [see E 36, E 43]. Paris: Librairie Théâtrale, 1977(?). 124 p.

64. Mémoires [Memoirs]. Trans. Maurice Pons & Michèle Witta. Paris: Robert Laffont, 1977 (copyright 1978). 310 p. ils.
Review: Homme, February 1978, pp. 102-103: Matthieu Galey.

GERMAN

65. Die Glasmenagerie: Ein spiel der Erinnerung [The Glass Menagerie]. Berlin: U. S. Military Government Information, n. d. 98 p.

66. "Begierde und der schwarz Masseur" ["Desire and the Black Masseur"]. Das Lot, 5 (May 1951), 11-17.

67. Mrs. Stone und ihr römanischer Frühling [The Roman Spring of Mrs. Stone]. Trans. Kurt Heinrich Hansen. Frankfurt: S. Fischer, 1953. 163 p.

68. "Der Algebrochene Aufenthalt, oder Das unbefriedigende Abendessen" ["The Long Stay Cut Short"]. Trans. Elisabeth Viertel. Perspektiven, 8 (Summer 1954), 119-128.

69. Camino Real: Ein Stücke in sechzehn Stationner. Trans. Berthold Viertel. Frankfurt: S. Fischer, 1954. 113 p.

70. "Sommerspiel zu dritt" ["Three Players of a Summer Game"]. Perspektiven, 11 (Spring 1955), 15-38.

71. "Sprich zu mir wie der Regen: Einakter" ["Talk to Me Like the Rain"]. Trans. Hans Sahl. Die neue Rundschau, 1 (1956).

72. "Frage und Antwort: Ein Selbst-Interview" ["The World I Live In"]. Monat, 104 (May 1957), 63-64.

73. Mississippi-melodie [one-act plays]. Trans. Hans Sahl. Frankfurt: S. Fischer, n. d. 152 p.

74. Der steinerne Engel [Summer and Smoke]. Frankfurt: S. Fischer, n. d. 209 p.

75. Plötzlich letzten Sommer [Suddenly Last Summer]. Trans. Hans Sahl. Almanach. Frankfurt: S. Fischer, 1958. Pp. 69-72.

76. "Bildnis eines Mädchens in Glas" ["Portrait of a Girl in Glass"]. Der Baum mit den bitteren Feigen. Edited by Elisabeth Schnack. Zurich: Diogenes, 1959. Pp. 377-392.

77. Die Katze auf dem heissen Blechdach [Cat on a Hot Tin Roof, trans. Hans Sahl]; Die Tätowierte rose [The Rose Tattoo, trans. Berthold Viertel]: zwei Theaterstücke. Frankfurt: S. Fischer, 1960. 196 p.

78. Sommer und Rauch [Summer and Smoke]. Theatrum mundi Amerikanische dramen der gegenwart. Frankfurt: S. Fischer, 1962. Pp. 217-295.

79. "Die letzte meiner echtgoldenen Uhren" ["The Last of My Solid Gold Watches"]. Trans. Hans Sahl. Almanach. Frankfurt: S. Fischer, 1962. Pp. 72-84.

80. Die Nacht des Leguan [The Night of the Iguana]. Frankfurt: S. Fischer, 1962. 189 p.

81. Plötzlich letzten Sommer [see E 75]; Orpheus steigt herab [Orpheus Descending, trans. Hans Sahl]. Frankfurt: S. Fischer, 1962. 160 p.

82. Süsser Vogel Jugend [Sweet Bird of Youth, trans. Hans Sahl]; Zeit der Anpassung, oder Hochpunkt über einer Höhle [Period of Adjustment, trans. Franz Höllering]. Frankfurt: S. Fischer, 1962. 168 p.

83. Sommerspiel zu dritt: Erzählungen [stories]. Trans. Paridam von dem Knesebeck. Frankfurt: S. Fischer, 1962. 262 p.

84. Endstation sehnsucht [A Streetcar Named Desire]; Die Glasmenagerie [see E 65]: zwei Theaterstücke. Trans. Berthold Viertel. Frankfurt: S. Fischer, 1963. 203 p.

85. Die Nacht des Leguan: Schauspiel in zwei Akten [The Night of the Iguana]. Trans. Franz Hollering. Theater Heuter, 3 (1963), iii-xx.

86. Die Nacht des Leguan [see E 80]: Porträt einer Madonna, und vier weitere Einakter [four one-act plays]. Frankfurt: S. Fischer, 1963. 177 p.

87. Die Katze auf dem heissen Blechdach [Cat on a Hot Tin Roof]. Trans. S. Melchinger. Frankfurt/Vienna/Zurich: Gulenberg, 1963.

88. Der Milchzug hält hier nicht mehr: ein Theaterstücke [The Milk Train Doesn't Stop Here Anymore, trans. Hans Sahl]; Königreich auf Erden: Ein Stück in sieben Szenen [Kingdom of Earth, trans. Jan Lustig]. Frankfurt: S. Fischer, 1969. 160 p.

89. Der fahrende Ritter und anders Erzählungen [The Knightly Quest]. Frankfurt: S. Fischer, 1970. 119 p.

89a. Endstation Sehnsucht; Die Glasmenagerie [see E 65, E 84]. Frankfurt: Fischer Taschensuch, 1976.

89b. Acht Damen [Eight Mortal Ladies Possessed]. Frankfurt: S. Fischer, 1977.

89c. Memoiren (Memoirs). Trans. Kai Molvig. Frankfurt: S. Fischer, 1977.

89d. Mrs. Stone und ihr römanischer Frühling (E 67). Frankfurt: S. Fischer, 1978.

GREEK

90. Theatrika erga: Kalokaira kai Katachnia [Summer and Smoke]; Triantaphyllo Sto Stēthos [The Rose Tattoo]; Hē Lyssasmene Gata [Cat on a Hot Tin Roof]. Trans. Marion Plōritē. Athens: Ekdoseie Gkone, 1962. 346 p.

HINDI

91. [The Glass Menagerie. Classics of American Literature: Selected Authors: Drama.] Delhi: Rajpal & Sons, 1965. Pp. 1-108.

HUNGARIAN

92. A vágy villamosa [A Streetcar Named Desire]. Nagyvilág, 6 (February 1961), 204-267.

93. Maeska a forró bádogtetön [Cat on a Hot Tin Roof]. Nagvilág, 7 (August 1962), 1146-1207.

94. "Két elbeszélés üvegkisasszony arcképe" [Portrait of a Girl in Glass"]. Nagyvilág, 8 (June 1963), 824-834.

95. Az ifjúság szép madara [Sweet Bird of Youth]. Nagyvilág, 9 (August 1964), 1162-1210.

96. Drámák [A Streetcar Named Desire (E 92); Summer and Smoke; "This Property Is Condemned"; "Talk to Me Like the Rain"; Cat on a Hot Tin Roof (E 93); Orpheus Descending; Suddenly Last Summer; Period of Adjustment]. Budapest: Európa Könyvkiadó, 1964. 615 p.

97. "Az eltiport petúniák esete" ["The Case of the Crushed Petunias"]. Nagyvilág, 10 (July 1965), 1016-1023.

98. Az Iguana éjazakája [The Night of the Iguana]. Nem félúnk a farkastól. Budapest: Európa Könyvkiadó, 1966. Pp. 5-129.

99. "Az uvegguyüjtu lány portréja" [see E 94]. Legjobb elbeszélések angolból. Edited by Mirka János Fordításai. Winnipeg, Manitoba: Canadian Hungarian News, 1966. Pp. 19-30.

100. Autóbusz és Iguána [collection]. Trans. Ottliki Géza. Budapest: Európa Kőnyvkiadó, 1968. 409 p.

ITALIAN

101. Lo zoo di vetro: Dramma in due atti [The Glass Menagerie]. Trans. Alfredo Segre. Milan: Garzanti, 1948. 142 p.

102. "Auto-da-Fé: Tragedia in un atto." Trans. Mino Roli. Il Dramma, 63 (15 July 1948), 61-66.

103. "La dama dell-insetticida Larkspur" ["The Lady of Larkspur Lotion"]. Trans. Mino Roli. Il Dramma, 65 (15 July 1948), 55-57.

104. "27 vagoni di cotone: Una commedia del delta del Mississippi in un atto e tre quadri" ["27 Wagons Full of Cotton"]. Trans. Gigi Cane. Il Dramma, 67/69 (1 August-1 September 1948), 79-88.

105. ["Hello from Bertha."] Trans. Gigi Cane. Il Dramma, 77 (15 January 1949), 37-41.

106. "Una lettera d'amore di Lord Byron" ["Lord Byron's Love Letter"]. Trans. Gigi Cane. Il Dramma, 85 (15 May 1949), 53-54.

107. "Il cristo di Guadalajara"; "Gli angeli dello sculpellino" ["The Christus of Guadalajara"; "The Stonecutter's Angels"]. Bottighe Oscure, 4 (1949), 37-40.

108. Un tram che se chiama Desiderio: Dramma in tre atti [A Streetcar Named Desire]. Sipario, 68 (December 1951), 49-72.

109. "Properieta espropriata: Un atto" ["This Property Is Condemned"]. Trans. Sergio Cenalino. Il Dramma, 161 (15 July 1952), 22-26.

110. "Gioco estivo" ["Three Players of a Summer Game"]. Prospetti, 11 (Spring 1955), 15-36.

110a. Visconti, Luchino. Senso. Edited by G. C. Cavallaro. Bologna: Cappelli, 1955.

111. Una lettera d'amore di Lord Byron: Opera in un atto [Lord Byron's Love Letter]. Milan: Ricordi, 1955. 39 p.

112. "Rinasco nelle fiamme gridava la fenice: Atto unios" ["I Rise in Flame, Cried the Phoenix"]. Sipario, 138 (October 1957), 53-56.

113. La gatta pul tetto che scotta: Tre atte [Cat on a Hot Tin Roof]. Sipario, 144 (April 1958), 40-58.

114. I blues [American Blues]. Trans. Gerardo Guerrieri. Torino: Giulio Einaudi, 1959. 84 p.

115. La primavera romana della Signora Stone [The Roman Spring of Mrs. Stone]. Trans. Bruno Tasso. Milan: Garzanti, 1961. 146 p.

116. Teatro [The Glass Menagerie (see E 101); A Streetcar Named Desire (see E 108); Summer and Smoke; Cat on a Hot Tin Roof (see E 113); Baby Doll; Orpheus Descending; and four one-act plays]. Trans. Gerardo Guerrieri. Torino: Einaudi, 1963. 529 p.

117. La notte dell'iguana [The Night of the Iguana]. Trans. Bruno Fonzi. Torino: Einaudi, 1965. 130 p.

118. Tutti i racconti [short stories]. Trans. Giuliana Beltrami Gadola & Nora Finzi. Torino: Einaudi, 1966. 260 p.

119. "La terra dei fagioli gigante (The Beanstalk Country)." Il Tarocco, 7/8 (1968), 39.

120. Un ospite indiscreto [The Knightly Quest]. Trans. Luciano Bianciardi. Milan: Rizzoli, 1970. 217 p.

JAPANESE

121. [A Streetcar Named Desire.] Trans. Tazima Horishi & Yamashita Osama. Tokyo: 1952. 320 p.

122. [The Rose Tattoo.] Trans. Suga Wara Takasi. Tokyo: 1956. 167 p.

123. [The Glass Menagerie.] Trans. Tazima Hiroshi. Tokyo: 1957. 177 p.

124. [The Roman Spring of Mrs. Stone.] Tokyo: Shincho Sha, n. d. 171 p.

125. [Suddenly Last Summer. In an unidentified anthology.] Tokyo: Orion, 1958. Pp. 195-244.

126. [Cat on a Hot Tin Roof.] Trans. Tazima Hiroshi. Tokyo: Shincho Sha, 1959. 304 p. Another edition, 337 p.

127. [Hard Candy.] Tokyo: Kinseido, 1961. 158 p. (In English and Japanese.)

128. [Orpheus Descending. In an unidentified anthology.] Tokyo: 1965. Pp. 56-107.

129. [Summer and Smoke. Contemporary American Literature, Vol. 2.] Tokyo: 1967. Pp. 523-618.

KOREAN

130. [A Streetcar Named Desire.] Trans. Il-Yong Moon. Seoul: Chong Su, 1957. 323 p.

131. [Cat on a Hot Tin Roof.] Trans. Yu Yeong. N. p.: 1959.

132. [The Glass Menagerie. American Masterpieces in Drama.] Trans. Wha-siye-Oh. Seoul: Capital Culture, 1963. Pp. 175-346.

133. [The Glass Menagerie (see E 132). The Masterpieces of the World.] Trans. Hwi Yung Lee & Uh Lyung Lee. Seoul: Lop-tong Sa, 1964. Pp. 307-311.

MARATHI

134. [The Glass Menagerie.] Bombay: Opular Prakashan, 1966.

135. Vassanaachakra [A Streetcar Named Desire]. Bombay: Popular Prakashan, 1966. 122 p.

NORWEGIAN

136. En sporvogn til begjaer: Skuespill i 11 Scener. [A Streetcar Named Desire]. Trans. Peter Magnus. Oslo: Gyldendal Norsk, 1950. 116 p.

137. Den tatoverte rosen: Skuespill i tre akter, ti scener. [The Rose Tattoo]. Oslo: Byldendal Norsk, 1951. 106 p.

138. Katt paa varmt blikktak: Skuespill i tre akter [Cat on a Hot Tin Roof]. Trans. Peter Magnus. Oslo: Gyldendal Norse Forlag, 1955. 104 p.

138a. Flyvende sommer [Summer and Smoke]. Oslo: Gyldendal Norse, 1956.

138b. Glassmenasjeriet: Skuespill i 2 avd [The Glass Menagerie]. Oslo: Gyldendal Norse, 1956.

POLISH

139. "Laka niebieskich dzieci" ["The Field of Blue Children"]. Tematy, 3 (1964), 102-111.

PORTUGUESE

140. A margem da vida [The Glass Menagerie]. Trans. Léo Gilson Ribeiro. Rio de Janeiro: Bloch, 1954. 191 p.

141. A rosa tatuada [The Rose Tattoo]. Trans. Eurico da Costa & Manuel Pina. Lisbon: Europa-America, 1956. 199 p.

142. A última primavera [The Roman Spring of Mrs. Stone]. Trans. José Estêvão Sasportes. Lisbon: Livros do Brasil, 1960. 146 p.

143. Fumo de verão [Summer and Smoke]. Trans. Luis de Stan Montiero. Lisbon: Europa-America, 1962. 131 p.

144. O anjo de pedra (Summer and Smoke) [see E 143]. Rio de Janeiro: Letras e Artes, 1964. 150 p.

145. A margem da vida [see E 140]. Rio de Janeiro: Letras e Artes, 1964. 150 p.

146. A rosa tatuado [see E 141]. Trans. R. Magalhães, Jr. Rio de Janeiro: BUP, 1964. 214 p.

147. Bruscamente no verão passado [Suddenly Last Summer]. Lisbon: Presença, 1964. 158 p.

148. A noite da iguana [The Night of the Iguana]. Trans. Idalina S. N. Piña Amaro. Rio de Janeiro: Europa-America, 1965. 129 p.

149. O anjo de pedra [see E 143 and E 144]. Rio de Janeiro: Bloch, 1968. 190 p.

ROMANIAN

150. Un tramvia numit Dorinta [A Streetcar Named Desire]. Trans. Dorin Dron. Teatra American Contemporan, Vol. 2. Bucharest: Pentru Literatură Universală, 1967. Pp. 109-216.

RUSSIAN

151. Stekljanny zverinets i eščë devjat' p'es [The Glass Menagerie and nine other plays]. Moscow: 1967. 721 p. il.

SLOVAKIAN

152. Sklenený zverinec hra v siedmich obrazoch [The Glass Menagerie]. Trans. Kaeol Dlouhy. Bratislava: Diliza, 1961.

153. Električka zvaná túžha [A Streetcar Named Desire]. Trans. Jan Trachta. Moderna svetová dráma. Bratislava: Slovenské Vydavatelstvo, 1964. Pp. 7-102.

154. Rimska pomlad gospe slonove [The Roman Spring of Mrs. Stone]. Trans. Maila Golob. Ljubljana: Mladinska Knjiga, 1965. 125 p.

155. Kralovstvo na zemi: hra v siedmich obrazuch. Trans. E. Castiglione. Bratislava: Diliza, 1969. 74 p.

156. Sladky vtak mladosti. Trans. E. Castiglione. Bratislava: Diliza, 1969. 57 p.

SPANISH

157. Teatro: Un tranvia llamado Deseo [A Streetcar Named Desire]; El zoologico de cristal [The Glass Menagerie]; Verano y humo [Summer and Smoke]. Trans. Léon Mirlas. Buenos Aires: Losado, 1951. 305 p.

158. Tres dramas [The Rose Tattoo; Cat on a Hot Tin Roof; Camino Real]. Trans. Floreal Mazia. Buenos Aires: Sudamericana, 1958.

159. Figuretes de vidre (The Glass Menagerie): Comedia en dos actos. Trans. B. Vallespinosa. Barcelona: Agrupació Dramatica de Barcelona, 1959. 32 p.

160. Orfeo desciende [Orpheus Descending]. Trans. Roberto Bixio. Buenos Aires: Sur, 1960. 163 p.

161. Un tranvia llamado Deseo (A Streetcar Named Desire): Tragedia en once cuadros, 1947. Trans. Juan García-Puerte. Teatro norteamericano contemporaneo. Madrid: Aguilar, 1961. Pp. 179-284.

162. La caída de Orfeo: Drama en tres actos [Orpheus Descending]. Trans. Antonio de Cabo. Madrid: Alfil, 1962. 112 p.

163. La gata sobre el tejado de zinc: Obra en tres actos, segundo y tercero sin interrupción [Cat on a Hot Tin Roof]. Trans. Antonio de Cabo & Luis Saenz. Madrid: Alfil, 1962. 80 p.

164. Un tranvia llamado Deseo: Comedia dividida en once cuadros [A Streetcar Named Desire]. Trans. José Méndez Herrera. Madrid: Alfil, 1962. 122 p.

165. Dulce pájaro de juventud [Sweet Bird of Youth]. Buenos Aires: Sur, 1962. 166 p.

166. Camino Real: Obra en tres actos divididas en dieciseis episodios. Trans. Diego Hurtado. Madrid: Alfil, 1963. 91 p.

167. Hasta llegar a entenderse (Period of Adjustment): Comedia en tres actos. Trans. Alfonso Paso & Julio Mathias. Madrid: Alfil, 1964. 83 p.

168. El zoo de cristal: Drama en dos actos [The Glass Menagerie]. Trans. José Gordón & José María de Quinto. Madrid: Alfil, 1964. 96 p.

169. La noche de la iguana [The Night of the Iguana]. Buenos Aires: Losada, 1964. 105 p.

170. La primavera romana de la Señora Stone [The Roman Spring of Mrs. Stone]. Trans. Martin Ezcurdia. Buenos Aires: Plaza & Janes, 1964. 175 p.

171. La noche de la iguana: Comedia en tres actos [see E 169]. Trans. José Méndez Herrera. Madrid: Alfil, 1965.

172. La noche de la iguano [see E 169 and E 171]. Lo que no se dice ["Something Unspoken"]; Súbitamente el ultimo verano [Suddenly Last Summer]; Período de ajuste [Period of Adjustment]. Trans. Manuel Barberá. Buenos Aires: Losada, 1966. 254 p.

173. Caramelo fundido [Hard Candy]. Trans. Roberto Bixio. Buenos Aires: Sur, 1966. 217 p.

174. Piezas cortas [one-act plays]. Madrid: Alianza, 1970. 201 p.

175. Un empeño caballeresco [The Knightly Quest]. Trans. Juan Ribalta. Barcelona: Lumen, 1972. 151 p.

176. El país del dragón [Dragon Country]. Trans. Alvarez Flórez & José Manuel. Madrid: Jucar, 1975. 390 p.

177. Ocho mujeres poseidas [Eight Mortal Ladies Possessed]. Trans. Pilar Giralt. Barcelona: Caralt, 1977. 164 p.

SWEDISH

178. Linje lusta: Skådespel i 3 akter. [A Streetcar Named Desire]. Stockholm: Albert Bonniers, 1949. 130 p.

179. Mrs. Stones Romerska Vaar [The Roman Spring of Mrs. Stone]. Trans. Th. Warburton. Stockholm: Albert Bonniers, 1951. 120 p.

179a. "Det kan man kalla kärlek" ["The Strangest Kind of Romance"]. Radiotjansts teaterbibliotek 97.

180. "Porträtt av en glasflicken" ["Portrait of a Girl in Glass"]. All Världers Berätare, 11 (November 1955), 8-15.

TAMIL

181. [The Glass Menagerie.] Trans. T. N. Suki Subramaniyam. Madras: Jothi Nilayam, 1966. 339 p.

TURKISH

182. Soğuk günes [The Roman Spring of Mrs. Stone]. Istanbul: Samim-Sadik Yayinlari, 1960.

183. Arzu tramvayi (A Streetcar Named Desire). Trans. Halit Cakir. Istanbul: Milli Egitim Basimevi, 1965. 148 p.

184. Iguana gecesi [The Night of the Iguana]. Istanbul: Altin Kitaplar, 1966. 288 p.

WELSH

185. Pethe brau [The Glass Menagerie]. Trans. Emyr Edwards. Llandysul, Wales: Gwasg y Gler, 1963. 74 p.

PART 2

WRITINGS, WITH NOTES ON COMPOSITION AND TEXTUAL VARIANTS

Introduction

Whereas in Part 1 Williams's works are listed in chronological order by type of publication, below they are subdivided by genre and listed alphabetically under their short title. Unpublished plays and screenplays that have been produced are also included here. I should like to thank Julian Olf and the Educational Theatre Journal, in whose pages an earlier version of Section F was published (see O 10).

Williams belongs to the great tradition of Whitman, James, Faulkner, Robert Lowell: instead of being satisfied with a work once it is in print, he constantly revises it. Thus, the textual editor of any definitive collection of his works is going to have an enormous problem. Although only a few of his poems, stories, and essays exist in more than one version, the situation is quite different with the plays. Of the forty-two that Williams has published since 1941, twenty have been printed in differing versions; only three of his seventeen full-length plays have not been revised at some point in print. Many other versions of all the plays, including screenplays, remain unpublished.

Critical attention to the revisions--save that directed to the almost notorious cases of Battle of Angels/Orpheus Descending and the third acts of Cat on a Hot Tin Roof--has been slight. Most critics have simply accepted the New Directions texts (which include these revisions of Orpheus and Cat) as definitive ones. But the versions published by Dramatists Play Service are often superior, and sometimes an earlier text published in a magazine still holds interest and is, in at least one case, the best text available.

In addition to these forty-two plays, Williams has written eleven that he has not yet published in any form but that have been produced, eight screenplays (only two of which have been published), and the libretto (published) for an opera. Information about productions of all these works is found in Section K. Although Williams is not often thought of as a writer of fiction, he has published at least thirty-seven short stories, several of great beauty and power, and two novels. He has also published at least 121 poems, 93 of which he has preserved in two collections. When we realize that his earliest successes with publishers were his poetry, we can forgive Williams for continuing to think of himself as a poet even though few of his lines are memorable (quite unlike the speeches in his plays). Finally, he has published a number of autobiographical pieces, including the eminently interesting Memoirs; unjustly neglected essays on a number of subjects, including some very interesting comments on fellow artists; and a few best-forgotten occasional pieces. Unfortunately, the recent collection of his essays does not serve him as well as it might have.

F. PLAYS AND SCREENPLAYS

1. "AT LIBERTY." American Scenes, ed. William Kozlenko. J. Day, 1941 (B 2). Also B 4.

   The play, the story of a trapped, frustrated actress dying of consumption, has been examined only by Weales (P 407).

2. "AUTO-DA-FE." Ms., Texas (J 9); 27 Wagons Full of Cotton. ND, 1945, 1953, 1966 (A 3, A 32, A 107); 27 Wagons Full of Cotton. J. Lehmann, 1949 (A 17). Also A 9, E 102.

3. BABY DOLL see "The Long Stay Cut Short" and "27 Wagons Full of Cotton"

4. BATTLE OF ANGELS/ORPHEUS DESCENDING/THE FUGITIVE KIND. Mss., Library of Congress (J 5), Texas (J 9).

   (a) Battle of Angels. Unpublished play in two acts and three scenes, 1940.

   (b) Battle of Angels. Pharos, spring 1945 (A 1); Orpheus Descending.... ND, 1958 (A 54); Theatre I. ND, 1971 (A 131).

   (c) Orpheus Descending.... ND, 1958 (A 54); Theatre Arts, September 1958 (C 92); Orpheus Descending. S&W, 1958 (A 59); The Fugitive Kind. NAL, 1960 (A 68); Orpheus Descending.... Penguin, 1961 (A 76); Five Plays. S&W, 1962 (A 80); The Night of the Iguana.... Penguin, 1968 (A 121); Theatre III. ND, 1971 (A 133); The Rose Tattoo.... Penguin, 1976 (A 156); Four Plays. NAL, 1976 (A 158). Also B 56, B 102, B 140, B 168a, E 12, E 14, E 44, E 45, E 46, E 50, E 81, E 96, E 116, E 128, E 151, E 160, E 162.

   (d) Orpheus Descending. DPS, 1959 (A 63).

   (e) The Fugitive Kind. Unpublished screenplay, with Meade Roberts, 1960.

   (f) Battle of Angels. DPS, 1975 (A 145).

   After Battle's fiasco in Boston in 1940, Williams revised the script, adding (as he often does when a play has been a failure) a prologue and an epilogue, and published it in 1945. He continued brooding over the story, making changes in characterization, development, and symbolism, but following always the same basic plot. In 1957 a new play, Orpheus Descending, was produced; it too quickly closed. Many critics, one of the best being Matthew (P 274), have compared the two New Directions versions.

   When Williams prepared Orpheus for the Dramatists Play Service in 1959, he reordered some of the material and turned out a text far superior to that published by New

Directions, though he marred the fire symbolism by omitting all references to the blowtorch in Act III. A revival of the play the same year was more successful. Williams also prepared the screenplay; the film was called The Fugitive Kind, the same title as an earlier but quite different play. Then in 1975 he returned to Battle, creating a script for Dramatists Play Service which retains the structure of the original Battle (minus the prologue and epilogue) but introduces some of the more telling scenes from Orpheus. It is by far the better version, though the script is blemished by careless editing.

Williams's essays "The History of a Play" (I 25) and "The Past, the Present, and the Perhaps" (I 44) concern the writing of the play. Critics who have looked specifically at the two plays are Chesler (P 59), Dickinson (P 87), Lee (P 251), Quirino (P 326), Thompson (P 378), and Traubitz (P 387). The production record is found in K 4. See also A 54 and A 59 for reviews.

5. BLOOD KIN see Kingdom of Earth

6. BOOM! see The Milk Train Doesn't Stop Here Anymore

7. "CAIRO, SHANGHAI, BOMBAY!" Ms., Texas (J 9); unpublished play, with Dorothy Shapiro, 1935.

This one-act comedy, about two sailors on leave who pick up two prostitutes, was Williams's first play to be produced.

8. CAMINO REAL. Mss., Texas (J 9).

(a) "Ten Blocks on the Camino Real." American Blues. DPS, 1948 (A 13).

(b) Camino Real. Unpublished play, 1953.

(c) Camino Real. ND, 1953, 1970 (A 31, A 130); Theatre Arts, August 1954 (C 73); Four Plays. S&W, 1956 (A 43); Camino Real. S&W, 1958 (A 53); The Rose Tattoo.... Penguin, 1958, 1976 (A 60, A 156); Three Plays. ND, 1964 (A 94); Camino Real. DPS, 1965 (A 102); Theatre II. ND, 1971 (A 132). Also B 78, B 86, B 90, B 96, B 131, B 137, E 69, E 158, E 166.

The shorter, Dramatists Play Service, version of the play was written in New Orleans in the winter of 1946. Elia Kazan urged Williams to expand it for a 1953 Broadway production simply called Camino Real. This was a failure, and Williams revised the play before allowing New Directions to publish it. Though much of the material from the short play remained intact, much was likewise omitted. The revision is tougher and more pessimistic; the dance-like rhythms of the first version changed into wild flight. Later productions in New York and London, using this text, were successful. When Whit Burnett (B 137) asked Williams to choose his best piece of writing for inclusion in an anthology, Williams picked Block 8 of the play.

Something of his intentions in the play can be gathered from his essays "Foreword" ("On the 'Camino Real'") and "Afterword" (I 21) and "Reflections on a Revival of a Controversal Fantasy" (I 53) and an interview (M 34). Critics Campbell (P 52), Coakley (P 65), Hill (P 183), Miller (P 280), Olley (P 300), Turner (P 388), and Wolf (Q 50, P 414) have looked at various aspects of the play. The production record is found in K 8. An interesting comment is by John Steinbeck (P 370).

9. CANDLES TO THE SUN. Ms., Texas (J 9); Unpublished play, 1936.

This melodrama, about Alabama coal miners and the injustices they suffer, was Williams's fourth play to be produced.

10. "THE CASE OF THE CRUSHED PETUNIAS." American Blues. DPS, 1948 (A 13). Also B 107, E 97.

11. CAT ON A HOT TIN ROOF. Mss., Texas (J 9).

(a) "Three Players of a Summer Game." Unpublished play, 1954.

(b) Cat on a Hot Tin Roof. ND, 1955 (A 38); Cat on a Hot Tin Roof. S&W, 1956 (A 44); Theatre Arts, June 1957 (C 89); Cat on a Hot Tin Roof. Penguin, 1957 (A 49); Cat on a Hot Tin Roof. NAL, 1958 (A 58); The Milk Train Doesn't Stop Here Anymore..., Penguin, 1969 (A 122); Theatre III. ND, 1971 (A 133); Cat on a Hot Tin Roof.... Penguin, 1976 (A 155). Also B 45, B 48, B 51, B 61, E 5, E 17, E 42, E 43, E 52, E 77, E 87, E 90, E 93, E 96, E 113, E 116, E 126, E 131, E 138, E 158, E 163.

(c) Cat on a Hot Tin Roof. DPS, 1958 (A 57).

(d) Cat on a Hot Tin Roof. ND, 1975 (A 146, A 147). Also B 171.

The materials which would evolve into Cat began with the short story "Three Players of a Summer Game" (G 37). It offers interesting insight into the way Williams develops characters and ideas, but it foreshadows the play rather distantly. Two studies of the relationship have been made by May (P 276) and Reck (P 332). Williams's direct dramatization of the story was produced in 1955 with little notice.

Cat was ready by 1954, but--as Williams has explained--Elia Kazan disliked the original third act, and at his urging the playwright rewrote it for the 1955 production. Williams was unhappy with this second version, however, and published both third acts in New Directions along with the note of explanation (but only the revision in Dramatists Play Service). All critics who have written about the play, and in particular Peterson (P 310), have mentioned the differences. In 1973 Williams prepared a final version of the third act, returning to the original version but maintaining the best moments from the Kazan version. He also made minor changes in the text of the first two acts and published this text in 1975.

See also Williams's essay "Critic Says 'Evasion,' Writer Says 'Mystery'" (I 14). Interesting comments about the first version of Cat were made by William Faulkner (P 164), Lillian Hellman (P 312), and Arthur Miller (P 54, P 377, P 378). The production record is found in K 11. Criticism is by Dukore (P 101), Funatsu (P 129), Gobnecht (Q 25), Hagopian (P 166), Isaac (P 198), Lolli (P 259), Sacksteder (P 346), and Young (P 417).

Williams did not work on the film version; the screenplay was prepared by James Poe and Richard Brooks, 1958.

12. "CONFESSIONAL" see Small Craft Warnings

13. CREVE COEUR.

(a) Creve Coeur. Unpublished play, 1978.

(b) A Lovely Sunday for Creve Coeur. Unpublished play, 1979.

The story concerns the frustrations of four women. See K 13 for reviews.

14. "THE DARK ROOM." American Blues. DPS, 1948 (A 13).

15. "THE DEMOLITION DOWNTOWN." Esquire, June 1971 (C 134).

This short play is about two couples caught in a revolution.

16. "DOS RANCHOS" see "The Purification"

17. THE ECCENTRICITIES OF A NIGHTINGALE see Summer and Smoke

18. "THE ENEMY: TIME" see Sweet Bird of Youth

19. "THE FROSTED GLASS COFFIN." Mss., Library of Congress (J 5), Texas (J 9); Dragon Country. ND, 1969 (A 127, A 128). Also E 176.

20. THE FUGITIVE KIND. Ms., Texas (J 9); unpublished play, 1936-1938.

This play, about derelicts in a flophouse, was Williams's fifth to be produced.

21. THE FUGITIVE KIND see Battle of Angels

22. GARDEN DISTRICT see "Something Unspoken" and Suddenly Last Summer

23. THE GLASS MENAGERIE. Mss., Texas (J 9).

(a) The Glass Menagerie. Random House, 1945 (A 2); The Glass Menagerie. J. Lehmann, 1948 (A 15); The Glass Menagerie. ND, 1949, 1966 (A 19, A 106); Four Plays. S&W, 1956 (A 43); A Streetcar Named Desire.... Penguin, 1959 (A 61); Sweet Bird of Youth.... Penguin, 1962 (A 79);

The Glass Menagerie. Braille edition, 1966 (A 108); The Glass Menagerie. ND, 1970 (A 129); Theatre I. ND, 1971 (A 131). Also A 33, A 88, A 89, A 117, B 9, B 13, B 19, B 21, B 24, B 27, B 30, B 32, B 37, B 41, B 44, B 48, B 49, B 50, B 54, B 55, B 73, B 75, B 77, B 89, B 91, B 100, B 103, B 110, B 113, B 117, B 118, B 121a, B 123, B 130, B 133, B 138, B 141, B 143, B 151, B 153, B 156, B 160, B 161, B 164, B 166, B 172, B 173, C 60, D 1, D 3, E 1, E 9, E 13, E 27, E 43, E 65, E 84, E 91, E 101, E 116, E 123, E 132, E 133, E 134, E 140, E 145, E 151, E 152, E 157, E 159, E 168, E 181, E 185.

(b) The Glass Menagerie. DPS, 1948 (A 14, A 66). Also B 68 (and possibly others in the above list).

(c) The Glass Menagerie. Unpublished screenplay, with Peter Berneis, 1950 (see C 62).

The play in 1943 developed out of the short story "Portrait of a Girl in Glass" (G 29) and some unpublished one-act plays (J 9); it was originally called "The Gentleman Caller." Williams has often said it began as a screenplay, and he made notes how it could be adopted for the screen (J 9); but his letters of the period (see A 167) would indicate he always thought of it primarily as a play.

For the Dramatists Play Service Williams omitted the screen device, added some dialogue, and somewhat changed the character of Jim. It is probably the better text, but it is somewhat disconcerting that critics routinely dismiss the screen device even though, so far as I can discover, no production has ever tried it out exactly as Williams imagined it. The development of the published versions has been rather thoroughly examined by Beaurline (P 19) and Watson (P 400); see also the article by Ellis (P 111).

Criticism specifically of the play is by Berkowitz (P 23), Bluefarb (P 32), Bryer (P 44), Casty (P 57), Cate and Presley (P 58), Debusscher (P 85), Howell (P 189), Ishizuka (P 205), King (P 235), Lees (P 252), Napieralski (P 290), Nolan (P 299), Rama Murthy (P 327), Ribey (P 335), Rowland (P 344), Scheye (P 335), Stein (P 369), Thompson (P 378), and an honors class in a New York high school (P 187). For the production record see K 23; reviews of the book are found A 2. Williams's screenplay has been examined by MacMullan (P 271).

24. "THE GNÄDIGES FRÄULEIN"/THE LATTER DAYS OF A CELEBRATED SOUBRETTE. Ms., Texas (J 9).

(a) Esquire, August 1965 (C 116); The Gnadiges Fraulein. DPS, 1967 (A 111); Dragon Country. ND, 1969 (A 127, A 128). Also E 176.

(b) The Latter Days of a Celebrated Soubrette. Unpublished play, 1974.

According to Leavitt (N 49) "Fräulein" was written under the influence of amphetamines; nothing else in the Williams canon is quite like it. There are a few minor textual variations between the Esquire and Dramatists Play Service scripts. The play was produced together with "The Mutilated" (F 43) under the collective title Slapstick Tragedy in 1966, but it was thus published, along with a preface (I 49), only in Esquire. Ishida (P 203) has examined the two plays. Reviews are listed in K 24.

Williams expanded the play as The Latter Days of a Celebrated Soubrette, and this version was produced in New York City. A review is found in K 24.

25. "HEADLINES." Unpublished sketch, 1936.

A plea for pacifism, the play was Williams's third to be produced.

26. "HELLO FROM BERTHA." Ms., Texas (J 9); 27 Wagons Full of Cotton. ND, 1945, 1953, 1966 (A 3, A 32, A 107); 27 Wagons Full of Cotton. J. Lehmann, 1949 (A 17). Also A 9, E 105.

27. "I CAN'T IMAGINE TOMORROW." Esquire, March 1966 (C 118); Dragon Country. ND, 1969 (A 127, A 128). Also B 146, E 176.

According to Curtiss (K 27c), the play was written in 1957. There are minor textual changes between the Esquire and New Directions versions: several speeches have been cut. Reviews are found in K 27.

28. "I RISE IN FLAME, CRIED THE PHOENIX." Ms., Texas (J 9).

(a) I Rise in Flame, Cried the Phoenix. ND, 1951 (A 25); New World Writing #1. NAL, 1952 (B 36); Ramparts, January 1968 (C 124).

(b) I Rise in Flame, Cried the Phoenix. DPS, 195- (A 41); Dragon Country. ND, 1969 (A 127, A 128). Also E 41, E 49, E 112, E 176 (I do not know which version).

The play was written in New Orleans in late summer 1941, after a visit to Mrs. Lawrence at Taos. Williams inexplicably marred one of his finest works by substituting a sentimental ending in the Dramatists Play Service version for his original, realistic view of human nature. He also translated the German scattered through Frieda's speeches. Reviews are found in K 28.

29. IN THE BAR OF A TOKYO HOTEL. Ms., Library of Congress (J 5); In the Bar of a Tokyo Hotel. DPS, 1969 (A 124); Dragon Country. ND, 1969 (A 127, A 128). Also E 176.

The play was inspired by Jackson Pollock. Williams wrote an interesting letter to the cast about the play's themes (B 170, C 127). Reviews are found in K 29.

30. KINGDOM OF EARTH. Mss., Library of Congress (J 5), Texas (J 9).

(a) Esquire, February 1967 (C 121).

(b) Kingdom of Earth. ND, 1968 (A 118); Kingdom of Earth. DPS, 1969 (A 123). Also E 60, E 88.

(c) Theatre V. ND, 1976 (A 151).

The play grew out of the 1954 short story of the same title (G 14). It was republished in 1966 and apparently stimulated Williams's imagination, for the next year he published a one-act dramatization, which sketched in the plot of the full-length play. The first New Directions and Dramatists Play Service texts are essentially the same, with a very few speeches reworked or shuffled. But in an attempt to get the play produced again after its New York failure (under the title, disliked by Williams, of The Seven Descents of Myrtle), he drastically cut it. This version was printed in the fifth volume of his collected plays, but unfortunately the editing has left some inconsistencies. Criticism is by Hirsch (P 184), Kalson (P 229), and Phillips (P 311). The production record is found in K 30. See also A 118.

Gore Vidal prepared the screenplay, 1969; the film was released under the title Last of the Mobile Hot-Shots in the United States and as Blood Kin abroad.

31. "THE LADY OF LARKSPUR LOTION." Ms., Texas (J 9); Best One-Act Plays of 1941, ed. Margaret Mayorga. Dodd, Mead, 1942 (B 3); 27 Wagons Full of Cotton. ND, 1945, 1953, 1966 (A 3, A 32, A 107); 27 Wagons Full of Cotton. J. Lehmann, 1949 (A 17). Also A 9, E 103.

Reviews are found in K 31.

32. "THE LAST OF MY SOLID GOLD WATCHES." Ms., Texas (J 9); Best One-Act Plays of 1942, ed. Margaret Mayorga. Dodd, Mead, 1943 (B 5); 27 Wagons Full of Cotton. ND, 1945, 1953, 1966 (A 3, A 32, A 107); 27 Wagons Full of of Cotton. J. Lehmann, 1949 (A 17). Also A 9, E 79.

Reviews are found in K 32.

33. LAST OF THE MOBILE HOT-SHOTS see Kingdom of Earth

34. THE LATTER DAYS OF A CELEBRATED SOUBRETTE see "The Gnädiges Fräulein"

35. "THE LONG GOODBYE." Ms., Texas (J 9); 27 Wagons Full of Cotton. ND, 1945, 1953, 1966 (A 3, A 32, A 107); 27 Wagons Full of Cotton. J. Lehmann, 1949 (A 17). Also A 9, B 161.

36. "THE LONG STAY CUT SHORT." Ms., Texas (J 9).

(a) "The Unsatisfactory Supper." Best One-Act Plays of 1945, ed. Margaret Mayorga. Dodd, Mead, 1945 (B 10); "The Long Stay Cut Short." American Blues. DPS, 1948 (A 13); Baby Doll. ND, 1956 (A 45). Also A 9, C 70, E 39, E 50, E 68.

(b) Baby Doll see "27 Wagons Full of Cotton"

(c) Tiger Tail see "27 Wagons Full of Cotton"

The play was combined with "27 Wagons" (F 71) to become

the basis for Williams's screenplay Baby Doll in 1956; this in turn was dramatized as Tiger Tail in 1978.

37. "LORD BYRON'S LOVE LETTER." Ms., Texas (J 9).

(a) 27 Wagons Full of Cotton. ND, 1945, 1953, 1966 (A 3, A 32, A 107); 27 Wagons Full of Cotton. J. Lehmann, 1949 (A 17). Also A 9, B 94, B 116, B 134, E 106.

(b) Lord Byron's Love Letter. Ricordi, 1955 (A 39). Also E 111.

The play was turned into an opera with music by Raffaello de Basfield. Reviews of the opera are found in K 37.

38. A LOVELY SUNDAY FOR CREVE COEUR see Creve Coeur

39. "THE MAGIC TOWER." Unpublished play, 1936.

This romantic drama about a young married couple was Williams's second play to be produced.

40. THE MIGRANTS.

This script for television was by Lanford Wilson, 1974. It was "based on an idea by Tennessee Williams." Reviews are found in K 40.

41. THE MILK TRAIN DOESN'T STOP HERE ANYMORE/BOOM! Mss., Columbia (J 4), Library of Congress (J 5), Texas (J 9).

(a) The Milk Train Doesn't Stop Here Anymore. Unpublished play in two acts and six scenes, 1962.

(b) Excerpts of second version in Best Plays of 1962-1963, ed. Henry Hewes. Dodd, Mead, 1963 (B 104).

(c) The Milk Train Doesn't Stop Here Anymore. ND, 1964 (A 90); The Milk Train Doesn't Stop Here Anymore. DPS, 1964 (A 91); The Milk Train Doesn't Stop Here Anymore. S&W, 1964 (A 92); The Milk Train Doesn't Stop Here Anymore..., Penguin, 1969 (A 122); Theatre V. ND, 1976 (A 151); Cat on a Hot Tin Roof.... Penguin, 1976 (A 155). Also E 60, E 88.

(d) The Milk Train Doesn't Stop Here Anymore. Unpublished play, 1965.

(e) Boom! Unpublished screenplay, 1968.

Williams has labored hard over Milk Train, but it has met repeated failures. The play grew out of the short story "Man Bring This Up Road" (G 19) and was already under way in 1959 (see M 19). The excerpts published in 1963 show enough to suggest it would be interesting to see all the variants. In earlier versions Mrs. Goforth accepts Chris Flanders; in the only published version and its rewrite she dies. Williams brings on "stagehands" for the third version and adds a prologue. A very brief passage in Scene 5 of the British editions does not appear in the American texts. Williams dropped the stagehands from the 1965 version and created a more humane Mrs. Goforth and a more mystical Chris, according to Taubman (K 41).

From comments of various persons who worked around the film (see N 68), it would seem that the screenplay was infinitely better than the film, which was released under the title Boom!

See Williams's interview (M 7). Specific criticism is by Armato (P 7) and McBride (P 265). The reviews are found in K 41.

42. "MOONY'S KID DON'T CRY." Ms., Texas (J 9); Best One-Act Plays of 1940, ed. Margaret Mayorga. Dodd, Mead, 1941 (B 1); American Blues. DPS, 1948 (A 13).

The play was written in November 1934. A review is found in K 42.

43. "THE MUTILATED." Ms., Texas (J 9).

(a) Esquire, August 1965 (C 116).

(b) The Mutilated. DPS, 1967 (A 112).

(c) Dragon Country. ND, 1969 (A 127, A 128). Also E 176.

The play was produced together with "The Gnädiges Fräulein" (F 24) under the title Slapstick Tragedy, but it was thus published only in Esquire, together with an interesting preface (I 49). Ishida (P 203) has examined the two plays. Since the Dramatists Play Service text follows the Esquire text but includes the variants to be worked into the New Directions text, it is quite rewarding to study. Reviews are found in K 24.

44. THE NIGHT OF THE IGUANA. Mss., Library of Congress (J 5), Texas (J 9).

(a) "The Night of the Iguana." Unpublished one-act play, 1959.

(b) The Night of the Iguana. Unpublished full-length play, 1960.

(c) Esquire, February 1962 (C 107); The Night of the Iguana. ND, 1962 (A 77); The Night of the Iguana. S&W, 1963 (A 85); The Night of the Iguana. NAL, 1964 (A 97); The Night of the Iguana. Penguin, 1964 (A 98); The Night of the Iguana. Braille edition, 1966 (A 110); The Night of the Iguana.... Penguin, 1968 (A 121); Theatre IV. ND, 1972 (A 134); Cat on a Hot Tin Roof.... Penguin, 1976 (A 155); Three by Tennessee. NAL, 1976 (A 159). Also B 95, B 102, B 142, B 159, C 115, E 6, E 59, E 80, E 85, E 86, E 98, E 100, E 117, E 148, E 169, E 171, E 172, E 184.

(d) The Night of the Iguana. DPS, 1963 (A 86).

Only the title, the central symbol, a storm, and a very different prototype for Hannah come from the short story of the same title (G 25). There are a few minor differences between the Esquire and New Directions texts. The Dramatists Play Service text is a severe cutting, especially of the third act; it removes much of the poetry and some purple prose. Probably it is better for the stage, but for reading I still prefer the New Directions version.

Williams discusses the origin of the play in his essay "A Summer of Discovery" (I 57); see also his interview (M 40). Criticism specifically of the play is by Adler (P 1), Armato (P 7), Embrey (P 112), Hendrick (P 177), Kahn (P 224), Leon (P 244), and Moorman (P 288). Production notes are found K 44. See also A 77.

The 1963 screenplay was the work of Tony Veiller, though Williams tinkered with it a little.

45. ORPHEUS DESCENDING see Battle of Angels

46. OUT CRY see The Two-Character Play

47. "A PERFECT ANALYSIS GIVEN BY A PARROT" see The Rose Tattoo

48. PERIOD OF ADJUSTMENT. Mss., Texas (J 9).
(a) Period of Adjustment. Unpublished play, 1958.
(b) Esquire, December 1960 (C 101).
(c) Period of Adjustment. ND, 1960 (A 70); Period of Adjustment. S&W, 1961 (A 72); Period of Adjustment. NAL, 1962 (A 83); Period of Adjustment.... NEL, 1963 (A 87); Theatre IV. ND, 1972 (A 134); Four Plays. NAL, 1976 (A 158). Also B 85, E 31, E 82, E 96, E 167, E 172.
(d) Period of Adjustment. DPS, 1961 (A 73).

The play was begun in 1957-1958. In each successive published script the dialogue and the action have been tightened and the satire sharpened. Consequently, the Dramatists Play Service script is the superior in every way. It also provides a more effective curtain for Act I. Goldfarb (P 149) is the only critic to have looked specifically at the play; reviews are found in K 48.

Isobel Lennart prepared the screenplay, 1962.

49. "PORTRAIT OF A MADONNA." 27 Wagons Full of Cotton. ND, 1945, 1953, 1966 (A 3, A 32, A 107); 27 Wagons Full of Cotton. J. Lehmann, 1949 (A 17). Also A 9, B 171, E 50, E 86.

Reviews are found in K 49.

50. "THE PURIFICATION." "Dos Ranchos." New Directions # 8. ND, 1944 (B 6); "The Purification." 27 Wagons Full of Cotton. ND, 1945, 1953, 1966 (A 3, A 32, A 107); 27 Wagons Full of Cotton. J. Lehmann, 1949 (A 17). Also A 9.

Williams's only play in verse, it was inspired by his visits to Taos, New Mexico. Reviews are found in K 50.

51. THE RED DEVIL BATTERY SIGN.
(a) Unpublished play in two acts and ten scenes, 1975.
(b) Unpublished play, 1976.

The play is an examination of American politics and sexuality. It takes place in Dallas on the day of Kennedy's assassination. See Williams's interviews (M 32, M 33, M 45). Reviews are found in K 51.

52. THE ROMAN SPRING OF MRS. STONE see Section G

53. THE ROSE TATTOO/"A PERFECT ANALYSIS GIVEN BY A PARROT." Mss., Texas (J 9).

(a) The Rose Tattoo Unpublished play, 1950.

(b) The Rose Tattoo. ND, 1951 (A 24); The Rose Tattoo. S&W, 1954 (A 37); Theatre Arts, May 1955 (C 79); The Rose Tattoo. NAL, 1955 (A 40); The Rose Tattoo.... Penguin, 1958, 1976 (A 60, A 156); Five Plays. S&W, 1962 (A 80); Three Plays. ND, 1964 (A 94); The Rose Tattoo. DPS, 1965 (A 103); Theatre II. ND, 1971 (A 132); Three by Tennessee. NAL, 1976 (A 159). Also B 31, B 61, B 69, B 93, B 114, B 163, D 5, E 3, E 10, E 16, E 22, E 36, E 37, E 43, E 77, E 90, E 122, E 137, E 141, E 146, E 158.

(c) The Rose Tattoo. Unpublished screenplay, adapted by Hal Kantor, 1955.

(d) "A Perfect Analysis Given by a Parrot." Esquire, October 1958 (C 93); A Perfect Analysis Given by a Parrot. DPS, n.d. (A 104); Dragon Country. ND, 1969 (A 127, A 128); Esquire, October 1973 (C 146, B 155). Also B 155, E 176.

The Rose Tattoo was begun in 1948 as a result of Williams's visit to Italy. It is one of his few plays for which only one published version exists; and, according to the copyright page, that was put together by Paul Bigelow. See Williams's essay "The Meaning of The Rose Tattoo" (I 36) and interview (M 25). Criticism is by Kolin (P 238), Starnes (P 367), and Thompson (P 378). Reviews are found in A 24 and K 53.

The characters and some of the dialogue of "A Perfect Analysis" appear in Act I, Scene 5 of Tattoo.

54. SENSO. Unpublished dialogue with Paul Bowles, based on screenplay by Camillo Alianello, Giorgio Bissani and Giorgio Prosperi, adapted by Luchino Visconti and Suso Cecci d'Amico, 1953 (but see E 110a).

The screenplay grew out of a story by Camillo Boito. It concerns a love affair in 1866 between a Venetian countess and an Austrian officer, whose mistress she becomes. During a war between the two countries, he abandons her, she denounces him as a deserter, and he is executed. The Visconti film was also released under the title The Wanton Countess. A review is given in K 54.

55. THE SEVEN DESCENTS OF MYRTLE see Kingdom of Earth

56. SLAPSTICK TRAGEDY see "The Gnädiges Fräulein" and "The Mutilated"

57. SMALL CRAFT WARNINGS/"CONFESSIONAL." Mss., Library of Congress (J 5), Texas (J 9).

(a) "Confessional." Dragon Country. ND, 1969 (A 127, A 128). Also B 152, E 176.

(b) Small Craft Warnings. ND, 1972 (A 136, A 137); Small Craft Warnings. S&W, 1973 (A 138); Theatre V. ND, 1976 (A 151); Also B 148.

The full-length play is more an expansion than a rewrite of "Confessional," and the earlier version is probably the better. Small Craft Warnings is too long, and the ending is sentimental. The character of Bobby has been changed: in "Confessional" he was more innocent, or ignorant, hardening into knowledge; in the revision he is experienced and, though perhaps a bit more believable, less interesting. Williams's essays "Too Personal?" (I 64) and "Notes after the Second Invited Audience" (I 40) and his letters on "Small Craft Warnings: Genius and Evolution" were published with the play. See also his interview (M 31). Reviews are found in A 136 and K 57.

58. "SOMETHING UNSPOKEN." Ms., Texas (J 9); 27 Wagons Full of Cotton. ND, 1953, 1966 (A 32, A 107); Garden District. S&W, 1959 (A 62); Orpheus Descending.... Penguin, 1961 (A 76); Five Plays. S&W, 1962 (A 80); Baby Doll.... Penguin, 1968 (A 120). Also B 53, B 76, B 132a, B 144, E 172.

The play was produced together with Suddenly Last Summer (F 62) under the collective title Garden District. Reviews are found in K 62.

59. STAIRS TO THE ROOF. Ms., Texas (J 9); unpublished play, 1940-1942.

The play is a fantasy set in a shirtmaker's factory; Nelson (P 296) has given a scene-by-scene résumé. Reviews are found in K 59.

60. "THE STRANGEST KIND OF ROMANCE." Ms., Texas (J 9); 27 Wagons Full of Cotton. ND, 1945, 1953, 1966 (A 3, A 32, A 107); 27 Wagons Full of Cotton. J. Lehmann, 1949 (A 17). Also A 9.

The play grew out of the short story "The Malediction" (G 17).

61. A STREETCAR NAMED DESIRE. Mss., Texas (J 9).

(a) A Streetcar Named Desire. ND, 1947 (A 11); A Streetcar Named Desire. J. Lehmann, 1949 (A 18); Four Plays. S&W, 1956 (A 43); A Streetcar Named Desire. S&W, 1957 (A 51); A Streetcar Named Desire.... Penguin, 1959 (A 61); Sweet Bird of Youth.... Penguin, 1962 (A 79). Also B 165, C 51.

(b) A Streetcar Named Desire. ND, n.d. (A 23); A Streetcar Named Desire, NAL, 1951 (A 26); A Streetcar Named

Desire. Braille edition, 1966 (A 109); Theatre I. ND, 1971 (A 131). Also A 99, B 15, B 35, B 40, B 48, B 121a, B 125, B 126, B 133, B 168a, D 6, D 7, E 2, E 8, E 12, E 33, E 43, E 52, E 63, E 84, E 92, E 96, E 100, E 108, E 116, E 121, E 130, E 135, E 136, E 150, E 153, E 157, E 161, E 164, E 178, E 183 (note: I cannot be sure which version was translated, so all translations are listed here).

(c) A Streetcar Named Desire. Screenplay, adapted by Oscar Saul, 1950: Film Scripts One, ed. G. P. Garrett et al. Appleton, 1971 (B 145).

(d) A Streetcar Named Desire. DPS, 1953 (A 30).

The play was begun in 1945. Dickson (P 88) has published a fascinating study of its development through the manuscripts. New Directions has published two slightly different texts of the play. The revision contains some rewriting of key speeches, but it is essentially a cutting of the original. The first edition begins with printed dialogue between Eunice and the Negro woman (see Leavitt, N 49, for some information about the origin of these speeches); it is this text that all British editions follow. The second edition begins with printed dialogue between Stanley and Stella. The speeches in the Dramatists Play Service edition and the second New Directions edition are practically the same, but the stage directions are often different. Thomas Hart Benton painted a scene from the first New York production, "The Polker Night" (K 61).

Williams's screenplay, written in the summer and fall of 1950, follows the play closely but omits mention of Allan Grey's homosexuality and suggests that Stella will not return to Stanley. See Kazin's interview (N 71). Valerie Bettis choreographed the ballet version of the play in 1952; music was Alex North's score for the film.

See Williams's essays "The Catastrophe of Success" (I 12) and "Let Me Hang It All Out" (I 35). Criticism includes that by Berkman (P 22), Berlin (P 25), Bernard (P 26), Bigsby (P 27), Cardullo (P 53), Efstate (P 108), Ehrlich (P 110), Farnsworth (P 116), Funatsu (P 128), Hirsch (P 186), Isaac (P 200), Kahn (P 225), Law (P 248), Mood (P 286), Oppel (P 301, P 302), Quijano (P 324), Quirino (P 325), Riddel (P 337), and Thomas (P 377). See also Chesler's summary (P 60). Collections of criticism have been edited by Hurrell (P 194) and Miller (P 282). The production record is found in K 61; reviews of the book are listed in A 11.

62. SUDDENLY LAST SUMMER. Mss., Texas (J 9).

(a) Suddenly Last Summer. ND, 1958 (A 55); Suddenly Last Summer. DPS, 1958 (A 56); Garden District. S&W, 1959 (A 62); Suddenly Last Summer. NAL, 1960 (A 67); Orpheus Descending.... Penguin, 1961 (A 76); Five Plays. S&W, 1962 (A 80); Baby Doll.... Penguin, 1968 (A 120); Theatre III. ND, 1971 (A 133); Four Plays. NAL, 1976

(A 158). Also A 116, B 135, E 50, E 75, E 81, E 96, E 125, E 147, E 172.

(b) Suddenly Last Summer. Unpublished screenplay, with Gore Vidal, 1959.

(c) Suddenly Last Summer. Unpublished play, 1976.

The play was produced together with "Something Unspoken" (F 58) under the collective title Garden District. In 1976 Williams revised the very ending. Vidal, in his comments (N 75 and elsewhere), would suggest that he did all the work on the screenplay. Specific criticism of the play is by Armato (P 7), Debusscher (P 83), Funatsu (P 130), Hurley (F 191), Hurt (P 195), Johnson (P 216), and Satterfield (P 350). Reviews are found in K 62.

63. SUMMER AND SMOKE/THE ECCENTRICITIES OF A NIGHTINGALE. Mss., Texas (J 9).

(a) Summer and Smoke. ND, 1948 (A 16); Summer and Smoke. J. Lehmann, 1952 (A 27); Four Plays. S&W, 1956 (A 43); Summer and Smoke. S&W, 1957 (A 52); Summer and Smoke. NAL, 1961 (A 74); Summer and Smoke.... NEL, 1963 (A 87); The Eccentricities of a Nightingale.... ND, 1964 (A 95); Theatre II. ND, 1971 (A 132); Four Plays. NAL, 1976 (A 158). Also A 100, B 35, B 39, B 65, B 121a, B 128, B 149, E 4, E 7, E 15, E 38, E 43, E 74, E 78, E 90, E 96, E 116, E 128, E 143, E 144, E 149, E 157.

(b) Summer and Smoke. DPS, 1950 (A 20).

(c) The Eccentricities of a Nightingale.... ND, 1964 (A 95); Theatre II. ND, 1971 (A 132).

(d) The Eccentricities of a Nightingale. DPS, 1977 (A 166).

Summer and Smoke has a passing relationship with the short story "The Yellow Bird" (G 42); Eccentricities has a somewhat stronger tie. The story should encourage the reader, however, to see that Alma's choice at the end of both versions of the play is a positive one, not tragic as too many critics, allowing their own puritan values to interfere with their vision of the play, have tried to assert. See also Williams's essay "Questions without Answers" (I 53).

The play was begun in 1945. Williams revised the New Directions text for Dramatists Play Service, omitting the prologue and the lines in Scene 1 about the microscope, shifting some material from one scene to another, and adding an entirely new scene with Alma and the older doctor between Scenes 1 and 2 (mentioning for the first time the aunt who figures so importantly in Eccentricities) and a prayer at the beginning of Scene 8. Unfortunately material in Scene 4 which he had introduced into the new scene was not deleted there. Specific criticism is by Brooking (P 37), Cottrell (P 287), and Moody (P 287). Reviews are found in A 16 and K 63.

The screenplay of Summer and Smoke was prepared by

James Poe and Meade Roberts, 1961. The libretto of the opera version (A 135, A 152) was made by Lanford Wilson in 1971; music was by Lee Hoiby. See Williams's and Hoiby's interview (M 17).

Williams rewrote the play so completely in 1951 that his choice of a new title is justified. Eccentricities is a more tightly structured and, in many ways, better work, but it is perhaps a less charming one. The Dramatists Play Service version adds some dialogue at the beginning of Act II, Scene 2; drops Act II, Scene 4; and radically rewrites Act III, bringing in some of the material from the omitted scene and adding much new dialogue. The Epilogue is the same in both texts. See Williams's essay "'I Have Rewritten a Play for Artistic Purity'" (I 29). For reviews, see, K 63.

64. SWEET BIRD OF YOUTH/"THE ENEMY: TIME." Mss., Library of Congress (J 5), Texas (J 9).

(a) "The Enemy: Time." Theatre, March 1959 (C 96).

(b) Sweet Bird of Youth. Unpublished play in two acts and eleven scenes, 1956.

(c) Sweet Bird of Youth. Esquire, April 1959 (C 96).

(d) Sweet Bird of Youth. ND, 1959 (A 65); Sweet Bird of Youth. NAL, 1962 (A 78); Sweet Bird of Youth.... Penguin, 1962 (A 79); Three Plays. ND, 1964 (A 94); Theatre IV. ND, 1972 (A 134); Three by Tennessee. NAL, 1976 (A 159). Also B 64, E 11, E 21, E 59, E 82, E 95, E 156, E 165.

(e) Sweet Bird of Youth. DPS, 1962 (A 84).

The play began as the one-act sketch "The Enemy: Time," written about 1952. In 1956 the full-length version was produced. Leavitt reproduces a part of the program for that production (B 170). The play caught the attention of Elia Kazan, who brought it to New York in 1959 and who was probably responsible for many alterations in the script. The version published in Esquire, particularly Act II, has already been far changed from the 1956 version and the horrible curtain line introduced, but it is still fairly close to Williams's original conception.

The New Directions and the Dramatists Play Service texts are messes. The New Directions text cuts one entire scene and parts of others from Act II and changes Act III still further. The Dramatists Play Service text has been so cut (yet another scene dropped from Act II, though an earlier Esquire scene was restored) that I can scarcely see how anyone could even follow the play. Act III has been rewritten for Dramatists Play Service, giving a more believable ending but one which destroys the entire thrust of the drama to that point. The whole problem is one of focus: the play is about Chance Wayne, but the Princess has taken over; and indeed Williams has thought about rewriting the drama to center on her (see A 154). Criticism is by Dukore (P 101), Hays (P 172), and Roulet (P 343). Reviews are found in A 65, A 71, and K 64.

65. "TALK TO ME LIKE THE RAIN AND LET ME LISTEN...." Ms., Texas (J 9); 27 Wagons Full of Cotton. ND, 1953, 1966 (A 32, A 107). Also E 50, E 71, E 96.

A review is found in K 65.

66. TENNESSEE WILLIAMS'S SOUTH.

This television tribute to Williams had a script by Harry Rasky, 1973.

67. THIS IS (AN ENTERTAINMENT). Unpublished play in two acts and several scenes, 1976.

Set in an imaginary mid-European country, the play examines the nature of sexuality and of fear; its mode is fantasy. Reviews are found in K 67.

68. "THIS PROPERTY IS CONDEMNED." Ms., Texas (J 9); American Scenes, ed. William Kozlenko. J. Day, 1941 (B 2); 27 Wagons Full of Cotton. ND, 1945, 1953, 1966 (A 3, A 32, A 107); 27 Wagons Full of Cotton. J. Lehmann, 1949 (A 17). Also A 9, C 66, E 50, E 96, E 109.

Reviews are found in K 68. Williams apparently worked to some extent on the screenplay made by Francis Ford Coppola, Fred Coe, and Edith Sommer, 1966, but demanded that his name be removed from the credits.

69. "THREE PLAYERS OF A SUMMER GAME" see Cat on a Hot Tin Roof

70. TIGER TAIL see " 27 Wagons Full of Cotton"

71. "27 WAGONS FULL OF COTTON"/BABY DOLL/TIGER TAIL. Mss., Library of Congress (J 5), Texas (J 9).

(a) "27 Wagons Full of Cotton." Best One-Act Plays of 1944, ed. Margaret Mayorga. Dodd, Mead, 1945 (B 8); 27 Wagons Full of Cotton. ND, 1945, 1953, 1966 (A 3, A 32, A 107); 27 Wagons Full of Cotton. J. Lehmann, 1949 (A 17); Baby Doll. ND, 1956 (A 45). Also A 9, B 14, B 57, B 60, B 83, B 85, E 50, E 104.

(b) Baby Doll. ND, 1956 (A 45); Baby Doll. NAL, 1956 (A 46); Baby Doll. S&W, 1957 (A 47); Baby Doll. Penguin, 1957 (A 48); Baby Doll..., Penguin, 1968 (A 120), Also E 50, E 61, E 116.

(c) Tiger Tail. Unpublished play, 1978.

"27 Wagons" was based on the short story of the same title (G 38). It, together with "The Long Stay Cut Short" (F 36), became the basis for Williams's first original screenplay, Baby Doll. He began work on it with Elia Kazan in 1952; the shooting script was finished in early 1956. The ending of the film, however, is not quite the same as that of the published script. See Williams's interview (M 14) and Kazan's (N 71). Criticism is by Dusenbury (P 106), Hilfer and Ramsey (P 182), and Kahn (P 222). In 1978 Williams turned the film script into a full-length play, Tiger Tail. Reviews of all three works are found in K 71.

72. THE TWO-CHARACTER PLAY/OUT CRY. Ms., Texas (J 9).
(a) The Two-Character Play. ND, 1969 (A 126).
(b) Out Cry. Unpublished play, 1971.
(c) Out Cry. ND, 1973 (A 139, A 140).
(d) The Two-Character Play. Theatre V. ND, 1976 (A 151).

The first version was performed in 1967. It lacked much of the symbolism of later versions and was without an intermission. Its structure is more satisfactory, but its development is less interesting. The second version was produced in 1971. The third version is perhaps the worst play Williams has ever written; the fourth, produced in 1975, is among his most interesting. In both these latter scripts the play within the play remains almost the same; it is the characters themselves and their response to their fate which have changed so radically. Both plays are too long, however. See Williams's interview (M 20). Criticism is by Ishida (P 204) and Stamper (P 365). Reviews are found in A 140 and K 72.

73. "THE UNSATISFACTORY SUPPER" see "The Long Stay Cut Short"

74. VIEUX CARRE.
(a) Unpublished play in two acts, 1977.
(b) Vieux Carré. ND, 1979 (A 170, A 171).

In the first version the first act was called "The Angel in the Alcove," after the short story (G 1); the second act was called "I Never Get Dressed Until After Dark on Sundays." The published version was first performed in 1978. Reviews are found in K 74.

75. THE WANTON COUNTESS see Senso

76. YOU TOUCHED ME. Mss., Texas (J 9).
(a) You Touched Me. Unpublished scripts, with Donald Windham, 1942-1943.
(b) You Touched Me! S. French, 1947 (A 8).

The play, Williams's second and last to be written in collaboration, is an adaptation of D. H. Lawrence's story of the same name, with touches of Lawrence's other works, particularly The Fox. Montgomery Clift hoped to turn out a screenplay, but he never finished it. Reviews are found in K 76.

G. SHORT STORIES AND NOVELS

1. "THE ANGEL IN THE ALCOVE." Ms., Texas (J 9); One Arm. ND, 1948, 1954, 1967 (A 12, A 36, A 113); Three Players of a Summer Game. S&W, 1960 (A 69); Three Players of a Summer Game. Penguin, 1965 (A 101). Also A 82, E 25, E 48, E 58, E 83.

   The story was written in October 1943 in Santa Monica, California. It became the basis for Act I of Vieux Carré (F 74).

2. "CAN A GOOD WIFE BE A GOOD SPORT?" Smart Set, May 1927 (C 2); Remember Me to Tom by Edwina D. Williams. Putnam's, 1963 (B 108).

   Disguised as an essay for a contest, this is really a work of fiction.

3. "CHRONICLE OF A DEMISE." Ms., Texas (J 9); One Arm. ND, 1948, 1954, 1967 (A 12, A 36, A 113); Three Players of a Summer Game. S&W, 1960 (A 69); Three Players of a Summer Game. Penguin, 1965 (A 101). Also A 82, E 25, E 48, E 58, E 83.

4. "THE COMING OF SOMETHING TO THE WIDOW HOLLY." Ms., Texas (J 9); New Directions # 14. ND, 1953 (B 42); Hard Candy. ND, 1954, 1959, 1967 (A 34, A 35, A 64, A 114); Three Players of a Summer Game. S&W, 1960 (A 69); Three Players of a Summer Game. Penguin, 1965 (A 101). Also A 115, B 112, E 55, E 83, E 127, E 173.

   The story was begun in 1943.

5. "COMPLETED." Eight Mortal Ladies Possessed. ND, 1974 (A 142, A 143); Eight Mortal Ladies Possessed. S&W, 1974 (A 144). Also E 176.

   The story was written in November 1973.

6. "DESIRE AND THE BLACK MASSEUR." Ms., Texas (J 9); New Directions # 10. ND, 1948 (B 16); One Arm. ND, 1948, 1954, 1967 (A 12, A 36, A 113); The Knightly Quest. S&W, 1968 (A 119). Also A 82, E 25, E 48, E 58, E 66.

   The story was begun in March 1942 in New York City and was finished in April 1946. It has been examined in detail by Hurley (P 193) and Schubert (P 356).

7. "THE FIELD OF BLUE CHILDREN." Ms., Texas (J 9); Story, September-October 1939 (C 29); One Arm. ND, 1948, 1954, 1967 (A 12, A 36, A 113); Three Players of a Summer Game. S&W, 1960 (A 69); Three Players of a Summer Game.

Penguin, 1965 (A 101). Also A 82, B 92, B 105, C 84, E 25, E 29, E 48, E 58, E 83, E 139.

8. "'GRAND'" see Section I

9. "HAPPY AUGUST THE TENTH." Antaeus, Winter 1971 (C 135); Esquire, December 1972 (C 138); Eight Mortal Ladies Possessed. ND, 1974 (A 142, A 143); Eight Mortal Ladies Possessed. S&W, 1974 (A 144). Also B 150, E 176.
The story was written in August 1970.

10. "HARD CANDY"/"THE MYSTERIES OF THE JOY RIO." Ms., Texas (J 9); Hard Candy. ND, 1954, 1959, 1967 (A 34, A 35, A 64, A 114); The Knightly Quest. S&W, 1968 (A 119). Also A 115, E 55, E 127, E 173.
The two stories, always published together, are variations on a theme. "Mysteries" is the earlier; "Hard Candy" was begun in Rome in August 1949 and finished in Key West in March 1953.

11. "THE IMPORTANT THING." Ms., Texas (J 9).
(a) Story, November-December 1945 (C 33). Also B 18.
(b) One Arm. ND, 1948, 1954, 1967 (A 12, A 36, A 113); Three Players of a Summer Game. S&W, 1960 (A 69); Three Players of a Summer Game. Penguin, 1965 (A 101). Also A 82, B 111, E 25, E 48, E 58, E 83.
In the first version Flora was called Laura. Some editorial changes, of a minor type, are also found.

12. "THE INVENTORY AT FONTANA BELLA." Playboy, March 1973 (C 142); Eight Mortal Ladies Possessed. ND, 1974 (A 142, A 143); Eight Mortal Ladies Possessed. S&W, 1974 (A 144). Also E 176.
The story was written in July 1972.

13. "THE KILLER CHICKEN AND THE CLOSET QUEEN." Christopher Street, July 1978 (C 159).
The story, written in November 1977, is a comedy about a middle-aged lawyer, his trying mother, and their encounter with an amoral adolescent.

14. "THE KINGDOM OF EARTH." Ms., Texas (J 9); Hard Candy. ND, 1954 (A 35); The Knightly Quest. ND, 1966 (A 105); The Knightly Quest. S&W, 1968 (A 119). Also E 57, E 89, E 120, E 175.
The story was begun in Macon, Georgia, in July 1942. It became the basis for the play of the same name (F 30).

15. "THE KNIGHTLY QUEST." The Knightly Quest. ND, 1966 (A 105); The Knightly Quest. S&W, 1968 (A 119). Also E 57, E 89, E 120, E 175.
Nelson (N 296) says the novella was begun in 1949.

16. "A LADY'S BEADED BAG." Ms., Texas (J 9); Columns, May 1930 (C 13).
A social protest story, the plot unfolds from a derelict's finding a rich woman's purse.

17. "THE MALEDICTION." Ms., Texas (J 9); Town and Country, June 1945 (C 31); One Arm. ND, 1948, 1954, 1967 (A 12, A 36, A 113); Three Players of a Summer Game. S&W, 1960 (A 69); Three Players of a Summer Game. Penguin, 1965 (A 101). Also A 82, E 25, E 48, E 58, E 83.
The story was begun in the summer of 1941. It was dramatized as "The Strangest Kind of Romance" (F 60).

18. "MAMA'S OLD STUCCO HOUSE." Esquire, January 1965 (C 112); The Knightly Quest. ND, 1966 (A 105); The Knightly Quest. S&W, 1968 (A 119). Also C 114, C 130, E 57, E 89, E 120, E 175.

19. "MAN BRING THIS UP ROAD." Mademoiselle, July 1959 (C 97); The Knightly Quest. ND, 1966 (A 105); The Knightly Quest. S&W, 1968 (A 119). Also B 99, C 113, E 56, E 57, E 89, E 120, E 175.
According to Williams (I 38), the story was written in the summer of 1953 in Italy. It was the basis for The Milk Train Doesn't Stop Here Anymore (F 41).

20. "THE MATTRESS BY THE TOMATO PATCH." Ms., Texas (J 9); London Magazine, October 1954 (C 74); Hard Candy. ND, 1954, 1959, 1967 (A 34, A 35, A 64, A 114); The Knightly Quest. S&W, 1968 (A 119). Also A 115, B 129, E 55, E 127, E 173.
The story was written in 1953.

21. "MISS COYNTE OF GREENE." Playboy, December 1973 (C 147); Eight Mortal Ladies Possessed, ND, 1974 (A 142, A 143); Eight Mortal Ladies Possessed, S&W, 1974 (A 144). Also E 176.
The story was written in November 1972.

22. MOISE AND THE WORLD OF REASON. Moise and the World of Reason, Simon & Schuster, 1975 (A 149); Moise and the World of Reason, W. H. Allen, 1976 (A 153); Moise and the World of Reason, Bantam, 1976 (A 161). Also E 62.
Reviews of the novel are found in A 149.

23. "MOTHER YAWS." Esquire, May 1977 (C 155).
The story concerns a slow-minded woman afflicted both by a disease and by an unfeeling family.

24. "THE MYSTERIES OF THE JOY RIO" see "Hard Candy"

25. "THE NIGHT OF THE IGUANA." Ms., Texas (J 9); One Arm.

ND, 1948, 1954, 1967 (A 12, A 36, A 113); Three Players of a Summer Game. S&W, 1960 (A 69); Three Players of a Summer Game. Penguin, 1965 (A 101). Also A 82, E 25, E 48, E 58, E 83.

The story was begun in April 1946 in New Orleans and was finished in February 1948 in Rome; it grew out of Williams's 1940 visit to Acapulco. It distantly foreshadows the play of the same name (F 44).

26. "ONE ARM." Mss., Texas (J 9); One Arm. ND, 1948, 1954, 1967 (A 12, A 36, A 113); Three Players of a Summer Game. S&W, 1960 (A 69); Three Players of a Summer Game. Penguin, 1965 (A 101). Also A 82, E 25, E 48, E 58, E 83.

The story was begun in May 1942 in New York City, was revised in October 1943 in Santa Monica, California, and was finished in August 1945 in Dallas. Williams has prepared a screenplay.

27. "ORIFLAMME." Ms., Texas (J 9); "Red Part of a Flag, or Oriflamme." Vogue, March 1974 (C 149); "Oriflamme." Eight Mortal Ladies Possessed. ND, 1974 (A 142, A 143); Eight Mortal Ladies Possessed. S&W, 1974 (A 144). Also E 176.

The story was written in January 1944.

28. "THE POET." One Arm. ND, 1948, 1954, 1967 (A 12, A 36, A 113); The Knightly Quest. S&W, 1968 (A 119); Also A 82, E 25, E 48, E 58, E 83.

29. "PORTRAIT OF A GIRL IN GLASS." Mss., Texas (J 9); One Arm. ND, 1948, 1954, 1967 (A 12, A 36, A 113); Three Players of a Summer Game. S&W, 1960 (A 69); Three Players of a Summer Game. Penguin, 1965 (A 101). Also A 82, B 115, E 25, E 48, E 58, E 76, E 83, E 94, E 99, E 180.

The story was begun in February 1941 in Key West and was finished in June 1943 in Santa Monica, California. It became The Glass Menagerie (F 23).

30. "A RECLUSE AND HIS GUEST." Playboy, January 1970 (C 129).

This allegorical story recounts an encounter between an androgynous traveller and a fearful hermit.

31. "RED PART OF A FLAG, OR ORIFLAMME" see "Oriflamme"

32. "THE RESEMBLANCE BETWEEN A VIOLIN CASE AND A COFFIN." Ms., Texas (J 9); Flair, February 1950 (C 56); Penguin New Writing # 40, ed. J. Lehmann. Penguin, 1950 (B 25); Hard Candy. ND, 1954, 1959, 1967 (A 34, A 35, A 64, A 114); Three Players of a Summer Game. S&W, 1960 (A 69); Three Players of a Summer Game. Penguin, 1965 (A 101). Also A 115, B 33, E 55, E 83, E 127, E 173.

The story was written in October 1949.

33. THE ROMAN SPRING OF MRS. STONE. Mss., Texas (J 9); *The Roman Spring of Mrs. Stone.* ND, 1950, 1969 (A 21, A 125); *The Roman Spring of Mrs. Stone.* J. Lehmann, 1950 (A 22); *The Roman Spring of Mrs. Stone.* NAL, 1952 (A 28); *The Roman Spring of Mrs. Stone.* S&W, 1957 (A 50); *The Roman Spring of Mrs. Stone.* NAL, 1961 (A 75); *The Roman Spring of Mrs. Stone.* Bantam, 1976 (A 162); *The Roman Spring of Mrs. Stone.* Panther, 1977 (A 165). Also E 18, E 20, E 23, E 26, E 28, E 32, E 34, E 35, E 51, E 53, E 67, E 115, E 124, E 142, E 154, E 170, E 179, E 182.

The novel began as an idea for a film; but the screenplay, when it was filmed, was written by Gavin Lambert, 1961. Criticism of the novel is by Gérard (P 142) and Hyman (P 197). Reviews of the book are found in A 21 and A 22. Reviews of the film are found in K 52.

34. "RUBIO Y MORENA." Ms., Texas (J 9); *Partisan Review*, December 1948 (C 46); *New Directions # 11.* ND, 1949 (B 20); *Hard Candy.* ND, 1954, 1959, 1967 (A 34, A 35, A 64, A 114); *The Knightly Quest.* S&W, 1968 (A 119). Also A 115, E 55, E 127, E 173.

Hyman (P 196) looks at the story in passing.

35. "SABBATHA AND SOLITUDE." *Playgirl*, September 1973 (C 148); *Eight Mortal Ladies Possessed.* ND, 1974 (A 142, A 143); *Eight Mortal Ladies Possessed.* S&W, 1974 (A 144). Also E 176.

The story was written in June 1973.

36. "SOMETHING ABOUT HIM." Ms., Texas (J 9); *Mademoiselle*, June 1946 (C 34).

This unjustly forgotten story tells about a librarian in love with a clerk whom nobody likes.

37. "THREE PLAYERS OF A SUMMER GAME." Mss., Texas (J 9); *New Yorker*, 2 November 1952 (C 68); *Hard Candy.* ND, 1954, 1959, 1967 (A 34, A 35, A 64, A 114); *Three Players of a Summer Game.* S&W, 1960 (A 69); *Three Players of a Summer Game.* Penguin, 1965 (A 101). Also A 115, B 38, B 81, B 120, C 76, E 24, E 29, E 40, E 55, E 70, E 83, E 110, E 127, E 173.

The story was written in Venice and Rome in the summer, 1951 and was revised in April 1952 (see N 39). It distantly foreshadows *Cat on a Hot Tin Roof* and was dramatized under its own name (F 11).

38. "TWENTY-SEVEN WAGONS FULL OF COTTON." Ms., Texas (J 9); *Manuscript*, August 1936 (C 22).

The story was dramatized under the same title (F 71).

39. "TWO ON A PARTY." Mss., Texas (J 9); Hard Candy. ND, 1954, 1959, 1967 (A 34, A 35, A 64, A 114); Three Players of a Summer Game. S&W, 1960 (A 69); Three Players of a Summer Game. Penguin, 1965 (A 101). Also A 115, B 162, E 55, E 83, E 127, E 173.

The story was begun in London and was finished in New Orleans in 1951-1952.

40. "THE VENGEANCE OF NITOCRIS." Weird Tales, August 1928 (C 3). Also B 132, B 139, C 111.

Written by Williams at age 16, the story tells of the revenge an Egyptian queen took against the murderers of her brother, though he was killed for having committed sacrilege.

41. "THE VINE." Mss., Texas (J 9); Mademoiselle, July 1954 (C 71); Hard Candy. ND, 1954, 1959, 1967 (A 34, A 35, A 64, A 114); The Knightly Quest. S&W, 1968 (A 119). Also A 115, B 67, E 55, E 127, E 173.

The story was begun in Laguna Beach, California, in May 1939, and was revised in Clayton, Missouri, in January 1944.

42. "THE YELLOW BIRD." Ms., Texas (J 9).

(a) Town and Country, June 1947 (C 38); One Arm. ND, 1948 (A 12).

(b) One Arm. ND, 1954, 1967 (A 36, A 113); Three Players of a Summer Game. S&W, 1960 (A 69); Three Players of a Summer Game. Penguin, 1965 (A 101). Also B 47, B 106, B 167, D 1, E 25, E 48, E 58, E 83.

Revisions are actually minor. The story foreshadows aspects of Summer and Smoke and The Eccentricities of a Nightingale (F 63). Williams has toyed with the idea of writing a screenplay.

H. POEMS

1. "ACROSS THE SPACE." Voices, September-December 1952 (C 65); In The Winter of Cities. ND, 1956, 1964 (A 42, A 96).

2. "AFTER A VISIT." Ms., Texas (J 9); Voices, August-September 1934 (C 19); Literary Digest, 1 September 1934 (C 20). Also A 81, B 108.

3. "ANDROGYNE, MON AMOUR." Ambit, 1977 (C 157); Androgyne, Mon Amour. ND, 1977 (A 163).
   The poem is dated "San Francisco, 1976."

4. "THE ANGELS OF FRUCTIFICATION." Ms., Texas (J 9).
   (a) Five Young American Poets. ND, 1944 (B 7).
   (b) In the Winter of Cities. ND, 1956, 1964 (A 42, A 96).
   Also E 54.
   The poem was written summer 1942. Only a line was changed when it was reprinted.

5. "APPARITION." Androgyne, Mon Amour. ND, 1977 (A 163).

6. "AVE ATQUE VALE." Alouette, October 1933 (C 18).

7. "THE BEANSTALK COUNTRY." Ms., Texas (J 9); Five Young American Poets. ND, 1944 (B 7); In the Winter of Cities. ND, 1956, 1964 (A 42, A 96). Also E 119.

8. "BLANKET ROLL BLUES." Unpublished poem.
   The poem was set to music by Kenyon Hopkins for the film The Fugitive Kind (F 4; K 4f).

9. "THE BRAIN'S DISSECTION." Androgyne, Mon Amour. ND, 1977 (A 163).

10. "CABIN." Ms., Texas (J 9); Blue Mountain Ballads. G. Schirmer, 1946 (A 6); In the Winter of Cities. ND, 1956, 1964 (A 42, A 96). Also B 127, D 2.
    The poem was set to music by Paul Bowles.

11. "CACTI." Ms., Texas (J 9); Voices, August-September 1934 (C 19).
    The poem was written in 1938 in Taos, New Mexico.

12. "CAMINO REAL" See "The Jockeys at Hialeah"

13. "CARROUSEL TUNE." Voices, September-December 1952 (C 65); In the Winter of Cities. ND, 1956, 1964 (A 42, A 96).

14. "THE CHRISTUS OF GUADALAJARA." Ms., Texas (J 9); Botteghe Obscura, 1949 (C 50); In the Winter of Cities. ND, 1956, 1964 (A 42, A 96). Also E 107.
The poem was written in June 1941 in Manhattan, but it grew out of Williams's 1940 trip to Mexico.

15. "CINDER HILL." Mss., Texas (J 9); Androgyne, Mon Amour. ND, 1977 (A 163).
Written and revised from 1941 in New Orleans until at least 1944 at Fire Island, New York, Williams thought of this poem as one of the "Blue Mountain Ballads."

16. "CLOVER." College Verse, January 1937 (C 24).

17. "LE COEUR A SES RAISONS." Ms., Texas (J 9); Eliot, December 1936 (C 23).

18. "THE COMFORTER AND THE BETRAYER." Mss., Texas (J 9); In the Winter of Cities. ND, 1964 (A 96).
The poem was written in October 1953 in Tangier and was revised in March 1954 in Key West.

19. "CORTEGE." Ms., Texas (J 9).
(a) Five Young American Poets. ND, 1944 (B 7).
(b) In the Winter of Cities. ND, 1956, 1964 (A 42, A 96). Also E 54.
The first version was written in Santa Monica in August 1943. Changes were many.

20. "COUNSEL." Ms., Texas (J 9).
(a) New Directions # 11. ND, 1949 (B 20).
(b) Androgyne, Mon Amour. ND, 1977 (A 163).
The poem was first written in Paris in May 1949. Changes are minor.

21. "THE COUPLE." Androgyne, Mon Amour. ND, 1977 (A 163).

22. "COVENANT." In the Winter of Cities. ND, 1964 (A 96).

23. "CREPE-DE-CHINE." New Yorker, 5 July 1969 (C 128); Androgyne, Mon Amour. ND, 1977 (A 163).

24. "CRIED THE FOX." Ms., Texas (J 9); Five Young American Poets. ND, 1944 (B 7); In the Winter of Cities. ND, 1956, 1964 (A 42, A 96). Also D 1.
Dedicated to D. H. Lawrence, the poem was written in Taos in 1939.

25. "THE DANGEROUS PAINTERS." Mss., Texas (J 9); Five Young

American Poets. ND, 1944 (B 7); In the Winter of Cities. ND, 1956, 1964 (A 42, A 96).

The poem was written in New York City, December 1942-January 1943.

26. "DARK ARM, HANGING OVER THE EDGE OF INFINITY." Mss., Texas (J 9).
(a) Five Young American Poets. ND, 1944 (B 7).
(b) Androgyne, Mon Amour. ND, 1977 (A 163).

The poem was written in Darian, Georgia, in April 1941 and was revised in New York City in May 1942. Stanza two of the first version was omitted in the 1977 printing.

27. "A DAYBREAK THOUGHT FOR MARIA." Androgyne, Mon Amour. ND, 1977 (A 163).

28. "THE DEATH EMBRACE." Five Young American Poets. ND, 1944 (B 7); In the Winter of Cities. ND, 1956, 1964 (A 42, A 96). Also E 54.

The poem was written in Acapulco in September 1940.

29. "DEATH IS HIGH." Ms., Texas (J 9); Five Young American Poets. ND, 1944 (B 7); In the Winter of Cities. ND, 1956, 1964 (A 42, A 96).

30. "DESCENT." Voices, September-December 1952 (C 65); In the Winter of Cities. ND, 1956, 1964 (A 42, A 96).

31. "THE DIVING BELL." Androgyne, Mon Amour. ND, 1977 (A 163).

32. "LES ETOILES D'UN CIRQUE." Androgyne, Mon Amour. ND, 1977 (A 163).

33. "EVENING." Androgyne, Mon Amour. ND, 1977 (A 163).

34. "EVENTS PROCEED." Androgyne, Mon Amour. ND, 1977 (A 163).

35. "EVERYMAN." Ms., Texas (J 9); Contemporary Poetry, Summer 1945 (C 32); In the Winter of Cities. ND, 1956, 1964 (A 42, A 96).

36. "THE EYES." Mss., Buffalo (J 2), Texas (J 9); New Directions #11. ND, 1949 (B 20); In the Winter of Cities. ND, 1956 1964 (A 42, A 96). Also E 54.

The poem was written for Professor Oliver Evans in Rome in July-August 1949.

37. "FAINT AS LEAF SHADOW." Ms., Texas (J 9); New Directions # 12, ND, 1959 (B 29); Voices, September-December 1952 (C 65); In the Winter of Cities. ND, 1956, 1964 (A 42,

A 96). Also E 54.
The poem was written in July 1949 in Rome.

38. "FEAR IS A MONSTER AS VAST AS NIGHT...." The Two-Character Play. ND, 1969 (A 126); Theatre V. ND, 1976 (A 151); Androgyne, Mon Amour. ND, 1977 (A 163).

39. "GOLD TOOTH BLUES." Ms., Texas (J 9); In the Winter of Cities. ND, 1956, 1964 (A 42, A 96). Also D 1.
The poem was set to music by Paul Bowles, but he lost his copy (see N 68).

40. "THE GOTHS." Ms., Texas (J 9); New Directions # 12. ND, 1950 (B 29).

41. "THE HARP OF WALES." Mss., Texas (J 9); Prairie Schooner, 1949 (C 49); Androgyne, Mon Amour. ND, 1977 (A 163).
The poem was written in August 1945 in Bethel, Connecticut, and was revised in September in Martha's Vineyard.

42. "HEAVENLY GRASS." Mss., Texas (J 9); Blue Mountain Ballads. G. Schirmer, 1946 (A 4); In the Winter of Cities. ND, 1956, 1964 (A 42, A 96). Also D 1, D 2.
The poem was written in March 1941 in Key West and was revised in May 1942. It was set to music by Paul Bowles. Williams uses it in Orpheus Descending (F 4) and in Kingdom of Earth (F 30).

43. "HER HEAD ON THE PILLOW." Ms., Texas (J 9); New Directions # 12. ND, 1950 (B 29); In the Winter of Cities. ND, 1956, 1964 (A 42, A 96).
The poem was set to music by Paul Bowles.

44. "HIS MANNER OF RETURNING." Androgyne, Mon Amour. ND, 1977 (A 163).

45. "I AM AN EXILE HERE, SOME OTHER LAND...." Voices, September-December 1952 (C 65).

46. "I CONFESS I CANNOT GUESS...." Voices, September-December 1952 (C 65).

47. "I THINK THE STRANGE, THE CRAZED, THE QUEER...." Ms., Texas (J 9).
(a) Tennessee Williams by Benjamin Nelson. Obolensky, 1961 (B 88).
(b) Esquire, August 1965 (C 116); The Mutilated. DPS, 1967 (A 112); Dragon Country. ND, 1969 (A 127, A 128).
The poem was first written in August 1941 in New York City. It was much expanded and used as a carol, set to music by Lee Hoiby, between scenes of "The Mutilated" (F 43).

48. "THE ICE-BLUE WIND." Mss., Texas (J 9).
(a) Five Young American Poets. ND, 1944 (B 7).
(b) Androgyne, Mon Amour. ND, 1977 (A 163).
The first version was written in Provincetown in July 1941 and was revised in St. Augustine during the summer 1942. Only five lines of the second version appeared in the first.

49. "IMPRESSIONS THROUGH A PENNSY WINDOW." Androgyne, Mon Amour. ND, 1977 (A 163).
This is really two poems: "Going Home" and "Rival Breathers." The second proves, if nothing else, that Williams is no botanist.

50. "IN JACK-O'-LATERN'S WEATHER"/"THE MARVELOUS CHILDREN." Ms., Texas (J 9).
(a) "The Marvelous Children." Five Young American Poets. ND, 1944 (B 7).
(b) "In Jack-o'-Lantern's Weather." In the Winter of Cities. ND, 1956, 1964 (A 42, A 96).
The poem was extensively rewritten for the second collection.

51. "INHERITORS." Ms., Texas (J 9); College Verse, April 1937 (C 26).

52. "THE INTERIOR OF THE POCKET." Mss., Texas (J 9); New Directions #13, ND, 1951 (B 34); In the Winter of Cities. ND, 1956, 1964 (A 42, A 96). Also B 154.
The poem was written in London and Paris in July 1948 and was revised in Italy during January-March 1949.

53. "INTIMATIONS." Mss., Texas (J 9).
(a) Five Young American Poets. ND, 1944 (B 7).
(b) In the Winter of Cities. ND, 1956, 1964 (A 42, A 96). Also E 54.
The first version was written in St. Louis in November 1941 and revised in Macon, Georgia, in July 1942.

54. "IRON IS THE WINTER." Ms., Texas (J 9); Five Young American Poets. ND, 1944 (B 7); In the Winter of Cities. ND, 1956, 1964 (A 42, A 96).
The poem was written in New York City in February 1942.

55. "THE ISLAND IS MEMORABLE TO US." Ms., Texas (J 9); New Directions #12, ND, 1950 (B 29); In the Winter of Cities. ND, 1956, 1964 (A 42, A 96).
The poem was written in Key West, its subject, in January 1950 for Frank Merlo.

56. "THE JOCKEYS AT HIALEAH"/"CAMINO REAL." Mss., Texas (J 9).
(a) "Camino Real." New Directions # 9, ND, 1946 (B 11).

(b) "The Jockeys at Hialeah." In the Winter of Cities. ND, 1956, 1964 (A 42, A 96).

The poem was begun in February 1945 in Chicago and was finished at Lake Chapala, Mexico, in July 1945; it was originally dedicated to "Jay." Only the title and subtitles were changed when it was collected. Part I was formerly called "The Jockeys at Hialeah"; Part II, "The Sunshine Special"; Part III, "The Doves of Aphrodite"; and Part IV, "Brass Bed."

57. "KITCHEN DOOR BLUES." Ms., Texas (J 9); Maryland Quarterly, 1944 (C 30); In the Winter of Cities. ND, 1956, 1964 (A 42, A 96). Also D 1.

58. "LADY, ANEMONE." Mss., Texas (J 9); New Directions # 9. ND, 1946 (B 11); In the Winter of Cities. ND, 1956, 1964 (A 42, A 96).

The poem was begun in Provincetown in June 1944 and was finished at Lake Chapala, Mexico, in July 1945.

59. "THE LADY WITH NO ONE AT ALL." Androgyne, Mon Amour. ND, 1977 (A 163).

60. "LAMENT." College Verse, January 1937 (C 24).

61. "LAMENT FOR THE MOTHS." Ms., Texas (J 9); Five Young American Poets. ND, 1944 (B 7); In the Winter of Cities. ND, 1956, 1964 (A 42, A 96).

The poem was written at Jacksonville, Florida, in October 1942.

62. "THE LAST WINE." Ms., Texas (J 9); Five Young American Poets. ND, 1944 (B 7); In the Winter of Cities. ND, 1956 1964 (A 42, A 96).

The poem was written in Memphis, Tennessee, in 1940.

63. "THE LEGEND." Ms., Texas (J 9); Five Young American Poets. ND, 1944 (B 7); In the Winter of Cities. ND, 1956, 1964 (A 42, A 96).

The poem was written at Taos, New Mexico, in 1940.

64. "LIFE STORY." Ms., Texas (J 9); In the Winter of Cities. ND, 1956, 1964 (A 42, A 96). Also E 49, E 54.

65. "LITTLE HORSE." Ms., Texas (J 9); In the Winter of Cities. ND, 1956, 1964 (A 42, A 96). Also D 1, B 79, B 170.

The poem was written for Frank Merlo.

66. "A LITURGY OF ROSES." Mss., Texas (J 9).

(a) Chicago Review, Summer 1946 (C 35).

(b) Androgyne, Mon Amour. ND, 1977 (A 163).

The poem was originally written in New York City in October 1945; it was revised in Rome in March 1948 and probably subsequently. Changes are extensive.

67. "LONESOME MAN." Ms., Texas (J 9); Blue Mountain Ballads. G. Schirmer, 1946 (A 5); In the Winter of Cities. ND, 1956, 1964 (A 42, A 96). Also D 2.
The poem was written in May 1942. It was set to music by Paul Bowles.

68. "LYRIC." College Verse, January 1937 (C 24).

69. "THE MAN IN THE DINING CAR." Ms., Texas (J 9); Five Young American Poets. ND, 1944 (B 7); In the Winter of Cities. ND, 1956, 1964 (A 42, A 96). Also E 49, E 54.

70. "THE MARVELOUS CHILDREN" see "In Jack-o'-Lantern's Weather"

71. "A MENDICANT ORDER." Androgyne, Mon Amour. ND, 1977 (A 163).

72. "THE MIND DOES NOT FORGET." Ms., Texas (J 9); Eliot, December 1936 (C 23).

73. "MISS PUMA, MISS WHO?" Antaeus, Autumn 1973 (C 145); Androgyne, Mon Amour. ND, 1977 (A 163).

74. "MODUS VIVENDI." Counterpoint, July 1933 (C 17).

75. "MORGENLIED." Ms., Texas (J 9); Five Young American Poets. ND, 1944 (B 7).
The poem was written in Washington, D. C., in the summer, 1941. It has been set to music by Joy Fetterman.

76. "MORNINGS ON BOURBON STREET." Ms., Texas (J 9); Five Young American Poets. ND, 1944 (B 7); In the Winter of Cities. ND, 1956, 1964 (A 42, A 96).
This poem about New Orleans was written in Santa Monica, California, in July 1943.

77. "MY LITTLE ONE." Ms., Texas (J 9); In the Winter of Cities. ND, 1956, 1964 (A 42, A 96). Also B 59, D 1.

78. "MY LOVE WAS LIGHT." Ms., Texas (J 9); Poetry, June 1937 (C 28). Also B 169.
The poem was written in St. Louis in 1936.

79. "NIGHT VISIT." Androgyne, Mon Amour. ND, 1977 (A 163).

80. "OCTOBER SONG." Ms., Texas (J 9); Neophyte, 1932-1933 (C 15).

81. "OF ROSES." The World of Tennessee Williams, ed. R. F. Leavitt. Putnam's, 1978 (B 170).

82. "OLD BEAUX AND FADED LADIES PLAY...." The Two-

Character Play. ND, 1969 (A 126); Androgyne, Mon Amour. ND, 1977 (A 163).

83. "OLD MEN ARE FOND." Ms., Texas (J 9); In the Winter of Cities. ND, 1964 (A 96).

84. "OLD MEN GO MAD AT NIGHT." Androgyne, Mon Amour. ND, 1977 (A 163).

85. "OLD MEN WITH STICKS." Ms., Texas (J 9).
(a) New Directions #12. ND, 1950 (B 29).
(b) In the Winter of Cities. ND, 1956, 1964 (A 42, A 96).

The poem was written in December 1949 in Key West. Lines 21-23 of the first version were changed.

86. "ONE AND TWO." Ms., Texas (J 9); Five Young American Poets. ND, 1944 (B 7); Androgyne, Mon Amour. ND, 1977 (A 163).

87. "ONE HAND IN SPACE." Ms., Texas (J 9); Five Young American Poets. ND, 1944 (B 7); Androgyne, Mon Amour. ND, 1977 (A 163).

The poem was written in December 1942 in New York City.

88-9. "ORPHEUS DESCENDING." Ms., Texas (J 9); Voices, September-December 1952 (C 65); In the Winter of Cities. ND, 1956, 1964 (A 42, A 96). Also E 54.

The poem was written in May 1951 in New York City.

90. "PART OF A HERO." Ms., Texas (J 9); London Magazine, February 1956 (C 82); In the Winter of Cities. ND, 1956, 1964 (A 42, A 96). Also E 54.

91. "PHOTOGRAPH AND PEARLS." Ms., Texas (J 9); In the Winter of Cities. ND, 1964 (A 96).

92. "PULSE." Mss., Texas (J 9); Five Young American Poets. ND, 1944 (B 7); In the Winter of Cities. ND, 1956, 1964 (A 42, A 96). Also E 54.

The poem was written in Santa Monica, California, in August-September 1943.

92a. "THE PURIFICATION" see Section F

93. "RECUERDO." Ms., Texas (J 9); New Directions # 9. ND, 1946 (B 11); In the Winter of Cities. ND, 1956, 1964 (A 42, A 96).

This autobiographical poem was written at Lake Chapala, Mexico, in July 1945.

94. "THE ROAD." Ms., Texas (J 9); Five Young American Poets.

ND, 1944 (B 7); In the Winter of Cities. ND, 1956, 1964 (A 42, A 96).

95. ROMAN SUITE.
Paul Bowles told Steen (N 68) that he had set a series of Williams's poems to music under this title. I have been unable to find out anything else.

96. "SACRE DE PRINTEMPS." College Verse, May 1937 (C 27).

97. "SAN SEBASTIANO DE SODOMA." Ms., Texas (J 9); New Directions # 12. ND, 1950 (B 29); In the Winter of Cities. ND 1956, 1964 (A 42, A 96).
The poem was written in Rome in 1949.

98. "A SEPARATE POEM." In the Winter of Cities. ND, 1956, 1964 (A 42, A 96).
According to Williams (I 38), the poem was written for Frank Merlo.

99. "SHADOW BOXES." Ms., Texas (J 9); Five Young American Poets. ND, 1944 (B 7); In the Winter of Cities. ND, 1956, 1964 (A 42, A 96).
The poem was written in July 1941 in Gloucester, Massachusetts.

100. "SHADOW WOOD."
(a) Period of Adjustment. DPS, 1961 (A 73).
(b) In the Winter of Cities. ND, 1964 (A 96).
The last stanza of the poem, with a changed last line, was used as the epigraph to the play.

101. "THE SIEGE." Ms., Texas (J 9); Five Young American Poets. ND, 1944 (B 7); In the Winter of Cities. ND, 1956, 1964 (A 42, A 96).
The poem was written in August 1941 in New York City.

102. "THE SOFT CITY." Mss., Texas (J 9).
(a) New Directions # 11. ND, 1949 (B 20).
(b) In the Winter of Cities. ND, 1956, 1964 (A 42, A 96).
The poem was first written in August 1941 in New York City and was then revised in Morocco in January 1949. Part II was substantially cut when the poem was collected.

103. "SONNETS TO THE SPRING (A SEQUENCE)." Ms., Texas (J 9); Wednesday Club Verse. 1946 (B 12); Remember Me to Tom by Edwina D. Williams. Putnam's, 1963 (B 108). Also (in part) B 170, C 21.

104. "SPEECH FROM THE STAIRS." Ms., Texas (J 9); Five Young American Poets. ND, 1944 (B 7); Androgyne, Mon Amour. ND, 1977 (A 163).
The poem was written in Boston in 1941.

105. "THE STONECUTTER'S ANGELS." Mss., Texas (J 9); Botteghe Obscura, 1949 (C 50). Also E 107.
The poem was written October-November 1941 in New Orleans.

106. "STONES ARE THROWN." Androgyne, Mon Amour. ND, 1977 (A 163).

107. "SUGAR IN THE CANE." Ms., Texas (J 9); Blue Mountain Ballads. G. Schirmer, 1946 (A 7); In the Winter of Cities. ND, 1956, 1964 (A 42, A 96). Also D 2.
The poem was written in May 1942. It was set to music by Paul Bowles.

108. "THE SUMMER BELVEDERE." Mss., Texas (J 9); Five Young American Poets. ND, 1944 (B 7); In the Winter of Cities. ND, 1956, 1964 (A 42, A 96). Also D 1, E 54.
The poem was begun in April 1943 in Clayton, Missouri, and was finished in May 1943 in Santa Monica, California.

109. "SWIMMER AND FISH GROUP." College Verse, March 1937 (C 25).

110. "TANGIER: THE SPEECHLESS SUMMER." Antaeus, Summer 1970 (C 133); Androgyne, Mon Amour. ND, 1977 (A 163).

111. "TENOR SAX TAKING THE BREAKS." Ms., Texas (J 9); Tennessee Williams by Benjamin Nelson. Obolensky, 1961 (B 88).
The poem was written in May 1939 in Laguna Beach, California.

112. "TESTA DELL'EFFEBO." Ms., Texas (J 9); Harper's Bazaar, August 1948 (C 44); New Directions # 12. ND, 1950 (B 29); In the Winter of Cities. ND, 1956, 1964 (A 42, A 96).
The poem was written in February 1948 in Rome.

113. "THIS HOUR." Ms., Texas (J 9); Poetry, June 1937 (C 28).

114. "THOSE WHO IGNORE THE PROPER TIME OF THEIR GOING." Ms., Texas (J 9); In the Winter of Cities. ND, 1956, 1964 (A 42, A 96). Also E 54.
The poem is dated summer 1955.

115. "THREE." Ms., Texas (J 9); Three. Hargail, 1947 (A 10).
The poem was written in May 1942. It was set to music by Paul Bowles.

116. "TOWNS BECOME JEWELS." Ms., Texas (J 9); Five Young American Poets. ND, 1944 (B 7); In the Winter of Cities. ND, 1956, 1964 (A 42, A 96).
The poem was written in Vero Beach, Florida, in April 1941.

117. "TUESDAY'S CHILD." Ms., Texas (J 9); Partisan Review, April 1949 (C 48); In the Winter of Cities. ND, 1956, 1964 (A 42, A 96).
The poem was written in July 1948 in Rome.

118. "TURNING OUT THE BEDSIDE LAMP." Androgyne, Mon Amour. ND, 1977 (A 163).

119. "UNDER THE APRIL RAIN." Inspiration, Spring 1933 (C 16).

120. "WHICH IS MY LITTLE BOY?" Ms., Texas (J 9); Experiment, Fall 1946 (C 36); Mademoiselle, July 1950 (C 57); In the Winter of Cities. ND, 1956, 1964 (A 42, A 96). Also D 1.

121. "THE WINE-DRINKERS." Ms., Texas (J 9); Five Young American Poets. ND, 1944 (B 7); Androgyne, Mon Amour. ND 1977 (A 163).
The poem was written in December 1941 in New Orleans.

122. "WINTER SMOKE IS BLUE AND BITTER." Androgyne, Mon Amour. ND, 1977 (A 163).

123. "WOLF'S HOUR." Androgyne, Mon Amour. ND, 1977 (A 163).

124. "A WREATH FOR ALEXANDRA MOLOSTVOVA." In the Winter of Cities. ND, 1956, 1964 (A 42, A 96).

125. "YOU AND I." Ms., Texas (J 9); Androgyne, Mon Amour. ND, 1977 (A 163).

126. "YOUNG MEN WAKING AT DAYBREAK." Evergreen Review, December 1967 (C 123); Androgyne, Mon Amour. ND, 1977 (A 163).

I. MEMOIRS, ESSAYS, AND OCCASIONAL PIECES

1. "THE AGENT AS CATALYST." Esquire, December 1962 (C 108). This tribute to his former agent, Audrey Wood, accompanied an article with the same title by Newman (N 59).

2. "AN ALLEGORY OF MAN AND HIS SAHARA." New York Times Book Review, 4 December 1949 (C 52). The review is about Paul Bowles's novel The Sheltering Sky.

3. "AN APPRECIATION." Ms., Texas (J 9); Derrière le Miroir, January 1949 (C 47). The essay concerns the painter Hans Hofmann.

4. "AN APPRECIATION." Ms., Texas (J 9); New York Times, 15 December 1946 (C 37); Women. 1948 (B 17); The World of Tennessee Williams, ed. R. F. Leavitt. Putnam's, 1978 (B 170). This eulogy was written on the death of the actress Laurette Taylor.

5. "THE AUTHOR" see "Biography of Carson McCullers"

6. "AUTHOR AND DIRECTOR: A DELICATE SITUATION." Playbill, 30 September 1957 (C 90); Where I Live. ND, 1978 (A 168, A 169).

7. "AUTHOR'S NOTE." The World of Tennessee Williams, ed. R. F. Leavitt. Putnam's, 1978 (B 170). This preface was written in Miami in April 1956 for the program of the first production of Sweet Bird of Youth (F 64).

8. "AUTHOR'S NOTE" see "A Preface"

9. "BIOGRAPHY OF CARSON McCULLERS"/"THE AUTHOR." Saturday Review, 23 September 1963 (C 104); Where I Live. ND, 1978 (A 168, A 169).

10. BLURBS AND SHORT COMMENTS. Williams has written blurbs for the works of Jane Bowles (B 119, B 122), Lewis Funke and John E. Booth (B 80), James Herlihy (B 70), James Purdy (C 103), Gore Vidal (B 58), Donald Windham (B 28, B 109), and Richard Yates (B 97, B 98). He has also written short comments about Licia Albanese (B 66), Gore Vidal (B 124, C 119), himself (B 2, B 108, C 80, E 49), the arts (C 151), books (C 40), film (C 56a, C 81a) and plays (C 160).

10a. "CAN A GOOD WIFE BE A SPORT?" see Section G.

11. "CANDIDA: A COLLEGE ESSAY." Ms., Texas (J 9); Shaw Review, May 1977 (C 157).
This theme was written by Williams while he was a student.

12. "THE CATASTROPHE OF SUCCESS"/"ON A STREETCAR NAMED SUCCESS." Ms., Texas (J 9).
(a) "On a Streetcar Named Success." New York Times, 30 November 1947 (C 39); A Streetcar Named Desire. NAL, 1951 (A 26). Also B 121.
(b) "The Catastrophe of Success." Story, Spring 1948 (C 41); The Glass Menagerie. J. Lehmann, 1948 (A 15); The Glass Menagerie. ND, 1949, 1966, 1970 (A 19, A 106, A 129); Theatre I. ND, 1971 (A 131); "On a Streetcar Named Success." Where I Live. ND, 1978 (A 168, A 169).
The first of Williams's New York Times essays to be written prior to the opening of a new play, this was for Streetcar (F 61). Story added a paragraph cut by the Times and changed the first sentence (as usually happened when one of these essays was collected with the play).

13. "CONCERNING EUGENE O'NEILL." Ahmanson's Theatre's Inaugural Season Program, 12 September 1967 (C 122).
A note about the problems of a playwright in general.

14. "CRITIC SAYS 'EVASION,' WRITER SAYS 'MYSTERY.'" New York Herald Tribune, 17 April 1955 (C 77); Where I Live. ND, 1978 (A 168, A 169).
The article is a response to Kerr's review of Cat on a Hot Tin Roof (K 11).

15. EUROPEAN TRIP REPORTS. U. City Pep, 30 October 1928-16 April 1929 (C 2 - C 4)

16. "FACTS ABOUT ME." Ms., Texas (J 9); Tennessee Williams Reading. Caedmon, 1952 (D 1); Facts About Me. 1952 (A 29); Twentieth Century Authors, ed. S. J. Kunitz. H. W. Wilson, 1955 (B 52); Where I Live. ND, 1978 (A 168, A 169).

17. "FIVE FIERY LADIES." Life, 3 February 1961 (C 102); Where I Live. ND, 1978 (A 168, A 169).
This gushing tribute was written to accompany photographs of Vivien Leigh, Geraldine Page, Anna Magnani, Katharine Hepburn, and Elizabeth Taylor.

18. "FOREWORD." Constructing a Play by Marian Gallaway. Prentice-Hall, 1950 (B 23).
In this introduction Williams speaks of the need for technique in writing.

19. "FOREWORD." Feminine Wiles by Jane Bowles. Black Sparrow, 1976 (B 163). These personal remembrances were written 11 November 1974.

20. "FOREWORD." Young Man with a Screwdriver by Oliver Evans. Nebraska, 1950 (B 22).

21. "FOREWORD" ("ON THE 'CAMINO REAL'") and "AFTERWORD." Ms., Texas (J 9).
(a) "On the 'Camino Real.'" New York Times, 15 March 1953 (C 69).
(b) "Foreword"; "Afterword." Camino Real. ND, 1953, 1970 (A 31, A 130); Theatre Arts, August 1954 (C 72); Four Plays. S&W, 1956 (A 43); Camino Real. S&W, 1958 (A 53); The Rose Tattoo.... Penguin, 1958, 1976 (A 60, A 156); Three Plays. ND, 1964 (A 94); Camino Real. DPS, 1965 (A 102); Theatre II. ND, 1971 (A 132); Where I Live. ND, 1978 (A 168, A 169). Also B 78, B 96.
The first essay was written for the opening of Camino Real (F 8); the second, dated 1 June 1953, was prepared for the book publication.

22. "FOREWORD" ("WILLIAMS' WELLS OF VIOLENCE"). "Williams' Wells of Violence." New York Times, 8 March 1959 (C 95); "Foreword." Sweet Bird of Youth. ND, 1959, 1975 (A 65, A 148); Sweet Bird of Youth. S&W, 1961 (A 71); Sweet Bird of Youth. NAL, 1962 (A 78); Sweet Bird of Youth.... Penguin, 1962 (A 79); Three Plays. ND, 1964 (A 94); Theatre III. ND, 1972 (A 134); Three by Tennessee. NAL, 1976 (A 159); Where I Live. ND, 1978 (A 168, A 169).
The essay was written for the opening of Sweet Bird (F 64) but is a review of many of his plays.

23. "'GRAND.'" Grand. House of Books, 1964 (A 93); Esquire, November 1966 (C 120); The Knightly Quest. ND, 1966 (A 105); The Knightly Quest. S&W, 1968 (A 119). Also E 57, E 89, E 120, E 175.
Though in the form of a short story, the work is a memoir of Williams's grandmother Mrs. Rose Dakin.

24. "'HAPPINESS IS RELEVANT.'" New York Times, 24 March 1968 (C 125).
This statement was written for the opening of Kingdom of Earth (F 30).

25. "THE HISTORY OF A PLAY (WITH PARENTHESES)." Ms., Texas (J 9); Battle of Angels. Pharos, Spring 1945 (A 1).
The essay, concerning not only Battle (F 4) but also his philosophy of writing, is an extremely important one for understanding Williams.

26. "HOMAGE TO KEY WEST." Harper's Bazaar, January 1973 (C 139); Where I Live. ND, 1978 (A 168, A 169).

27. "THE HUMAN PSYCHE--ALONE." Saturday Review, 23 December 1950 (C 61); Where I Live. ND, 1978 (A 168, A 169).
The review is of Paul Bowles's stories collected in The Delicate Prey.

28. "'I AM WIDELY REGARDED AS THE GHOST OF A WRITER.'" New York Times, 8 May 1977 (C 155).
This statement was written for the opening of Vieux Carré (F 74).

29. "'I HAVE REWRITTEN A PLAY FOR ARTISTIC PURITY.'" New York Times, 21 November 1976 (C 152).
The essay concerns The Eccentricities of a Nightingale (F 63).

30. "INTRODUCTION." The World of Tennessee Williams, ed. R. F. Leavitt. Putnam's, 1978 (B 170).

31. "INTRODUCTION" see "The Writing Is Honest"

32. "INTRODUCTION: THIS BOOK." Ms., Texas (J 9); Reflections in a Golden Eye by Carson McCullers. ND, 1950 (B 26); Where I Live. ND, 1978 (A 168, A 169). Also B 72.

33. "LET ME HANG IT ALL OUT." New York Times, 4 March 1973 (C 143).
This very important essay, written for the New York performance of Out Cry (F 72), is largely concerned with Streetcar (F 61) and Cat (F 11).

34. LETTERS. Tennessee Williams Letters to Donald Windham. Campbell, 1976 (A 157). Tennessee Williams Letters to Donald Windham. Holt, 1977 (A 167).
Many of Williams's letters, public and private, have been published (A 136-A, 138, A 151, A 157, A 167, B 88, B 108, B 136, B 137, B 170, C 14, C 42, C 59, C 81, C 83, C 86, C 109, C 127, C 131, C 139, C 153, C 158).

35. "THE MEANING OF THE ROSE TATTOO." Vogue, 15 March 1951 (C 64); Where I Live. ND, 1978 (A 168, A 169).
The essay was written for the opening of the play (F 53).

36. MEMOIRS/"SURVIVAL NOTES: A JOURNAL."
(a) "Survival Notes." Esquire, September 1972 (C 137); London Times Saturday Review, 20 January 1973 (C 141).
(b) Memoirs. Doubleday, 1975 (A 150); Memoirs. Bantam, 1976 (A 160). Also B 167, C 150, E 64.
(c) Memoirs. W. H. Allen, 1976, 1977 (A 154, A 164).
"Survival Notes" was incorporated into Chapters 1, 4, and 5 of the Memoirs. Since Doubleday has been accused of cutting so much of the manuscript, perhaps it is worth saying that only two cuts were made in the original journal

(one of which, however, explained the reference to "leaves" which opens Chapter 5) and much was added. However, there is no doubt that someone edited the manuscript. Williams added four pages to the London edition. Reviews are found in A 150 and A 154.

37. "THE MISUNDERSTANDINGS AND FEARS OF AN ARTIST'S REVOLT." Where I Live. ND, 1978 (A 168, A 169).

38. "A MOVIE CALLED 'LA TERRA TREMA.'" '48 Magazine, June 1948 (C 43).
The review is of a film by Luchino Visconti.

39. [NOTE ON HART CRANE]. Tennessee Williams Reads Hart Crane. Caedmon, 1965 (D 4).

40. "NOTES AFTER THE SECOND INVITED AUDIENCE: (AND A TROUBLED SLEEP)." Small Craft Warnings. ND, 1972 (A 136, A 137); Small Craft Warnings, S&W, 1973 (A 138); Theatre V. ND, 1976 (A 151).
The notes concern Small Craft (F 57).

41. "ON A STREETCAR NAMED SUCCESS" see "The Catastrophe of Success"

42. "ON MEETING A YOUNG WRITER." Harper's Bazaar, August 1956 (C 85).
The essay concerns Françoise Sagan.

43. "ON THE 'CAMINO REAL'" see "Foreword"

44. "THE PAST, THE PRESENT, AND THE PERHAPS." Ms., Texas (J 9); New York Times, 17 March 1957 (C 87); Orpheus Descending.... ND, 1958 (A 54); Orpheus Descending. S&W, 1958 (A 59); The Fugitive Kind. NAL, 1960 (A 68); Orpheus Descending.... Penguin, 1961 (A 76); Five Plays. S&W, 1962 (A 80); The Night of the Iguana.... Penguin, 1968 (A 121); Theatre III. ND, 1971 (A 133); The Rose Tattoo.... Penguin, 1976 (A 156); Four Plays. NAL, 1976 (A 158); Where I Live. ND, 1978 (A 168, A 169).
Written for the opening of Orpheus (F 4), the essay gives much information about his life in the 1930's and Battle of Angels.

45. "PERSON-TO-PERSON." New York Times, 20 March 1955 (C 75); Cat on a Hot Tin Roof. ND, 1955 (A 38); Cat on a Hot Tin Roof. S&W, 1956 (A 44); Cat on a Hot Tin Roof. Penguin, 1957 (A 49); Cat on a Hot Tin Roof. NAL, 1958 (A 58); Five Plays. S&W, 1962 (A 80); The Milk Train Doesn't Stop Here Anymore.... Penguin, 1969 (A 122); Theatre III. ND, 1971 (A 133); Cat on a Hot Tin Roof.... Penguin, 1976 (A 155); Where I Live, ND, 1978 (A 168, A 169).
The essay was written for the opening of Cat (F 11).

46. "THE PLEASURES OF THE TABLE." Where I Live. ND, 1978 (A 168, A 169).

47. "PRAISE TO ASSENTING ANGELS." Ms., Texas (J 9); The Mortgaged Heart by Carson McCullers; introduction by M. G. Smith (excerpts). Houghton Mifflin, 1971 (B 147).

48. "A PREFACE"/"AUTHOR'S NOTE." I Rise in Flame, Cried the Phoenix. ND, 1951 (A 25); New World Writing # 1. NAL, 1952 (B 36); I Rise in Flame, Cried the Phoenix. DPS, 195- (A 41); Ramparts, January 1968 (C 124); Dragon Country. ND, 1969 (A 127, A 128).

Dated September 1941 in New Orleans, the note concerns D. H. Lawrence and his paintings.

49. "PREFACE." Esquire, August 1965 (C 116).

Though written as an introduction to Slapstick Tragedy (F 56), the essay also concerns other works and Williams's philosophy of writing in general.

50. "PREFACE TO MY POEMS." Five Young American Poets. ND, 1944 (B 7); Where I Live. ND, 1978 (A 168, A 169).

51. "PRELUDE TO A COMEDY." New York Times, 6 November 1960 (C 100); Where I Live. ND, 1978 (A 168, A 169).

The essay was written for the opening of Period of Adjustment (F 48).

52. "QUESTIONS WITHOUT ANSWERS." New York Times, 3 October 1948 (C 45); Where I Live. ND, 1978 (A 168, A 169).

The essay was written for the opening of Summer and Smoke (F 63).

53. "REFLECTIONS ON A REVIVAL OF A CONTROVERSIAL FANTASY." New York Times, 15 May 1960 (C 98); Where I Live. ND, 1978 (A 168, A 169).

The essay concerns Camino Real (F 8).

54. "SOME WORDS BEFORE." Go Looking by Gilbert Maxwell, B. Humphries, 1954 (B 43).

This introduction to a collection of poems by a friend contains a note on Hart Crane. Maxwell dedicated the book to Williams and others.

55. "SOME WORDS BEFORE." The Lonely Hunter by V. S. Carr. Doubleday, 1975 (B 157).

The introduction is about Carson McCullers.

56. "SOMETHING WILD...." New York Star, c. 1949 (C 53); 27 Wagons Full of Cotton. ND, 1953, 1966 (A 32, A 107); Where I Live. ND, 1978 (A 168, A 169).

The essay is a tribute to the Little Theater of his youth.

57. "A SUMMER OF DISCOVERY." New York Herald Tribune, 24 December 1961 (C 106); Where I Live. ND, 1978 (A 168, A 169).
The essay was written for the opening of Iguana (F 44). It contains much about the background of the play.

58. "SURVIVAL NOTES: A JOURNAL" see Memoirs

59. "T. WILLIAMS'S VIEW OF T. BANKHEAD." New York Times, 29 December 1963 (C 111); Where I Live. ND, 1978 (A 168, A 169).
This tribute to Tallulah Bankhead was written for the second New York opening of Milk Train (F 41). (Note: if there was an essay written for the first opening, it was not printed because of a newspaper strike, and it has never surfaced.)

60. "'TENNESSEE, NEVER TALK TO AN ACTRESS.'" New York Times, 4 May 1969 (C 126).
The essay, written for the opening of In the Bar of a Tokyo Hotel (F 29), is about rehearsals.

61. "TENNESSEE WILLIAMS PRESENTS HIS POV." New York Times Magazine, 12 June 1960 (C 99); Where I Live. ND, 1978 (A 168, A 169). Also B 74.
Williams's "point of view" is a response to an essay by Marya Mannes (P 273).

62. "THE TIMELESS WORLD OF A PLAY." Ms., Texas (J 9); New York Times, 14 January 1951 (C 63); The Rose Tattoo. ND, 1951 (A 24); The Rose Tattoo. S&W, 1954 (A 37); Theatre Arts, May 1955 (C 79); The Rose Tattoo. NAL, 1955 (A 40); The Rose Tattoo.... Penguin, 1958, 1976 (A 60, A 156); Five Plays. S&W, 1962 (A 80); Three Plays. ND, 1964 (A 94); The Rose Tattoo. DPS, 1965 (A 103); Theatre II. ND, 1971 (A 132); Three by Tennessee. NAL, 1976 (A 159); Where I Live. ND, 1978 (A 168, A 169). Also B 84, B 114, B 117, B 121.
The essay was written for the opening of Tattoo (F 53).

63. "TO WILLIAM INGE: AN HOMAGE." New York Times, 1 July 1973 (G 144).

64. "TOO PERSONAL?" Small Craft Warnings. ND, 1972 (A 136, A 137); Small Craft Warnings. S&W, 1973 (A 138); Theatre V. ND, 1976 (A 151); Where I Live. ND, 1978 (A 168, A 169).
The essay was written for the Times for the opening of Small Craft (F 57), but the newspaper chose to publish an interview instead.

64a. "W. H. AUDEN: A FEW REMINISCENCES." Harvard Advocate, 1975 (C 150a).

65. "WE ARE DISSENTERS NOW." Harper's Bazaar, January 1972 (C 136).

The article is a series of notes about the political situation in America.

66. "WHAT'S NEXT ON THE AGENDA, MR. WILLIAMS?" Mediterranean Review, Winter 1971 (C 132).

This autobiographical piece about his 1969 confinement to a St. Louis mental hospital was read at the 1970 London Poetry Festival.

67. "WILLIAMS' WELLS OF VIOLENCE" see "Foreword"

68. "THE WOLF AND I." New York Times, 20 February 1966 (C 117).

An autobiographical piece, the story was retold in Memoirs (I 35).

69. "THE WORLD I LIVE IN." London Observer, 7 April 1957 (C 88); Where I Live. ND, 1978 (A 168, A 169). Also E 72.

70. "A WRITER'S QUEST FOR A PARNASSUS." Ms., Texas (J 9); New York Times Magazine, 13 August 1950 (C 58); Where I Live. ND, 1978 (A 168, A 169).

71. "THE WRITING IS HONEST"/"INTRODUCTION." "The Writing Is Honest." New York Times, 16 March 1958 (C 91); "Introduction." The Dark at the Top of the Stairs by William Inge. Random House, 1958 (B 62); "If the Writing Is Honest." Where I Live. ND, 1978 (A 168, A 169). Also B 63, B 71, B 78.

The essay, dated January 1958 in Key West, was written for Dark.

PART 3

WILLIAMS'S MANUSCRIPTS

Introduction

In 1963 Williams gave the University of Texas at Austin his manuscripts. Andreas Brown and the staff of the Humanities Research Center catalogued the enormous number of unpublished works and drafts of published works, as well as a huge holding of published editions. One day the Texas Tower series will publish an annotated catalogue of all these materials, but the very wealth of books and manuscripts precludes an early date for that bibliography.

Meanwhile, scholars have started to examine the manuscripts, especially of those plays directed by Elia Kazan. Ellen Dunlap, the research librarian at the center, tells me, however, that the collection is by no means one of the more popular ones in the library. So far only one study of a play's evolution has been published: Vivienne Dickinson's examination of the various stages of A Streetcar Named Desire.

I list the title of the greater part of the manuscripts on file, but I make no attempt to indicate how many drafts of any work exist nor what state they are in. Nor do I attempt to list letters, untitled works, or such. There are also manuscripts, mostly letters, in various other libraries.

J. LISTINGS BY INSTITUTION

1. AMERICAN ACADEMY OF ARTS AND LETTERS
   Letters

2. UNIVERSITY OF BUFFALO: LOCKWOOD MEMORIAL LIBRARY
   *The Eyes (poem)

3. UNIVERSITY OF CHICAGO: JOSEPH REGENSTEIN LIBRARY
   Letters
   *My Love Was Light (poem)
   *This Hour (poem)

4. COLUMBIA UNIVERSITY
   *The Milk Train Doesn't Stop Here Anymore (play)
   Plenty of Zip (play)

5. LIBRARY OF CONGRESS
   *Baby Doll (screenplay)
   *Confessional (play)
   The Fugitive Kind (screenplay)
   *In the Bar of a Tokyo Hotel (play)
   *Kingdom of Earth (play)
   *The Milk Train Doesn't Stop Here Anymore (play)
   *The Night of the Iguana (play)
   The Night of the Iguana (screenplay by Anthony Veiller)
   The Parade (play)
   *Old Folks at Home, or The Frosted Glass Coffin (play)
   *Orpheus Descending (play)
   *Sweet Bird of Youth (play)

6. HARVARD UNIVERSITY; HOUGHTON LIBRARY and HARVARD THEATRE COLLECTION
   *Cat on a Hot Tin Roof (play)
   *Dos Ranchos (play)
   Letters
   *The Night of the Iguana (play)
   *Period of Adjustment (play)
   *Slapstick Tragedy (one-act plays)
   *A Streetcar Named Desire (play)

7. UNIVERSITY OF MISSOURI
   Beauty Is the Word (play)

8. UNIVERSITY OF ROCHESTER
   Letters

9. UNIVERSITY OF TEXAS: HUMANITIES RESEARCH CENTER
   The Accent of a Coming Foot (story)
   Accidents (poems)
   Acknowledgement (poem)
   Act of Love (play)
   Act of Love (story)
   Adam and Eve on a Ferry [about D. H. Lawrence] (play)
   *After a Visit (poem)
   An Afternoon Off for Death (poem)
   Age of Retirement (story)
   Alice at the Country Club

---

*Indicates a work has been published.

9. UNIVERSITY OF TEXAS (cont.)
(play)
The Alien Heart: A Group of Sonnets (poems)
All Kinds of Salvation (story)
"All the words have been spoken" (poem)
"All through the night" (poem)
Alladin in the Orchard of Jewels (poem)
An Allegory in Pink (play)
An American Chorus (dialogue)
American Gothic: A One-Act Play (play)
Amor Perdida, or How It Feels to Become a Professional Playwright (essay)
"And all the while Armand kept smiling"
"And I would have in my hands" (poem)
*The Angel in the Alcove (story)
*The Angels of Fructification (poem)
Apt. F 3rd Flo. So. (play)
Apt. F 3rd Flo. So. (story)
Apocalypse (poem)
Apostrophe to Peace (poem)
*An Appreciation [Laurette Taylor] (essay)
Apricots Too Sweet (poem)
An April Rendezvous (story)
An April Sermon (poem)
April Song (poem)
"The armed have always their weapons" (poem)
The Art of Acting and Anna (essay)
The Artist (poem)
As a Man Thinketh (essay)
"Ask the man who dies in the electric chair" (poem)
"At break of dawn" (poem)
At Daybreak (poem)
"At seven o'clock or eleven"
Ate Toadstools But Didn't Quite Die (story)
August Evening: Lindell Blvd. (poem)
*Auto-da-Fé: A Tragedy in One Act (play)
An Autobiographical Note (poem)
An Autumn Song (poem)
Autumn Sunlight (story)
*Baby Doll (screenplay)
Ballad of an Old War (poem)
The Ballad of Billy the Kid (screenplay for ballet)
*Battle of Angels (play)
*The Beaded Bag (story)
*The Beanstalk Country (poem)
Beauty Is No Cheap Thing (poem)
Beauty Is the Word (photocopy of play, J 7)
Beauty the Cross (poem)
The Beetle of the Sun: A Lyric Play (play)
Beginning and End of a Story, or Souvenir for Bennie and Eva (story)
"Being in a foreign nation" (poem)
Being Man (poem)
Big Black: A Mississippi Idyll
The Big Flashy Tiffany Diamond Blues (poem)
The Big Game: A One-Act Play (play)
The Big Time Operators (play)
Biography: Sonnet (poem)
The Black Cygnet (story)
Black Faced Comedians Blown Out of Smoking Room
The Black Nurse (poem)
Blood of the Wolf (poems)
Blood on the Snow (poem)

9. UNIVERSITY OF TEXAS (cont.)
- Blossoms' Treat
- Blue Mountain Blues: A Collection of Folk-Verse (twelve poems)
- The Blue Ornament: A Christmas Play (play)
- Blue Roses (story)
- The 'Boss' Complex (essay)
- The Bottle of Brass (story)
- A Branch for Birds (poem)
- Bride of the Night (poem)
- The Bridegroom's Song (poem)
- "Burn me! Burn me" (poem)
- "But play it sweetly"
- "But that iron master heard no bells" (poem)
- "But the lady in the little milk house" (poem)
- "But thou as the moon" (poem)
- "By your hand's miracle" (poem)
- Byron (story)
- *Cabin (poem)
- *Cacti (poem)
- Cairo, Shanghai, Bombay!: A One-Act Melodrama (play)
- *Camino Real (play)
- Camino Real (television script edited by Hugh Leonard)
- Camino Real, or The Rich and Eventful Death of Oliver Winemiller (play)
- "The campfire flickers" (poem)
- "Can it be again" (poem)
- Candles to the Sun (play)
- Il Canne Incantando delle Divina Costiera: 1-Act Sketch (play: basis for The Rose Tattoo)
- The Carnival (poem)
- Carnival Night (story)
- Carol's Song (poem)
- *Cat on a Hot Tin Roof (play)
- The Cataract (poem)
- The Caterpillar Dogs (story)
- Cathedral (poem)
- Celebration of Mass (poem)
- Cellophane Boxes (story)
- Change and Resistance and Change (poem)
- Changling (poem)
- Chant (poem)
- A Chant for My Former Companions (poem)
- Chaplinesque, or the Funniest Pair of Lovers (play)
- The Chart (poem)
- "Cheap silks and perfumes" (poem)
- A Chicken Farm in Idaho (story)
- The Christmas Blocks
- *The Christus of Guadalajara (poem)
- *The Chronicle of a Demise (story)
- *Cinder Hill: A Narrative Poem (poem)
- Cinquains (poem)
- "Clothed in seventy years of love and sorrow" (poem)
- *La Coeur A Ses Raisons: Sonnet (poem)
- Cold Stream (story)
- College essays
- Combination Forgotten (television play)
- *The Comforter and the Betrayer (poem)
- *The Coming of Something to the Widow Holly (story)
- "Commencing at meridian" (poem)
- Compass (poem
- Compromise
- *Confessional (play)
- Convenience (poem)
- Conversion (story)
- Corduroy Pants (story)

9. UNIVERSITY OF TEXAS (cont.)
*Cortege (poem)
*Counsel (poem)
Crazy Night (story)
*Cried the Fox (poem)
Crooked (poem)
Crooked Blues (poem)
The Crowded Street (poem)
"Cruel the Torture" (poem)
Cupid on a Corner
Curtains for the Gentleman: A One-Act Play (play)
Cut Out (story)
Dago Hill (story)
"Daisy Lanier was eight minutes" (poem)
*The Dangerous Painters (poem)
Danse Macabre (poem)
*Dark Arm, Hanging over the Edge of Infinity (poem)
The Dark Pine Wood (poem)
The Dark Room (story)
The Darkling Plain (essay)
Daughter of Revolution
The Day Is Not Enough (poem)
De Preacher's Boy (story)
A Dead Hero and the Living (story)
Dead Planet, the Moon (play)
Dear Diary (story)
*Dear Silent Ghost (poem)
Death: Celebration (poem)
Death Is a Word
*Death Is High (poem)
Death of a God (play)
The Death of Venus (poem)
Decision (poem)
"Deep in distant waters" (poem)
Deepest Instinct, or Fate (essay)
Definition of Verbs (poem)
Delle (story)
Departure (poem)
Desertion
*Desire and the Black Masseur (story)
"Destroy me" (poem)
Dialogue between Dances (play)
Diver (poem)
A Do-It-Yourself Interview (essay)
The Doctor's Waiting Room (play)
The Dog Can Speak (poem)
Dolores Sleeps under the Roses (story)
Dos Ranchos (poem)
Down Shropshire Lane (poem)
The Drab of Jericho (poem)
Dragon Country (play)
The Dream of Permanence (poem)
Driftwood: For Hart Crane (poem)
The Drunken Faun of Herculaneum (poem)
The Drunken Fiddler (poem)
The Dual Angel (poem)
Dynamics of Play (essay)
Early Frost (poem)
"The earth will seduce me" (poem)
Earth's Brief Passion (poem)
"E'en before noonday, neighbor" (poem)
Elégis Matinale (poem)
Elegy for an Artist (poem)
Elegy for Rose (poem)
End of Summer
*The Enemy: Time (play)
Envoi
Episode (poem)
Episode: Cafeteria (poem)
Episode in Connecticut (poem)
Epitome (poem)
Epode (poem)
Eros: Metropolis (poem)
Escape (play)
Every Friday Nite Is Kiddies Nite (story)
Every Twenty Minutes: A Satire (play)
*Everyman (poem)
Exaltations (poem)
An Extraordinary Disaster (poem)

9. UNIVERSITY OF TEXAS (cont.)
The Eye That Saw Death (story)
*The Eyes (poem)
*Facts about Me (essay)
*Faint as Leaf Shadow (poem)
Fallen Leaves (story)
Family Pew (play)
The Fat Man's Wife (play)
Fatal Moment (poem)
Fate and the Fishpole: A One-Act Play (play)
Fear (poem)
*The Field of Blue Children (story)
Field of Gold (poem)
*A Film in Sicily (essay)
Fin du Monde: A Postscript to the Casualty list (story)
First Syllable (poem)
"Fish have colors that are pale" (poem)
Flight (poem)
Floor Show Every Saturday Nite (story)
The Flower-Girl of Carthage (story)
Flowers (story)
Fontana Vecchia: A Masque
For My Grandmother Rosina Maria Francesca von Albertzart-Otte Larkin (or Rose) (play)
For Spain (poem)
For the Punishment or Rage
"For those impossible things" (poem)
"For you are not stars" (poem)
For You, Pygmalion (poem)
The Foreign Country (poem)
The Form of Fern (poem)
The Four-Leaf Clover (story)
Français Deux
Frieze: Les Bos
The Front Porch Girl (play)
Frost
*The Frosted Glass Coffin (play)
The Fugitive Kind (play)
The Fugitive Kind (screenplay)
A Gallantry of Maidens (play)
Gambler's Song (poem)
The Garden of Emiel Kroger (story)
Garden Scene: Recitation after a Painting by Pierre Bonnard (poem)
Gatto Romano
The Gay Cat (poem)
A Gentleman behind the Bars (story)
Gethsemane (poem)
Gift of an Apple (story)
"A Gilded cock upon a steeple" (poem)
La Gioconda
Girl (poem)
Girl from Joe's (play)
*The Glass Menagerie (play)
The Glass Menagerie (screenplay)
The Glass Menagerie (television adaptation by Hugh Leonard)
Go Down, Moses (play)
Goat Song (play)
God in the Free Ward (story)
Gods Passed This Way (poem)
*Gold Tooth Blues (poem)
The Good Time House (play)
Goofer Song (poem)
*The Goths (poem)
The Gravedigger's Speech (poem)
Green Shade
The Green Situation (poem)
Grenanda to West Plains (story)
A Guest at the Gables
Gunner Jack (poem)
"A hand that makes medival stones" (poem)
*Hans Hofmann: An

9. UNIVERSITY OF TEXAS (cont.)

Appreciation (essay)
*Hard Candy (story)
The Harlequin of the Dance (poem)
*The Harp of Wales (poem)
"The hawk that high in heaven wheels" (poem)
"The hawthorn is withered" (poem)
"He fingered his vest" (poem)
Heart Continues
The Heaven Tree
Heavenly (story)
*Heavenly Grass (poem)
Heavenly Grass, or The Miracle at Granny's (play)
"Hefts, hifts and whatnots" (poem)
Helen before Troy (poem)
Hell: An Expressionistic Drama Based on the Prison Atrocity in Philadelphia County (play)
*Hello from Bertha (play)
Her Admired Exaltation (story)
"Her body swims in passion" (poem)
*Her Head on the Pillow (poem)
Here It Is Winter (poem)
"Here was love's pain" (poem)
The Hill (poem)
His Father's Home (story)
His Mark on You (poem)
Histoire du Cirque (poem)
*The History of a Play (with Parentheses) (essay)
Homage to Ophelia: A Pretentious Foreword (essay)
Honor the Living (play)
Hot Milk at Three in the Morning (play)
The House of Stone (poem)
House of the Heart's Early Wonder (play)
House of Vines: A Period Play (play)
Housing Problem (poem)
"How like a caravan" (poem)
"How shall I speak to you" (poem)
How Sleeps My Lord (poem)
"How straight my love lies on her bed" (poem)
Hyacinths in the Window Bloom (poem)
Hymns to Eros (poem)
"I am in debt to you" (poem)
"I came upon a fragment of a speech"
"I cannot deny I have lost in crossing" (poem)
I Cannot Tell (poem)
"I did not elect this problem" (poem)
"I don't know how a woman gets an idea" (poem)
"I envy you, Thomas" (poem)
I Fly My Colors (poem)
"I give my love" (poem)
I Got Fired (poem)
I Got Pneumonia in the Heart (poem)
"I had a warnin'" (poem)
"I have a vast traumatic eye" (poem)
I Have Concluded Lately (poem)
"I have kept this love" (poem)
I Have Not Long to Love (poem)
"I have put my passion" (poem)
I haven't an Open Car (poem)
"I must depend on you" (poem)
"I once observed the mechanical antics" (poem)
"I remained there" (poem)
*I Rise in Flame, Cried

9. UNIVERSITY OF TEXAS (cont.)

the Phoenix: A Play about D. H. Lawrence (play)
"I said to myself, said I" (poem)
"I saw how the green sea's denial" (poem)
"I think I am beginning to remember death more kindly" (poem)
"I think I have heard you" (poem)
"I think it is time" (poem)
*"I think the strange, the crazed, the queer" (poem)
I, Vaslev (play)
I Walk through the City (poem)
"I walked down five steps to hell" (poem)
"I walked this morning along the esplanade" (poem)
I Want to Go Away (play)
"I want to go down to the sea" (poem)
"I wanted music" (poem)
I Would Dance (poem)
"I would like to infect you with the excitement of living" (poem)
"I wounded a man I know" (poem)
Ice and Roses (poem)
*The Ice-Blue Wind (poem)
Ice-Edge (poem)
The Iceberg (poem)
An Idea of Life (poem)
Idillio (poem)
Idiot and Spinner (poem)
"If ever the bell" (poem)
"If I could march" (poem)
If I Wore (poem)
"If you be wanton in my arms" (poem)
If You Breathe It Breaks, or Portrait of a Girl in Glass: A One-Act Play (play: basis for The Glass Menagerie)
"If you should return" (poem)
The Image of the Bell and Dove (poem)
Imaginary Interview, re Orpheus Descending (essay)
Imagism Old and New (essay)
*The Important Thing (story)
In a Mood of Wistful Tenderness (story)
In Memory of a Rose (poem)
In Memory of an Aristocrat (play)
In Memory of an Aristocrat, or Disturbance at the Spring Display (story)
In Our Profession (play)
In Praise of Zinnias, and Similar Flora (poem)
In Spain There Was Revolution (story)
"In terraces the buried city lies" (poem)
"In the beginning there was the word" (poem)
"In the middle of the crazed painter's hair" (poem)
"In this precints the holy light is held" (poem)
"The indifference to life or death"
*Inheritors (poem)
*The Interior of the Pocket (poem)
Interior: Panic (play)
Interval (poem)
The Interval (story)
*Intimations (poem)
The Inventory (story)
*Iron Is the Winter (poem)
Ironweed (story)
Is Fives
Ishtar: A Babylonian Fantasy (play)
*The Island Is Memorable to Us (poem)
It Can Turn (poem)
Its Light Is Longer (poem)

9. UNIVERSITY OF TEXAS (cont.)

Jean Qui Pleur ou Jean Qui Rit?
*The Jockeys at Hialeah (poem)
Joe Clay's Fiddle (poem)
John's Bird (poem)
Joy Rio (play)
"Joyous was I" (poem)
Jungle (play)
"The juniper is dead" (poem)
Katharsis (story)
The Kewpie Doll (play)
*The Kingdom of Earth (story)
*The Kitchen Door Blues (poem)
Knowledge (poem)
*Lady, Anemone (poem)
The Lady from the Village of Falling Flowers: A Japanese Fantasy in One Act (play)
Lady Misunderstood (poem)
*The Lady of Larkspur Lotion (play)
*Lament for the Moths (poem)
Last March (poem)
Last Night When I was Young (poem)
*The Last of My Solid Gold Watches (play)
Last Star (poem)
The Last Verse: A Fantasy in One Act (play)
*The Last Wine (poem)
Laugh Not So Proudly (poem)
Laughter (poem)
Laurel (poem)
"Law, law! She never had no 'ligion!" (poem)
*The Legend (poem)
The Lemon Tree (poem)
"Let me review once more" (poem)
"Let the gloomy bards deny it" (poem)
"Let us go tight-lipped" (poem)
A Letter from the See (poem)
A Letter of Explanation and Apology (poem)
Letter to an Old Friend (poem)
Letter to an Old Love (poem)
A Letter to Irene (essay)
Letters
Life Is for the Living
The Life of a Sitting Target
*Life Story (poem)
Light (poem)
Lily and la vie, or One of Picasso's Blues (play)
A Literary Clicque (story)
Little Eva's Dilemma
*Little Horse (poem)
The Little Town (poem)
The Little White Lady of Tsarko-Toye: A One-Act Tragedy of the Russian Revolution (play)
*A Liturgy of Roses (poem)
The Log Book
*Lonesome Man (poem)
*The Long Goodbye (play)
A Long Road with Pines (story)
The Long Stay Cut Short (poem)
*The Long Stay Cut Short, or The Unsatisfactory Supper (play)
*Look Both Ways Before Crossing Streets (poem)
Lord Buddha Speaks to the Novice (poem)
*Lord Byron's Love Letter (play)
The Lost Girl (poem)
Loudspeaker
Love Having Owned You (poem)
The Love Is Never (poem)
Love, O Literary Love! (story)
Love Song (poem)
The Love Trip (story)
The Lovers (story)
Lyric (several poems of

9. UNIVERSITY OF TEXAS (cont.)

that title)
Madrigal (poem)
The Magic Tower: One-Act Play (play)
*The Malediction (story)
*The Man in the Dining Car (poem)
Marine (poem)
The Mark of the Mahki (story)
Marriage Is a Private Affair (screenplay)
Mars (poem)
*The Marvelous Children (poem)
*The Mattress by the Tomato Patch (story)
Me, Vashya (play)
The Mebby's Cabin (story)
The Meeting of People (play)
The Meeting of People (story)
Memories of War
The Mercury
Meridian
Mesalliance (poem)
Message (poem)
Middle West (poem)
A Military Funeral (poem)
*The Milk Train Doesn't Stop Here Anymore (play)
*The Mind Does Not Forget (poem)
The Minstrel Jack (poem)
Mirrors and Metals (poem)
Miss Jelkes Recital (poem)
Miss Wilkins and Archie
Mr. Paradise (play)
A Moment in a Room (poem)
Monotony (poem)
Moon (poem)
Moon of My Delight: A One-Act Play (play)
Moon Song: Key West (poem)
*"Moony's Kid Don't Cry" (play)
More Poetry Than Truth (poem)
*Morgenlied (poem)
Morning (poem)
Morning at Midnight
Morning with Martial Music (story)
*Mornings on Bourbon Street (poem)
Mrs. Young (play)
"Much green water" (poem)
"Much shall they suffer" (poem)
Las Muchachas (story)
The Mutilated (poem)
My Escape
"My feasting is among the damned" (poem)
My Grandmother's Favorite Color (story)
"My grandmother's name was Rosina Maria Francesca" (poem)
My Joy Killing Roomie (story)
*My Little One (poem)
*My Love Was Light (poem)
"My sister is discretion's self" (poem)
"My wife is a white lady" (poem)
Myra My Brother's Wife
The Mystery of Your Smile (poem)
The Mystery Play at Chat Noire (story)
"Neighing warning of early disaster"
Never Completely (poem)
Never Spit Against the Wind
The New Boarder
The New Home
The New Poet (poem)
Night Before Sailing: A One-Act Play (play)
A Night in Madrid (story)
*The Night of the Iguana (play)
*The Night of the Iguana (story)
The Night of the Zeppelin (play)
Night Passage (poem)

9. UNIVERSITY OF TEXAS (cont.)

Nirvana (story)
"No compliments or apologies are called for" (poem)
No Warmer Garment (poem)
None But the Lonely Heart
Not about Nightingales (play)
"Not long of leave, this residence" (poem)
"Not that I should or that it matters much" (poem)
"Not with the curved remembrance of the hand" (poem)
Notes for a Coffin Maker (poem)
November Grief (poem)
"Now a memory that's painful" (poem)
"Now I am a logical sailor" (poem)
"Now I divide again the already split particles" (poem)
"O I am burning" (poem)
"O shallow, glittering, unarrested, profound" (poem)
Oak Leaves (story)
Observe His Heart: A Choral Elegy (play)
*October Song (poem)
"Oh, the long marvelous letters"
"Oh, they complain, they complain" (poem)
Old Ladies' Skulls (poem)
An Old Lady Falls with Two Books (essay)
*Old Men Are Fond (poem)
*Old Men with Sticks (poem)
Old Shoe (poem)
Old Wife's Warning (poem)
Ole 'Sephus: Monologue to a Coon Dog (poem)
Omer (poem)
*On a Streetcar Named Success (essay)
On Summer Evenings (poem)
On the Beat (story)
Once in a Life Time (play)
*One and Two (poem)
*One Arm (story)
*One Hand in Space (poem)
One Morning in May
"One that thunders" (poem)
"The opaque casions were raided" (poem)
The Orchard
The Orchards of Night (poem)
Orpheus among the Shades (screenplay)
*Orpheus Descending (play)
*Orpheus Descending (poem)
"Our daughter was Evelyn" (poem)
"Our death was yesterday" (poem)
Our Faith (play)
"Our hearts are damaged" (poem)
"Our new and very tender guest" (poem)
*Out Cry (play)
Ozark (poem)
The Painted Masque (poem)
Las Palomas (story)
The Palooka (play)
A Panic Renaissance in the Lobos Mountains (play)
The Paper Lantern: A Dance Play for Martha Graham
Parentheses (poem)
*Part of a Hero (poem)
The Partner of the Acrobat (play)
*The Past, the Present, and the Perhaps (essay)
"Peace bought at fifteen cents a glass" (poem)
The Pearl of Greater Price (story)
"The pediment of our land" (poem)
Penates (poem)
Pensée Cyníque (poem)

9. UNIVERSITY OF TEXAS (cont.)

*A Perfect Analysis Given by a Parrot (play)
"Perhaps I should tell you" (poem)
*Period of Adjustment (play)
Period of Adjustment (story)
The Pet of Princess Angh (poem)
*Photograph and Pearls (poem)
Pierrot and Pierrette (play)
Pieta
The Pink Bedroom (play)
The Pink Bedroom (story)
Plato's Address to the United Artists of America
The Play of Character (essay)
Poem (several poems of this title)
Poor Katie with Her Crystal Gone (poem)
The Poppy Paradise (story)
Portrait (poem)
*Portrait of a Girl in Glass (story)
*Portrait of a Madonna (play)
Pragmatic Compendium: 1936 (poem)
*Praise to Assenting Angels (essay)
Prayer (poem)
The Preacher's Boy (story)
Preface to Action (play)
A Preface to Browning's 'My Last Duchess' (play)
The Private Hedge (poem)
The Problems of a Long Run (essay)
The Prodigal Race (poem)
The Puppets of the Levantine (play)
Psyche: Letter to an Old Friend (poem)
*Pulse (poem)
The Purification (story)
Quest
*The Radiant Guest (poem)
The Rebellion (poem)
The Recital (poem)
Recollection
*Recuerdo (poem)
*The Red Part of a Flag (story)
Remember Me as One of Your Lovers (poem)
Rendezvous (story)
A Reply to Mr. Nathan (essay)
Reprieve (poem)
*The Resemblance between a Violin Case and a Coffin (story)
Return to Dust (essay)
Reviews
Rhapsody: Columbus Circle (poem)
The Ring (poem)
*The Road (poem)
The Road: Sunrise (play)
*The Roman Spring of Mrs. Stone (novel)
The Roman Spring of Mrs. Stone (screenplay by Gavin Lambert)
*The Rose Tattoo (play)
The Rose Tattoo (screenplay)
Roses (poem)
Rose's Song (poem)
Rousseau: Bord de l'Oise (poem)
*Rubio y Morena (story)
Sacre de Printemps: A One-Act Play (play)
Said the Chinese Nightingale
Sailor Jack (poem)
Salome (poem)
*San Sebastiano de Sodoma (poem)
Sanctuary
Sand (story)
Sand Shark (poem)
Scenario (essay)
Scene (poem)
Sea Grapes: A Parable (poem)

9. UNIVERSITY OF TEXAS (cont.)

Sea Shell (play)
The Sea without Water (story)
Season of Grapes (story)
Secret Wisdom (poem)
"Seek her again in the garden" (poem)
Semaphone (poem)
Sentimental Story (poem)
Sentiments for the Second Sunday in May (poem)
*The Seven Descents of Myrtle (play)
*Shadow Boxes
"Shall I wear a decoration on my dress" (poem)
A Shallow Cup (story)
The Shallow Pool (poem)
She Loved Him: A One-Act Play (play)
"She never wanted more than this" (poem)
She That Comes Late to the Dance (poem)
She Walks in Beauty (poem)
Sheep Trail (poem)
Show Me the Way to Go Home (story)
Side Light on a Convention (play)
Sideshoed
*The Siege (poem)
Silently, Invisibly (story)
'Silver Dollar' West (poem)
"A simple ring can hold together" (poem)
The Simplification (poem)
Sissy (story)
Situation Wanted
*Slapstick Tragedy (plays)
Slide Area (play)
The Smooth Black Lake and the Swan (play)
So Glad! (play)
"So, let the sweet singers laugh"
So Long, Moon (play)
"So we'll go no more a roving" (poem)
A Social Problem (poem)
*The Soft City (poem)
Sold for a Penny (poem)
Soldier's Memoranda (poem)
"Some folks are niggardly of love" (poem)
"Some look for destiny within a cup" (poem)
*Some Notes on 'Camino Real' (essay)
*Something about Him (story)
Something by Tolstoi
*Something Unspoken (play)
"Sometimes the space between" (poem)
Son of ____ (story)
Song (two poems of this title)
Song among Leaves (poem)
Song for the Damned (poem)
Sonnet (poem)
Sonnet for a Prodigal (poem)
Sonnet to a Fool in Love (poem)
Sonnet to Pygmalion (poem)
*Sonnets for the Spring: A Sequence (poems)
Sonnets in My Sixteenth Year (poem)
"Soon after the event is past" (poem)
Speech (poem)
*Speech from the Stairs (poem)
The Spinning Song (play)
The Spinning Song (story)
"Spreading havoc among them while on the subject" (poem)
"Spring from the west" (poem)
Spring Night: Adventure (poem)
Spring Storm (play)
Springfield, Illinois (play outline, based on life of Vachel Lindsay)
Square Pegs
The Stage Play

9. UNIVERSITY OF TEXAS (cont.)

Stains of a Tender Outrage
Stairs to the Roof (play)
Stairs to the Roof (story)
Stars Are Candles for the Dead (poem)
Stella for Star (story)
Still Waters (poem)
Stone and Plaster (poem)
*The Stonecutter's Angels (poem)
Storm Clouds over the Wheat
The Stranger (story)
Stranger in Yellow Gloves
The Strangers (radio play)
"The strangers pass me on the street" (poem)
*The Strangest Kind of Romance (play)
The Street (poem)
Street Music
*A Streetcar Named Desire (play)
*A Streetcar Named Desire (screenplay)
Sub Terra (poem)
Suburbs (poem)
Such a Reverence for Tea-Cups: A Dramatic Monologue
*Suddenly Last Summer (play)
*Sugar in the Cane (poem)
*Summer and Smoke (play)
Summer and Smoke (screenplay by James Poe)
Summer and Smoke (story)
Summer at the Lake/Escape: A Play in One Act (play)
*The Summer Belvedere (poem)
A Summer Husbandry (poem)
Summer: Manhattan (poem)
Summer: Meridian (poem)
Summer Night (poem)
Summer Notes and Some Ain't
Sun Flower (poem)
The Swan (story)
Swan Song (poem)
*Sweet Bird of Youth (play)
A System of Wheels (story)
A Tale of Two Writers, or The Ivory Tower (story)
Talisman of Roses (poem)
Talisman Roses (play)
*Talk to Me Like the Rain and Let Me Listen (play)
The Talk Went On (poem)
Te Moraturi Salutamus (essay)
"The tears that pass" (poem)
The Temple of Yama and Yu (story)
Temples to the Red Earth Shook (poem)
Ten Minute Stop (story)
The Tender Ones (poem)
Tennessee Williams: The Author (autobiographical essay)
*Tenor Sax Taking the Breaks (poem)
*Testa dell'Effebo (poem)
Testament (poem)
Thank You, Kind Spirit (play)
That Horse (play)
That Red-Headed Woman of Mine (story)
"Their distance asserts your dereliction" (poem)
"Then I must twist and turn (poem)
"Then I must weave my thread" (poem)
"There is a wistful shepherd-girl" (poem)
There Was Light (play)
These in the Sun's Temple (poem)
A Thing Called 'Personal Lyricism' (essay)

9. UNIVERSITY OF TEXAS (cont.)

Thinking Our Thoughts (essay)
*This Book (essay)
This Can't Last Forever (story)
This Cryptic Bone (poem)
*This Hour (poem)
"This is at once his pride and his disgrace" (poem)
*This Property Is Condemned (play)
This Spring (story)
This Year's Debutante: A Three-Act Farce (play)
*Those Who Ignore the Appropriate Time of Their Going (poem)
*Three (poem)
Three against Grenada
Three Myths and a Malediction
Three Players of a Summer Game (play)
*Three Players of a Summer Game (story)
Three Songs for the Damned (poem)
"The tide runs full" (poem)
Till One or the Other Gits Back
Time and Life and Dance (essay)
Time in Motion
Time of the Locust (poem)
*The Timeless World of a Play (essay)
Timothy the Tinker: A Puppet Farce (play)
"The tinkling of glasses" (poem)
To a Lost Friend (poem)
To Me Who Loved You Once (poem)
To Mr. Ustinov: A Gentle Objection (essay)
Tomorrow Is Another Day (play)
The Tongue (poem)
"The too limpid streets have grown narrow" (poem)
Tourists
*Towns Become Jewels (poem)
The Treadmill (story)
A Tree of Gold Apples (play)
*Tuesday's Child (poem)
*Twenty-Seven Wagons Full of Cotton (story)
*27 Wagons Full of Cotton (play)
Twenty-Three (story)
Two Friends (play)
*Two Metaphysical Sonnets (poems)
*Two on a Party (story)
Two out of Three
The Uglie Queen
Unarmed (poem)
Under the April Rain (poem)
Unemployment (poem)
"The unexpressed and ever wonderful" (poem)
Unidentified works and fragments
The Union With (poem)
Unresigned (poem)
Until the Man Jumped (poem)
Unwilling Hero (poem)
An Urban Fantasy (poem)
Useless (story)
The Valediction (poem)
Valentine's Story of Vivien
The Valkyr's Ride (poem)
Venito Adoremus (story)
Victim of a Hunter
Vieux Carré (poem)
*The Vine (story)
The Vine (play)
La Violletta Romane
The Virgin (poem)
Virgin's Dream
Virgo (poem)
A Vision of Tyre (poem)
Visions (poem)
The Vocal Dead: An Act in Verse (play)
"Waiting in line for bread" (poem)
Waiting Room (play)
A Walk through Snow (poem)
Warning (poem)

9. UNIVERSITY OF TEXAS (cont.)
   - "The wayward flash has made me wise" (poem)
   - "We are coming here to die" (poem)
   - We Have Not Long to Love (poem)
   - "We were the pioneers" (poem)
   - Wedding Day
   - The Weight of a Stone: A Verse Play for Dancers (play)
   - "What did he think of as he died?" (poem)
   - "What does the bird in his eyrie sing?" (poem)
   - What Harp Unmangled (poem)
   - "What have you done" (poem)
   - "What ornament will be upon your breast?" (poem)
   - "What would you like for lunch? they ask" (poem)
   - When (poem)
   - When Love Went Out (poem)
   - *"When will the sleeping tiger stir" (poem)
   - *Which Is My Little Boy? (poem)
   - The Whisper of the Marsh (story)
   - The White Cafe (poem)
   - "Who goes between their awful world and ours" (poem)
   - "Who is able to breathe?" (poem)
   - Who Possibly Will (poem)
   - Why Did Desdemona Love the Moor? (story)
   - Why Do You Smile So Much, Lilly? (play)
   - Why Do You Smile So Much, Lilly? (story)
   - "Why should I seek the lofty things" (poem)
   - Wild Girl (poem)
   - Will You Believe (story)
   - Wind of the Night (poem)
   - The Windows of the Blue Hotel (play)
   - *The Wine-Drinkers (poem)
   - Wings in the Night (poem)
   - Winter Is Death's Season (poem)
   - A Winter Song
   - "With a necklace of amber and agate" (poem)
   - "With the first crocus" (poem)
   - The Woman from Alice Regan's (play)
   - Woman Key: A Melodrama for Tallulah Bankhead (play)
   - Woman of the Hills (story)
   - Woman of the Winter Wood (poem)
   - The Wooden Cross
   - Words to the Wise (poem)
   - World of Light and Shadow (story)
   - The Wounds of Vanity (essay)
   - *A Writer's Quest for a Parnassus (essay)
   - The Years of Vision (poem)
   - *The Yellow Bird (story)
   - "Yes, I suppose that art was a form of misogyny" (poem)
   - *You and I
   - You Could Not Understand (poem)
   - "You never saw him" (poem)
   - *You Touched Me (play)

10. WASHINGTON UNIVERSITY LIBRARY
    - Letters

11. STATE HISTORICAL SOCIETY OF WISCONSIN
    - Letters

12. YALE UNIVERSITY
    - Letters

PART 4

IMPORTANT PRODUCTIONS

Introduction

Williams has been both spectacularly successful and equally unlucky in his production record. He has often attracted the best directors Broadway had to offer and set off dramatic fireworks. But they did not always give him the best production possible, and thus many a play fizzled, only to have a successful revival off-Broadway. Williams, contrary to his own high expectations and that apparently of a number of reviewers, cannot always turn out a masterpiece. His greatest fault has been his incessant return to Broadway and the full-length play after his equally incessant annoucements that he would never write for that market again. Williams's natural bent is increasingly for the short play as he explores new forms. But on Broadway lie acclaim, money, and even critical success. Reviewers for years have announced the presence of a new genius off Broadway; critical attention is still paid mostly to those like Williams, Miller, and Albee who have made it on Broadway.

Williams's record began badly with the now famous closing of Battle of Angels in Boston. Then for seventeen years he alternated between a great and a lesser success. The Glass Menagerie played 561 performances; You Touched Me closed after 109. A Streetcar Named Desire ran for 855 performances; Summer and Smoke barely made it to 100. The Rose Tattoo had 306; Camino Real, 60. Cat on a Hot Tin Roof, 694; Orpheus Descending, 68. (Suddenly Last Summer opened off-Broadway, and I have never been able to discover how many performances it had.) Sweet Bird of Youth had 383; Period of Adjustment, 132. The Night of the Iguana, 316; The Milk Train Doesn't Stop Here Anymore, 65.

Then Williams's record went steadily downhill. A revised version of Milk Train closed after only 4 performances; Slapstick Tragedy, after 7; Kingdom of Earth, after 29; In the Bar of a Tokyo Hotel, after 25. Not until Small Craft Warnings did Williams have another successful run: 200 performances. There then followed Out Cry, 12; The Red Devil Battery Sign, which closed in Boston; The Eccentricities of a Nightingale, 24, Vieux Carré, 5. Revivals, however, were more successful: a production of Glass in the mid-sixties ran for 175 performances; the revised Cat had 160 performances in the mid-seventies. Williams began to seem like a period piece to some.

While the sixties and the seventies were proving generally so unkind to him, Williams's earlier plays still carried his reputation around the country. Otis Guernsey, Jr., in the Best Plays series noted an average of seven professional productions of Williams's plays a year during the period 1967-1973. And in 1975-1976 he had thirteen productions of ten different plays; in 1976-1977, sixteen of seven different plays. Throughout the bicentennial Williams was repeatedly greeted by the theater as one of our living treasures.

Williams has written eight screenplays which have been filmed and has had eight works adapted to the screen by others. Though many of these seemed quite daring when they appeared, they are now being shown on evening television. Eleven of Williams's one-act plays have been televised; Glass has been seen twice; Cat and Eccentricities, once each; and a special, which included excerpts from different plays, was made for Canadian television.

His works have had an enormous popularity abroad, though not enough to win him the Nobel Prize. A recent reprint of the Signet edition of Streetcar records that "the play has also been produced in England, France, Italy, Germany, Austria, Switzerland, Holland, Poland, Norway, Sweden, Denmark, Belgium, Cuba, and Mexico." From my foreign students I have learned that it has also been presented in several East Asian countries. Yet standard American references ignore almost all these productions, and the user of this bibliography will find the production record, save for the States, England, France, and Germany, sadly incomplete.

Gore Vidal has remarked (N 75, p. 144) that Williams's "literary peers" have commented on his work only on "rare occasions." These occasions have always been in the form of interviews or reviews. And, as Vidal further remarked, the results have often been "depressing." Their level of commentary is often lower than that of the professional reviewer. A huge number of critics have either felt compelled to downgrade Williams constantly or have praised even his lesser plays meaninglessly. The fact that he has been so popular on stage and screen is suspect to many. Few have been able to look at him calmly, steadily, and in perspective. From the more liberal attitudes toward language and life-styles which presently prevails, it is easy to forget that Williams was one of the most important warriors in gaining freedom for the stage and screen to treat formerly forbidden matters. Reviewers often reacted (or felt they had to react) with shock to works now routinely taught in colleges. Shades of Joyce, Lawrence, and O'Neill!

"Homophobia" has often played its part in bad reviewing. Any sensitive reader could have guessed as early as 1948 that Williams was probably gay. Throughout the fifties reviewers twitched as they approached the fact. Some undoubtedly feared the discovery of their undisclosed homosexuality; others felt called upon to display all the fear and loathing the American culture can breed about individual sexual preference; and some probably wanted to titillate their own audiences. Thus knowing allusions have been brought in on flimsy pretenses. Even as late as 1973 one reviewer felt he must write the following incredible statement about Out Cry (New York Theatre Critics' Reviews, p. 344):

> The relationship between the brother and sister is never developed beyond the basic fact of its being incestuous. Even that is suspect since the sister is plainly a homosexual-substitute, Williams evidently feeling that incest is more palatable to general audiences than homosexuality. In these days of gay liberation, such theatrical subterfuge is even more absurd than it always was!

The reasoning here is apparently no gay playwright can write about women; therefore, any woman in his plays must be a man in disguise. Is it too much to hope that such absurd asides will end? (1979 note: It is. The New York Times reviewer of A Lovely Sunday for Creve Coeur, not satisfied with the lesbian undertones in the play, felt compelled to suggest the four women are really men in disguise.)

There follows a list of all the major productions I have been able to find, with reviews of each production listed alphabetically by journal. I have listed the name of the reviewer whenever it was given, but I have omitted, as largely meaningless, the title of the review. (In a way I regret that I have not thus demonstrated how many copy editors have felt "A Crass Menagerie" was witty and fresh.) As far as possible I have tried to indicate which text a production used. Small letters of the alphabet within parentheses after the production title refer back to Section F. At the end of this part, in Section L, I have listed collections of reviews.

K. PRODUCTIONS (WITH JOURNAL REVIEWS)

1. "AT LIBERTY."

I have found no record of a professional production, but an experimental theatre group in New York City presented the play in September 1976.

2. "AUTO-DA-FE."

Again, I have found no record of a professional production. I have seen the play on university stages and found it quite as effective as some more often produced works by Williams.

3. BABY DOLL see "27 Wagons Full of Cotton"

4. BATTLE OF ANGELS/ORPHEUS DESCENDING/THE FUGITIVE KIND.

Battle of Angels (a*). Theatre Guild. Boston: Wilbur Theatre, 30 December 1940-11 January 1941. Margaret Webster, director. Cleon Throckmorton, designer. Music by Colin McPhee. With Wesley Addy (Val), Mirian Hopkins (Myra), Doris Dudley (Cassandra), Katherine Raht (Vee).

Reviews:

Boston Herald, 31 December 1940, p. 10: Alexander Williams. Reprint: Leavitt (N 49), p. 46.

New York Times, 31 December 1940, p. 18 (NYTTR 4).

________, 5 January 1941, sec. 2, p. 1 (NYTTR 4).

Orpheus Descending (c). Producers Theatre. New York: Martin Beck Theatre, 21 March-18 May 1957 (68 performances). Harold Clurman, director. Boris Aronson, Lucinda Ballard, Feder, designers. With Cliff Robertson (Val), Maureen Stapleton (Lady), Lois Smith (Carol), Joanna Roos (Vee).

Reviews:

America, 97 (6 April 1957), 4.

________, 97 (27 April 1957), 148-150: Theophilus Lewis.

Catholic World, 185 (June 1957), 226-227: Euphemia Van Rensselaer Wyatt.

Christian Century, 74 (10 April 1957), 455-456: Tom F. Driver.

Commonweal, 66 (26 April 1957), 94-97: Richard Hayes.

Harper's, 214 (May 1957), 76-77.

Nation, 184 (6 April 1957), 301-302: Robert Hatch.

New Republic, 135 (8 April 1957), 21: Margaret Marshall.

*Parenthetical letters following production titles refer to those used in Section F.

New York Theatre Critics' Reviews, 18 (1957), 310-313:
Daily Mirror, 22 March 1957: Robert Coleman.
Daily News, 22 March 1957: John Chapman.
Herald Tribune, 22 March 1957: Walter Kerr.
Journal American, 22 March 1957: John McClain.
Post, 22 March 1957: Richard Watts, Jr.
World Telegram & Sun, 22 March 1957: Tom Donnelly.
New York Times, 22 March 1957, p. 28 (NYTTR 6): Brooks Atkinson.
_______, 31 March 1957, sec. 2, p. 1 (NYTTR 6): Brooks Atkinson.
New Yorker, 33 (30 March 1957), 84-86: Wolcott Gibbs.
Newsweek, 49 (1 April 1957), 81.
Reporter, 16 (18 April 1957), 43: Marya Mannes.
Saturday Review, 40 (30 March 1957), 26: Henry Hewes.
Theatre Arts, 41 (May 1957), 20.
Time, 69 (1 April 1957), 61.

La descente d'Orphée (adaptation by Raymond Rouleau). Paris: Théâtre de l'Athénée, 16 March 1959. Raymond Rouleau, director. Lila de Nobili, designer. With Jean Babilée (Val), Arletty (Lady), Claude Génia (Carol), Andrée Tainsy (Vee).
Reviews:
Etudes, 301 (June 1959), 381-385: R. Abirached.
French Review, 33 (May 1960), 551-557: Thomas W. Bishop.
New York Times, 18 March 1959, p. 44 (NYTTR 6).
Nouvelles Litteraires, 1647 (26 March 1959), 10: Gabriel Marcel.
Paris Herald Tribune, 19 March 1959: Thomas Quinn Curtiss.
Revue de Paris, 4 (April 1959), 136-139: Thierry Maulnier.

Orpheus Descending. London: Royal Court Theatre, 14 May 1959. Tony Richardson, director. With Gary Cockrell (Val), Isa Miranda (Lady).
Reviews:
Catholic World, 189 (June 1959), 192-193: Richard A. Duprey.
New Statesman, 57 (23 May 1959), 721-722: A. Alvarez.
New York Times, 15 May 1959, p. 23 (NYTTR 6).
Times, 15 May 1959, p. 6.

Orpheus Descending (d). New York: Gramercy Arts Theatre, 5 October 1959; Greenwich News Theatre, 10 February 1960. Adrian Hall, director. Robert Soules, designer. With John Rasmondetta (Val), Ann Hamilton (Lady), Diane Ladd (Carol).
Review:
New York Times, 6 October 1959, p. 45 (NYTTR 6): Louis Calta.

The Fugitive Kind (e). United Artists film, 8 April 1960. Sidney Lumet, director. Boris Kaufman, cameraman. Richard Sylbert, art director. Music by Kenyon Hopkins. With Marlon Brando (Val), Anna Magnani (Lady), Joanne Woodward (Carol), Maureen Stapleton (Vee).

Production notes:

Nason, Richard. "'Fugitive' Is Shot." New York Times, 5 July 1959, sec. 2, p. 5.

Gelb, Arthur. "Williams Booed at Film Preview." New York Times, 8 December 1959, p. 58.

Bogdanovich, Peter. "An Interview with Sidney Lumet," Film Quarterly, 13 (Winter 1960), 18-23.

Reviews:

America, 103 (30 April 1960), 201.

Commonweal, 72 (29 April 1960), 127-128: Philip T. Hartung.

Film Quarterly, 13 (Summer 1960), 47-49: Parker Tyler.

Illustrated London News, 237 (17 September 1960), 494.

McCalls, 87 (June 1960), 179-180: Richard Marek.

New Republic, 142 (2 May 1960), 21-22: Stanley Kauffmann.

Reprint: World on Film (L 17), pp. 83-85.

New Statesman, 60 (10 September 1960), 336: William Whitebait.

New York Times, 15 April 1960, p. 1e (NYTFR): Bosley Crowther.

_______, 24 April 1960, sec. 2, p. 1: Bosley Crowther.

New Yorker, 36 (23 April 1960), 147-148: John McCarten.

Newsweek, 55 (25 April 1960), 115.

Saturday Review, 43 (23 April 1960), 28: Hollis Alpert.

Spectator, 205 (9 September 1960), 372-374.

Time, 75 (18 April 1960), 81.

[Orpheus Descending.] Moscow: 27 August 1961. Irina Anisimova-Wolf, producer. Music by Kirill Molchanov. With Vera Maretskaya (Lady).

Battle of Angels (f). Circle Repertory Company. New York: Circle Theatre, 3 November 1974 (32 performances). Marshall W. Mason, director. John Lee Beatty, Dennis Parichy, Jennifer von Mayrhauser, designers. Music by Norman L. Berman. With Max (Val), Tanya Berezin (Myra), Trish Hawkins (Cassandra), Conchata Ferrell (Vee).

Reviews:

New York Times, 4 November 1974, p. 51: Mel Gussow.

_______, 17 November 1974, sec. 2, p. 5: Walter Kerr.

5. BLOOD KIN see Kingdom of Earth

6. BOOM! see The Milk Train Doesn't Stop Here Anymore

7. "CAIRO, SHANGHAI, BOMBAY!" "Cairo, Shanghai, Bombay!" Garden Players. Memphis, Tenn.: Rose Arbor Playhouse, 12 July 1935. Arthur B. Scharff, director.

8. CAMINO REAL.
Camino Real (b). New York: Martin Beck Theatre, 19 March-9 May 1953 (60 performances). Elia Kazan, Anna Sokolow, directors. Lemuel Ayers, designer. Music by Bernardo Ségall. With Eli Wallach (Kilroy), Jo Van Fleet (Marguerite), Joseph Anthony (Casanova), Barbara Baxley (Esmeralda), Frank Silvera (Gutman), Hurd Hatfield (Byron).
Reviews:
America, 89 (4 April 1953), 25: Theophilus Lewis.
________, 89 (11 April 1953), 59-60: Theophilus Lewis.
Catholic World, 197 (May 1953), 148: Euphemia Van Rensselaer Wyatt.
Commonweal, 58 (17 April 1953), 51-52: Richard Hayes.
Look, 17 (5 May 1953), 17: Stephen White.
Nation, 176 (4 April 1953), 293-294: Harold Clurman.
Reprints: Lies (L 10), pp. 83-86; Divine Pastime (L 9), pp. 21-23.
New Republic, 128 (30 March 1953), 30-31: Eric Bentley.
Reprints: Dramatic Event (L 1), pp. 107-110; What (L 3), pp. 74-78.
New York Theatre Critics' Reviews, 14 (1953), 330-332.
Daily Mirror, 20 March 1953: Robert Coleman.
Daily News, 20 March 1953: John Chapman.
Herald Tribune, 20 March 1953: Walter F. Kerr.
Journal-American, 20 March 1953: John McClain.
Post, 20 March 1953: Richard Watts, Jr.; Response: 10 April 1953: John Steinbeck; Reprint: Life (P 370), pp. 441-442.
World-Telegram, 20 March 1953: William Hawkins.
New York Times, 20 March 1953, p. 26 (NYTTR 6): Brooks Atkinson.
________, 29 March 1953, sec. 2, p. 1 (NYTTR 6): Brooks Atkinson; Response: 5 April 1953, sec. 2, p. 3 (including Edith Sitwell); Reprint: Leavitt (N 49), p. 102; Response: 3 May 1953, sec. 2, p. 3.
New Yorker, 29 (28 March 1953), 69-70: Wolcott Gibbs.
Newsweek, 41 (30 March 1953), 63.
Saturday Review, 26 (18 April 1953), 28-30: John Mason Brown.
Theatre Arts, 37 (June 1953), 14, 88: George Jean Nathan.
Reprint: Theatre (L 24), pp. 109-112.
Time, 61 (30 March 1953), 46.
Times, 15 May 1953, p. 10.

Camino Real (adaptation by Berthold Viertel). Darmstadt: Hessischen Landestheater, 6 November 1954. Gustav Rudolf Sellner, director. Franz Mertz, designer. With Claus Hofer (Kilroy), Brigitte König (Marguerite), Alwin Michael Rueffer (Casanova), Julia Costa (Esmeralda), Max Noack (Gutman).

Camino Real. Boch, Germany: Festival of American Drama, 19 March 1955.

Camino Real (c). London: Phoenix Theatre, 8 April-1 June 1957 (63 performances). Peter Hall, director. With Denholm Elliott (Kilroy), Diana Wynyard (Marguerite), Harry Andrews (Casanova), Elisabeth Seal (Esmeralda), Harold Kasket (Gutman), Robert Hardy (Byron).

Production Note:

"'Camino Real' to Be Withdrawn." Times, 17 May 1957, p. 3.

Reviews:

English, 11 (Summer 1957), 186.

Illustrated London News, 230 (27 April 1957), 702: J. C. Trewin.

New Statesman, 53 (13 April 1957), 473-474: T. C. Worsley.

New York Times, 9 April 1957, p. 41 (NYTTR 6).

Spectator, 198 (12 April 1957), 488: David Watt.

Camino Real (adaptation by Berthold Viertel). Hannover: Landestheater, 1959. Günther Fleckenstein, director. Friedhelm Strenger, designer. With Rosemary Gerstenberg (Marguerite).

Camino Real (c). Circle-in-the-Square. New York: St. Marks Playhouse, 16 May 31-July 1960 (89 performances). José Quintero, director. Keith Cuerden, Patricia Zipprodt, Patricia Collins, designers. With Clinton Kimbrough (Kilroy), Nan Martin (Marguerite), Addison Powell (Casanova), David Doyle (Gutman), Lester Rowlins (Byron).

Reviews:

America, 103 (2 July 1960), 422-424: Theophilus Lewis.

Educational Theatre Journal, 12 (October 1960), 227: John Gassner.

Reprint: Dramatic Soundings (L 12), p. 585.

New York Times, 12 May 1960, p. 42 (NYTTR 7): Brooks Atkinson.

________, 29 May 1960, sec. 2, p. 1 (NYTTR 7): Brooks Atkinson.

New Yorker, 36 (28 May 1960), 92-94: Donald Malcolm.

"Ten Blocks on the Camino Real" (a). National Educational Television Playhouse. PBS-TV, 7 October 1966. Jack Lendan, director. With Mark Sheehan (Kilroy), Lotte Lenya, Albert Dekker, Carrie Nye, Hurd Hatfield, Janet Margolin (Esmeralda).

Review:

New York Times, 8 October 1966, p. 63: Jack Gould.

Camino Real (c). Los Angeles: Center Theatre Group of Mark Taper Forum, 21 August 1968 (61 performances).

Milton Katselas, director. Peter Wexler, Peter J. Hall, Designers. With Frank Schofield, Karen Black.

Camino Real (c). New York: Vivian Beaumont Theatre, 8 January-21 February 1970 (52 performances). Milton Katselas, director. Peter Hexler, John Gleason, designers. Music by Bernardo Ségall. With Al Pacino (Kilroy), Jessica Tandy (Marguerite), Jean-Pierre Aumont (Casanova), Susan Tyrrell (Esmeralda), Victor Buono (Gutman), Clifford Davis (Byron).

Reviews:

America, 122 (7 February 1970), 140-142: Theophilus Lewis.
Commentary, 49 (March 1970), 22-24: Jack Richardson.
Nation, 210 (26 January 1970), 93-94: Harold Clurman.
New York Theatre Critics' Reviews, 31 (1970), 395-399:
ABC-TV, 8 January 1970: John Bartholomew Tucker.
CBS-TV, 8 January 1970: Leonard Harris.
NBC, 8 January 1970: Edwin Newman.
Daily News, 9 January 1970: Lee Silver.
Post, 9 January 1970: Richard Watts, Jr.
Wall Street Journal, 12 January 1970: John J. O'Connor.
Women's Wear Daily, 9 January 1970: Martin Gottfried.
New York Times, 9 January 1970, p. 42 (NYTTR 8): Clive Barnes.
_______, 18 January 1970, sec. 2, p. 1 (NYTTR 8): Walter Kerr.
Reprint: God (L 19), pp. 172-176.
New Yorker, 45 (17 January 1970), 50-52: Brendan Gill.
Newsweek, 75 (19 January 1970), 82:
Saturday Review, 53 (24 January 1970), 24: Henry Hewes.
Time, 95 (19 January 1970), 61.

9. CANDLES TO THE SUN. Candles to the Sun. Mummers. St. Louis: Wednesday Club Auditorium, 18 & 20 March 1937. Willard H. Holland, director.

10. "THE CASE OF THE CRUSHED PETUNIAS." This must be one of Williams's most popular plays for amateur productions, but I have found record of only one professional production: Cincinnati: Shelterhouse Theater, 31 May 1973. Pirie MacDonald, director.

11. CAT ON A HOT TIN ROOF/"THREE PLAYERS OF A SUMMER GAME."

Cat on a Hot Tin Roof (c). Playwrights' Company. New York: Morosco Theatre, 24 March 1955-17 November 1956 (694 performances). Elia Kazan, director. Jo Mielziener, Lucinda Ballard, designers. With Ben Gazzara (Brick), Barbara Bel Geddes (Maggie), Burl Ives (Big Daddy), Mildred Dunnock (Big Mama), Madeleine Sherwood (Mae). Winner of Pulitzer Prize for Drama, New York Drama Critics' Circle Award, and Donaldson Award.

Production notes:

"Play Loses Anecdote." New York Times, 7 April 1955, p. 23.

Mitgang, Herbert. "Burl Ives: Ballads to Big Daddy" [interview]. New York Times, 17 April 1955, sec. 2, p. 3.

Hewes, Henry. "Critics on a Tin Roof." Saturday Review, 38 (30 April 1955), 26.

Grutzner, Charles. "Pulitzer Winners." New York Times, 3 May 1955, pp. 1, 28.

"Drama Critics Circle Makes Award." New York Times, 16 May 1955, p. 27.

Downing, Robert. "From the Cat-Bird Seat: The Production Stage Manager's Notes on Cat on a Hot Tin Roof." Theatre Annual, 14 (1956), 46-50.

Reviews:

Catholic World, 181 (May 1955), 147-148: Euphemia Van Rensselaer Wyatt.

Collier's, 137 (2 March 1956), 6: John O'Hara.

Commonweal, 62 (3 June 1955), 230-231: Richard Hayes.

Hudson Review, 8 (Summer 1955), 268-272: William Becker.

Response: 8 (Winter 1956), 633-635.

Kenyon Review, 18 (Winter 1956), 125-126: Mary Hivnor.

Life, 38 (18 April 1955), 137-142.

Nation, 180 (9 April 1955), 314-315: Robert Hatch.

New Republic, 132 (11 April 1955), 28: Eric Bentley.

Reprint: What (L 3), pp. 224-231.

Response: 132 (18 April 1955), 22-23; 132 (25 April 1955), 23.

New York Theatre Critics' Reviews, 16 (155), 342-344:

Daily Mirror, 25 March 1955: Robert Coleman.

Daily News, 25 March 1955: John Chapman.

Herald Tribune, 25 March 1955: Walter F. Kerr.

Journal-American, 25 March 1955: John McClain.

Post, 25 March 1955: Richard Watts, Jr.

World-Telegram, 25 March 1955: William Hawkins.

New York Times, 25 March 1955, p. 18 (NYTTR 6): Brooks Atkinson.

_______, 3 April 1955, sec. 2, p. 1 (NYTTR 6): Brooks Atkinson.

New Yorker, 31 (2 April 1955), 68: Wolcott Gibbs.

Newsweek, 45 (4 April 1955), 54.

Reporter, 12 (15 May 1955), 41-43: Marya Mannes.

Response: 12 (30 June 1955), 4.

Saturday Review, 38 (9 April 1955), 32-33: Henry Hewes.

Spectator, 196 (2 March 1956), 284: John Rosselli.

Theatre Arts, 39 (June 1955), 18-19.

_______, 39 (June 1955), 22-23, 93: Maurice Zolotow.

_______, 39 (July 1955), 74-77.

Time, 65 (4 April 1955), 98.

Times, 22 April 1955, p. 16.

Three Players of a Summer Game (a). Westport, Conn.: White Barn Theatre, 19 July 1955.

Die Katze auf dem heissen Blechdach (adaptation by Hans Sahl). Dusseldorf: Schauspielhaus, 26 November 1955. Leo Mittler, director. With Peter Mosbacher (Brick), Ida Kroftendorf (Maggie), Alfred Schieske (Big Daddy), Gerda Maurus (Big Mama).

Cat on a Hot Tin Roof (c). Washington: National Theatre, 26 November 1956. With Alex Nicol (Brick), Marjorie Steele (Maggie), Thomas Gomez (Big Daddy), Mary Bell (Big Mama).

La chatte sur un toit brûlant (adaptation by André Obey). Paris: Théâtre Antoine, 18 December 1956. Peter Brook, director. With Paul Guers (Brick), Jeanne Moreau (Maggie), Antoine Balpêtré (Big Daddy), Jane Marken (Big Mama).

Reviews:

New York Times, 20 December 1956, p. 37.

Nouvelle Revue Française, 4 (February 1957), 312-316: Jacques Lemarchand.

Paris Herald Tribune, 27 December 1956: Thomas Quinn Curtiss.

Cat on a Hot Tin Roof. San Francisco: Geary Theatre, 24 October 1957. Albert Lipton, director.

Cat on a Hot Tin Roof (b). London: Comedy Theatre, 30 January 1958. Peter Hall, director. With Paul Massie (Brick), Kim Stanley (Maggie), Leo McKern (Big Daddy).

Reviews:

New Statesman, 55 (8 February 1958), 166: T. C. Worsley.

New York Times, 31 January 1958, p. 24 (*NYTTR* 6).

Planned Irish Production, 1958.

Production note:

"Dublin Booking of Play Cancelled." *Times*, 5 June 1958, p. 16.

Cat on a Hot Tin Roof. Liverpool: May 1958. Sam Wanamaker, director.

Production note:

"Critical Views on Unlicensed Play." *Times*, 6 June 1958, p. 6.

Cat on a Hot Tin Roof (screenplay by James Poe and Richard Brooks). Avon Productions. MGM film, 6 August 1958. Richard Brooks, director. William Daniels, cameraman. William A. Horning, Urie McCleary, art directors. With Paul Newman (Brick), Elizabeth Taylor (Maggie), Burl Ives (Big Daddy), Judith Anderson (Big Mama), Madeleine Sherwood (Mae).

Production notes:

"M-G-M Buys 'Cat on a Hot Tin Roof' as a Starring Vehicle for Grace Kelly." New York Times, 10 July 1955, sec. 1, p. 52.

Reviews:

America, 99 (27 September 1958), 679:

Catholic World, 188 (November 1958), 153:

Commonweal, 68 (26 September 1958), 637: Philip T. Hartung.

Cosmopolitan, 145 (September 1958), 18.

Film Quarterly, 12 (Winter 1958), 54-55: Albert Johnson.

Illustrated London News, 233 (18 October 1958), 660.

Library Journal, 83 (1 October 1958), 2667: Charlotte Bilkey Speicher.

Nation, 187 (11 October 1958), 220: Robert Hatch.

New Republic, 139 (29 September 1958), 21-23: Stanley Kauffmann.

Reprint: World (L 18), pp. 79-81.

New York Times, 19 September 1958, p. 24 (NYTFR): Bosley Crowther.

________, 21 September 1958, sec. 2, p. 1: Bosley Crowther.

New York Times Magazine, 30 August 1958, p. 34.

New Yorker, 34 (27 September 1958), 141: John McCarten.

Newsweek, 52 (1 September 1958), 56.

Saturday Review, 41 (13 September 1958), 58: Hollis Alpert.

Spectator, 201 (17 October 1958), 516:

Time, 72 (15 September 1958), 92.

Uma gata sobre um teato quente. Lisbon: 21 October 1959. With Laura Alves (Maggie).

Review:

New York Times, 23 October 1959, p. 23.

Cat on a Hot Tin Roof. London: Eblana Theatre, 1962.

Die Katze auf dem Blechdach. Zurich: Schauspielhaus, 1966. Werner Düggelin, director. Günther Walbeck, designer. With Peter Arens (Brick), Zonja Ziemann (Maggie).

Cat on a Hot Tin Roof (d). West Springfield, Mass.: Stage West Theater, 9 November 1973. John Ulmer, director. Charles G. Stockton, Susan Glenn, Harvout, designers. With Armand Assante (Brick), Linda Selman (Maggie), Maury Cooper (Big Daddy), Charlotte Jones (Big Mama).

Review:

New York Times, 12 November 1973, p. 50: Mel Gussow.

Cat on a Hot Tin Roof (d). Stratford, Conn.: American Shakespeare Theatre, 10 July 1974 (26 performances); New York: ANTA Theatre, 24 September 1974-8 February 1975

(160 performances). Michael Kahn, director. John Conklin, Marc B. Weiss, Jane Greenwood, designers. With Keir Dullea (Brick), Elizabeth Ashley (Margie), Fred Gwynne (Big Daddy), Kate Reid (Big Mama).

Production notes:

Barthel, Joan. "A 'Cat' in Search of Total Approval" [interview with Elizabeth Ashley]. New York Times, 22 September 1974, sec. 2, pp. 1, 3.

Reviews:

America, 131 (12 October 1974), 194: Catherine Hughes.

Nation, 219 (12 October 1974), 349-350: Harold Clurman.

New Republic, 171 (19 October 1974), 16: Stanley Kauffmann.

New York Theatre Critics' Reviews, 35 (1974), 242-246:

CBS-TV, 24 September 1974: Pat Collins.

NBC-Radio, 25 September 1974: Leonard Probst.

Christian Science Monitor, 27 September 1974: Louis Snyder.

Daily News, 25 September 1974: Douglas Watt.

Post, 25 September 1974: Martin Gottfried.

Wall Street Journal, 27 September 1974: Edwin Wilson.

Women's Wear Daily, 25 September 1974: Christopher Sharp.

New York Times, 22 July 1974, p. 40: Mel Gussow.

________, 28 July 1974, sec. 2, p. 3: Julius Novick.

________, 25 September 1974, p. 40: Clive Barnes.

________, 6 October 1974, sec. 2, pp. 1, 3: Walter Kerr.

New Yorker, 50 (7 October 1974), 73: Brendan Gill.

Newsweek, 84 (7 October 1974), 73: Jack Kroll.

Plays and Players, 22 (October 1974), 45: Catherine Hughes.

Time, 104 (7 October 1974), 107: T. E. Kalem.

Cat on a Hot Tin Roof. A Tribute to American Theater. NBC-TV, 6 December 1976. With Robert Wagner (Brick), Natalie Wood (Maggie), Laurence Olivier (Big Daddy), Maureen Stapleton (Big Mama).

Review:

New York Times, 5 December 1976, sec. 2, p. 29: John J. O'Connor.

12. "CONFESSIONAL" see Small Craft Warnings

13. CREVE COEUR.

Creve Coeur (a). Charleston, S. C.: Spoleto Festival U. S. A., 5 June 1978. Keith Hack, director. Steve Rubin, Craig Miller, designers. With Shirley Knight (Dorothea), Jan Miner (Bodey), Charlotte Moore (Helena).

Reviews:

Educational Theatre Journal, 30 (December 1978), 552-553: Albert E. Kalson.

New York, 11 (26 June 1978), 60-61: John Simon.
New York Times, 7 June 1978, sec. C, p. 19: Mel Gussow.
Time, 111 (12 June 1978), 84: T. E. Kalem.

A Lovely Sunday for Creve Coeur (b). New York: Hudson Guild Theater, 21 January 1979. Keith Hack, director. John Conklin, Craig Miller, Linda Fisher, designers. With Shirley Knight (Dorothea), Peg Murray (Bodey), Charlotte Moore (Helena).

Reviews:
Advocate, 22 March 1979, p. 40: Robert Chesley.
America, 140 (24 February 1979), 135: C. Hughes.
Christian Science Monitor, 26 June 1979: John Beaumont.
Commonweal, 106 (16 March 1979), 146-147: G. Weales.
Nation, 228 (10 February 1979), 156-157: H. Clurmon.
New York Times, 22 January 1979, sec. C, p. 15: Richard Eder.
New Yorker, 54 (5 February 1979), 99-101: E. Oliver.
Newsweek, 93 (5 February 1979), 68: Jack Kroll.

14. "THE DARK ROOM."
I have found no record of any professional production.

15. "THE DEMOLITION DOWNTOWN."
I have found no record of any production at all.

16. "DOS RANCHOS" see "The Purification"

17. THE ECCENTRICITIES OF A NIGHTINGALE see Summer and Smoke

18. "THE ENEMY: TIME" see Sweet Bird of Youth

19. "THE FROSTED GLASS COFFIN."
"The Frosted Glass Coffin." Key West Players. Key West, Fla.: Waterfront Playhouse, 1 May 1970. Tennessee Williams, director.

20. THE FUGITIVE KIND.
The Fugitive Kind. Mummers. St. Louis: Wednesday Club Auditorium, December 1937. Willard H. Holland, director.

21. THE FUGITIVE KIND see Battle of Angels

22. GARDEN DISTRICT see Suddenly Last Summer and "Something Unspoken"

23. THE GLASS MENAGERIE.
The Glass Menagerie (b). Chicago: Civic Theatre, 26 December 1944; New York: Playhouse Theatre, 31 March 1945-3 August 1946 (561 performances). Eddie Dowling, Margo Jones, directors. Jo Mielziner, designer. Music by Paul

Bowles. With Laurette Taylor (Amanda), Julie Haydon (Laura), Eddie Dowling (Tom), Anthony Ross (Jim). Winner of New York Drama Critics Circle Award, Sidney Howard Memorial Award, and Donaldson Award.

Production notes:

Mielziner, Jo. "Scene Designs for The Glass Menagerie." Theatre Arts, 29 (April 1945), 211.

"'Glass Menagerie' Is Best Play of Year, Drama Critics Decide." New York Times, 11 April 1945, p. 18.

Nichols, Lewis. "Critics in a Menagerie." New York Times, 15 April 1945, sec. 2, p. 1.

"Winner: Season's Best American Play." Time, 45 (23 April 1945), 88. Reprint: Leavitt (N 49), p. 58.

"To Honor Three Iowa Alumni." New York Times, 9 May 1945, p. 27.

Zolotow, Sam. "Playwright's Prize Goes to Williams." New York Times, 6 June 1945, p. 17.

Donaldson Winners Listed for Awards." New York Times, 1 July 1945, sec. 1, p. 19.

Goldsmith, Theodore. "The Gentleman Caller" [interview with Anthony Ross]. New York Times, 1 July 1945, sec. 2, p. 1.

[Photograph, special Washington performance.] New York Times, 27 January 1946, sec. 2, p. 1.

Reviews:

Catholic World, 161 (May 1945), 166-167: Euphemia Van Rensselaer Wyatt.

________, 161 (June 1945), 263-264: Euphemia Van Rensselaer Wyatt.

Commonweal, 42 (20 April 1945), 16-17: Kappo Phelan.

Life, 18 (30 April 1945), 81-83.

________, 18 (11 June 1945), 12-14.

Nation, 160 (14 April 1945), 424: Joseph Wood Krutch.

New Republic, 112 (16 April 1945), 505: Stark Young. Reprint: Immortal Shadows (L 33), pp. 249-253; Oppenheimer (L 28), pp. 488-591.

New York Theatre Critics' Reviews, 6 (1945), 234-237.

Daily News, 2 April 1945: John Chapman.

Herald Tribune, 2 April 1945: Otis L. Guernsey, Jr.

Journal-American, 2 April 1945: Robert Garland.

PM, 2 April 1945: Louis Kronenberger.

Post, 2 April 1945: Wilella Waldorf.

World-Telegram, 2 April 1945: Burton Rascoe.

New York Times, 14 January 1945, sec. 2, p. 2: Lloyd Lewis.

________, 2 April 1945, p. 15 (NYTTR 5): Lewis Nichols.

________, 8 April 1945, sec. 2, p. 1 (NYTTR 5): Lewis Nichols.

________, 31 March 1946, sec. 2, p. 1.

_______, 2 June 1946, sec. 2, p. 2.
New York Times Magazine, 4 March 1945, pp. 28-29.
New Yorker, 21 (7 April 1945), 40: Wolcott Gibbs.
Newsweek, 25 (2 April 1945), 86.
Player's Magazine, 22 (September-October 1945), 5, 17: Barnard Hewitt.
Saturday Review, 28 (14 April 1945), 34-36: John Mason Brown.
Reprint: Seeing Things (L 7), pp. 224-230.
Theatre Arts, 29 (May 1945), 263.
_______, 29 (June 1945), 325-328: Rosamond Gilder.
Reprint: Theatre Arts Anthology, pp. 657-661.
_______, 29 (October 1945), 554.
Theatre Book of the Year, 1944-1945 (New York: Alfred A. Knopf, 1946), pp. 324-327: George Jean Nathan.
Time, 45 (9 April 1945), 86-88.

Die Glasmenagerie (adaptation by Berthold Viertel). Basel: Theater der Stadt, November 1946. Kurt Horwitz, director. With Therese Giehse (Amanda), Margrit Winter (Laura), Leopold Biberti (Tom), James Meyer (Jim).

Zoo di vetro (adaptation by Alfredo Segre). Rome: Theatro Eliseo, 12 December 1946. Luchino Visconti, director. Mario Chiari, Uberto Petrassi, Renato Morozzo, Amleto Neoccia, designers. Music by Paul Bowles. With Tatiana Pavlova (Amanda), Nina Morelli (Laura), Paolo Stoppa (Tom), Girgio de Lullo (Jim).
Review:
Theatre Arts, 31 (August 1947), 38-39.

La ménagerie de verre (adaptation by Marcel Duhamel). Compagnie de Genève. Paris: Théâtre du Vieux-Colombier, 18 April 1947. Claude Maritz, director. With Jane Marken (Amanda), Hélène Vita (Laura), Claude Maritz (Tom), Daniel Ivernel (Jim).
Review:
Theatre Arts, 31 (August 1947), 39.

[The Glass Menagerie.] Stockholm: Royal Dramatic Theater, 1947. With Nancy Dalunde (Laura), Olof Bergström (Jim).
Review:
Theatre Arts, 31 (August 1947), 38-39.

The Glass Menagerie (b). London: Theatre Royal, Haymarket, 28 July 1948. John Gielgud, director. Jo Mielziner, designer. Music by Paul Bowles. With Helen Hayes (Amanda), Frances Heflin (Laura), Phil Brown (Tom), Hugh McDermott (Jim).
Reviews:
Illustrated London News, 213 (28 August 1948), 250: J. C. Trewin.
New Statesman, 36 (7 August 1948), 113: T. C. Worsley.

New York Times, 29 July 1948, p. 17 (NYTTR 5).
Spectator, 181 (6 August 1948), 173: Peter Fleming.

The Glass Menagerie (c). Warner Brothers film, 7 September 1950. Irving Rapper, director. Robert Burke, cameraman. Robert Haas, art director. Music by Max Steiner. With Gertrude Lawrence (Amanda), Jane Wyman (Laura), Kirk Douglas (Tom), Arthur Kennedy (Jim).

Production notes:

Bradt, Thomas F. "Hollywood Digest." New York Times, 22 January 1950, sec. 2, p. 5.

Hayes, J. J. "'Glass Menagerie' in Ireland." Christian Science Monitor Magazine, 15 April 1950, p. 8.

Aldrich, Richard Stoddall. Gertrude Lawrence as Mrs. O: An Intimate Biography of the Great Star. New York: Greystone Press, 1954. Chap. 17.

Reviews:

Christian Century, 67 (22 November 1950), 1407.

Commonweal, 52 (6 October 1950), 631-632: Philip T. Hartung.

Good Housekeeping, 131 (August 1950), 215.

Holiday, 8 (August 1950), 14-16: Al Hine.

Library Journal, 75 (15 October 1950), 1843: Frances Clark Sayers.

New Republic, 123 (23 October 1950), 22: Robert Hatch.

New York Times, 29 September 1950, p. 51 (NYTFR): Bosley Crowther.

________, 8 October 1950, sec. 2, p. 1: Bosley Crowther.

New York Times Magazine, 4 June 1950, p. 58.

New Yorker, 26 (30 September 1950), 60: John McCarten.

Newsweek, 36 (9 October 1950), 90.

Rotarian, 78 (January 1951), 38: Jane Lockhart.

Saturday Review, 33 (14 October 1950), 32-33: Richard Griffith.

Scholastic, 57 (18 October 1950), 28.

Time, 56 (2 October 1950), 74.

The Glass Menagerie (b). New York: City Center Theatre, 21 November 1956. Alan Schneider, director. Peggy Clark, designer. With Helen Hayes (Amanda), Lois Smith (Laura), James Daly (Tom), Lenny Chapman (Jim).

Reviews:

Catholic World, 184 (January 1957), 307: Euphemia Van Rensselaer Wyatt.

New York Theatre Critics' Reviews, 17 (1956), 190-193:

- Daily Mirror, 22 November 1956: Robert Coleman.
- Daily News, 22 November 1956: John Chapman.
- Herald Tribune, 22 November 1956: Walter Kerr.
- Journal-American, 23 November 1956: John McClain.
- Post, 23 November 1956: Richard Watts, Jr.
- World-Telegram, 23 November 1956: Tom Donnelly.

New York Times, 22 November 1956, p. 50 (NYTTR 6): Brooks Atkinson.

_______, 2 December 1956, sec. 2, p. 1 (NYTTR 6): Brooks Atkinson.
Saturday Review, 39 (8 December 1956), 29: Henry Hewes.
Theatre Arts, 41 (February 1952), 24.

The Glass Menagerie (b). Theatre Guild American Repertory Company. Washington: National Theatre, March 1961; European and South American tour, spring-summer 1961. With Helen Hayes (Amanda), Nancy Coleman (Laura), James Broderick (Tom), Leif Erikson (Jim).

Production notes:
Zolotow, Sam. "Announcement by Langer." New York Times, 25 August 1960, p. 24.

Reviews:
New York Times, 6 March 1961, p. 30 (NYTTR 7): Howard Taubman.
_______, 20 March 1961, p. 32 [Brussels].
_______, 28 March 1961, p. 32 [Belgrade].
_______, 1 April 1961, p. 11 (NYTTR 7) [Athens].
_______, 11 April 1961, p. 43 (NYTTR 7) [Tel Aviv].
_______, 21 April 1961, p. 29 (NYTTR 7) [Vienna].
_______, 1 May 1961, p. 35 (NYTTR 7) [West Berlin].
_______, 19 May 1961, p. 22 (NYTTR 7) [Stockholm].
_______, 31 May 1961, p. 28 (NYTTR 7) [Rome].
_______, 16 June 1961, p. 27 (NYTTR 7) [Paris].
_______, 21 August 1961, p. 20 (NYTTR 7) [Bogotá].

Planned American tour, 1962.

Production notes:
"Williams Cancels Bids for 'Glass Menagerie.'" New York Times, 21 September 1962, p. 35.

Le ménagerie de verre (adaptation by Robert Antelme). Communauté Théâtrale Mouffetard. Paris: Théâtre de la Bruyère, 29 March 1963.

The Glass Menagerie. Caedmon recording, 1964 (D 3). Howard Sackler, director. With Jessica Tandy (Amanda), Julie Harris (Laura), Montgomery Clift (Tom), David Wayne (Jim).

The Glass Menagerie (b). Minnesota Theater Company. Minneapolis: Tyrone Guthrie Theatre, summer 1964. Alan Schneider, director. Lois Brown, designer. Music by Herbert Pilhofer. With Ruth Nelson (Amanda), Ellen Gweer (Laura), Lee Richardson (Tom), Ed Flanders (Jim).

Reviews:
Nation, 199 (10 August 1964), 60: Harold Clurman. Reprint: Naked Image (L 11), pp. 142-143.
New York Times, 20 July 1964, p. 18 (NYTTR 7): Howard Taubman.

Die Glas menagerie. Vienna: Akademietheater, 1965. Willi Schmidt, director & designer. With Paula Wessely (Amanda), Annemarie Düringer (Laura).

The Glass Menagerie (b). New York: Brooks Atkinson Theatre, 4 May-2 October 1965 (175 performances). George Keathley, director. James A. Taylor, Robert T. Williams, Patton Campbell, V. C. Fuqua, designers. Music by Paul Bowles. With Maureen Stapleton (Amanda), Piper Laurie (Laura), George Gizzard (Tom), Pat Hingle (Jim).

Production notes:

Stang, Joanne. "Maureen into Amanda" [interview with Maureen Stapleton]. New York Times, 16 May 1965, sec. 2, pp. 1, 3.

Reviews:

America, 112 (19 June 1965), 888-889: Theophilus Lewis.
Commonweal, 82 (9 June 1965), 356-357: Wilfred Sheed.
Life, 58 (28 May 1965), 16: Claudia Cassidy.
New York Theatre Critics' Reviews, 26 (1965), 332-335:
Daily News, 5 May 1965: Douglas Watt.
Herald Tribune, 5 May 1965: Walter Kerr.
Journal-American, 5 May 1965: John McClain.
Post, 5 May 1965: Richard Watts, Jr.
World-Telegram & Son, 5 May 1965: Norman Nadel.
New York Times, 5 May 1965, p. 53 (NYTTR 7): Howard Taubman.
______, 16 May 1965, sec. 2, p. 1 (NYTTR 7): Howard Taubman.
New Yorker, 41 (15 May 1965), 158: John McCarten.
Newsweek, 65 (17 May 1965), 92.
Reprint: Gilman, Common and Uncommon Modes (L 13), pp. 148-149.
Time, 85 (14 May 1965), 64.

El zoologico de cristal. Mexico City: Casa de la Paz, 5 July 1965. Juan López Moctezuma, Sergio Guzik, directors. Roberto Donis, Roberto Cirou, Raúl Díaz González, designers. Music by Juan José Calatayud. With María Socorro Cano de Delgado (Amanda), Virginia O. de Gutiérrez (Laura), Juan López Moctezuma (Tom), Constantino Gutiérrez (Jim).

Die Glassmenagerie (adaptation by Berthold Viertel). Ulmer Theatre, 1966. Kai Braak, director. Ekkehard Köhn, designer. With Tilli Breidenbach (Amanda), Wiebke Paritz (Laura).

The Glass Menagerie (cut by Williams). CBS-TV, 8 December 1966. Michael Elliott, director. John Clements, designer. With Shirley Booth (Amanda), Barbara Loden (Laura), Hal Holbrook (Tom), Pat Hingle (Jim).

Review:

New York Times, 9 December 1966, p. 95: Jack Gould.

The Glass Menagerie (b). New Haven, Conn.: Long Wharf Theatre, 20 October 1967. Arvin Brown, director. James Gohl, Rosemary Ingham, designers. With Mildred Dunnock (Amanda), Joyce Ebert (Laura), Charles Cioffi (Tom), Joseph Hindy (Jim).

Review:

Saturday Review, 50 (25 November 1967), 71: Henry Hewes.

The Glass Menagerie. ABC-TV, 16 December 1973. Anthony Harvey, director. With Katharine Hepburn (Amanda), Joanna Miles (Laura), Sam Waterston (Tom), Michael Moriarty (Jim).

Production notes:

Higham, Charles. "Private and Proud and Hepburn" [interview with Katharine Hepburn]. New York Times, 9 December 1973, sec. 2, pp. 3, 21.

Reviews:

New York Times, 14 December 1973, p. 94: John J. O'Connor.

New Yorker, 49 (31 December 1973), 50-51: Pauline Kael.

Reprint: Reeling, pp. 246-247.

Newsweek, 82 (17 December 1973), 61: Harry F. Waters.

The Glass Menagerie (b). New York: Circle-in-the-Square Theater, 18 December 1975-22 February 1976 (78 performances). Theodore Mann, director. Ming Cho Lee, Thomas Skelton, Sydney Brooks, designers. Music by Craig Wasson. With Maureen Stapleton (Amanda), Pamela Playton-Wright (Laura), Rip Torn (Tom), Paul Rudd (Jim).

Reviews:

America, 134 (31 January 1976), 75: Catherine Hughes.

Nation, 222 (3 January 1976), 28: Harold Clurman.

New Republic, 174 (17 January 1976), 28: Stanley Kauffmann.

New York Theatre Critics' Reviews, 36 (1975), 125-128:

NBC, 18 December 1975: Leonard Probst.

Christian Science Monitor, 26 December 1975: John Beaufort.

Daily News, 19 December 1975: Douglas Watt.

Post, 19 December 1975: Martin Gottfried.

Wall Street Journal, 23 December 1975: Edwin Wilson.

Women's Wear Daily, 19 December 1975: Howard Kissel.

New York Times, 19 December 1975, p. 52: Walter Kerr.

_______, 28 December 1975, sec. 2, p. 5: Walter Kerr.

Time, 107 (12 January 1976), 61: T. E. Kalem.

La ménagerie de verre (adaptation by Marcel Duhamel).

Paris: Théâtre 347, winter 1977. M. Lupovici, director. With Odille Varsois or Hélène Vallier (Amanda), Anne Saint-Mor (Laura), Daniel Colas (Tom), Bernard Crommbey (Jim).

The Glass Menagerie (b). Dolphin Theatre Company. London: Shaw Theatre, 13 June-13 August 1977. Jonathan Lynn, director. Saul Radomsky, Michael Onthwaite, designers. Music by Ray Cook. With Maxine Audley (Amanda), Connie Booth (Laura), James Aubry (Tom), Angus Macinnes (Jim).

Review:

Plays and Players, 24 (September 1977), 26-27: Charles Marowitz.

24. "THE GNÄDIGES FRÄULEIN"/THE LATTER DAYS OF A CELEBRATED SOUBRETTE.

Slapstick Tragedy (a). New York: Longacre Theater, 22-26 February 1966 (7 performances). Alan Schneider, director. Ming Cho Lee, Noel Taylor, Martin Aronstein, designers. Music by Lee Hoiby. With Margaret Leighton (Fräulein), Zoe Caldwell (Polly), Kate Reid (Molly).

Reviews:

Commonweal, 84 (8 April 1966), 82: Wilfred Sheed.

Nation, 202 (14 March 1966), 309: Harold Clurman.
Reprint: Stanton (P 366), pp. 71-73.

New Republic, 154 (26 March 1966), 34-36: Robert Brustein.

New York Theatre Critics' Reviews, 27 (1966), 359-362:
- Daily News, 23 February 1966: Douglas Watt.
- Herald Tribune, 23 February 1966: Walter Kerr.
- Journal-American, 23 February 1966: John McClain.
- Post, 23 February 1966: Richard Watts, Jr.
- World-Telegram & Sun, 23 February 1966: Norman Nadel.

New York Times, 23 February 1966, p. 42 (NYTTR 7): Stanley Kauffmann.

________, 6 March 1966, sec. 2, p. 1 (NYTTR 7): Stanley Kauffmann.

New Yorker, 42 (5 March 1966), 83-84: John McCarten.

Newsweek, 67 (7 March 1966), 90.
Reprint: Gilman, Common and Uncommon Modes (L 13), pp. 150-151.

Reporter, 34 (24 March 1966), 49-50: Gerald Weales.

Saturday Review, 49 (12 March 1966), 28: Henry Hewes.
Reprint: Leavitt (N 49), p. 145.

Tamarack Review (Toronto), 39 (Spring 1966), 52-58: Barry Callaghan.

Time, 87 (4 March 1966), 88.

Vogue, 147 (1 April 1966), 109: Anthony West.

The Latter Days of a Celebrated Soubrette (b). New York: Central Arts Cabaret Theater, 16 May 1974. Luis Lopez-Cepero, director. With Anne Meacham (Fräulein), Robert Frink (Molly), William Pritz (Polly).

Review:
New York Times, 29 May 1974, p. 48: Mel Gussow.

25. "HEADLINES."
Curtain raiser for Irwin Shaw's Bury the Dead. Mummers. St. Louis: Wednesday Club Auditorium, 11 November 1936. Willard H. Holland, director.

26. "HELLO FROM BERTHA."
Four by Tennessee. Play of the Week. PBS-TV, 6 February 1961. With Maureen Stapleton (Bertha), Eileen Heckart (Goldie), Salome Jens (Lena).
Review:
New York Times, 7 February 1961, p. 67: John P. Shaley.

27. "I CAN'T IMAGINE TOMORROW."
"I Can't Imagine Tomorrow." PBS-TV, 3 December 1970. Glenn Jordan, director. With Kim Stanely (One), William Redfield (Two).
Review:
New York Times, 4 December 1970, p. 95: Jack Gould.

"I Can't Imagine Tomorrow." New York: WPA Theater, 1975. Craig Barish, director.

"Je n'imagine pas ma vie demain." Paris: Le Coupe Chou, spring 1976. Andreas Voutsines, director. With Reine Bartere (One), François Nocher (Two).
Review:
International Herald Tribune, 30 April 1976: Thomas Quinn Curtiss.

28. "I RISE IN FLAME, CRIED THE PHOENIX."
Two Short Plays. New York: Theatre de Lys, 14 April 1959. Tom Brennan, director. With Alfred Ryder (Lawrence), Viveca Lindfors (Frieda) Nan Martin (Brett).
Reviews:
New York Times, 15 April 1959, p. 30 (NYTTR 6): Louis Calta.
Saturday Review, 42 (25 April 1959), 23: Henry Hewes.

Four by Tennessee. Play of the Week. PBS-TV, 6 February 1961. With Alfred Ryder (Lawrence), Jo Van Fleet (Frieda).
Review:
New York Times, 7 February 1961, p. 67: John P. Shanley.

The play was performed in London during the 1970-1971 season and again during the 1971-1972 season.

29. IN THE BAR OF A TOKYO HOTEL.
In the Bar of a Tokyo Hotel. New York: Eastside Playhouse,

11 May-1 June 1969 (22 previews, 25 performances). Herbert Machiz, director. Neil Peter Jampolis, Stanley Simmons, Hayward Morris, designers. With Anne Meacham (Miriam), Donald Madden (Mark), Jon Lee (Barman), Lester Rawlins (Leonard).

Reviews:

Life, 66 (13 June 1969), 10: Stefan Kanfer.
Nation, 208 (2 June 1969), 709-710: Harold Clurman.
New York Times, 12 May 1969, p. 54 (NYTTR 8): Clive Barnes.
_______, 25 May 1969, sec. 2, p. 5 (NYTTR 8): Walter Kerr.
Newsweek, 73 (26 May 1969), 133: Jack Kroll.
Saturday Review, 52 (31 May 1968), 18: Henry Hewes.
Time, 93 (23 May 1969), 75.

The play was produced in London during the 1974-1975 season.

30. KINGDOM OF EARTH.

The Seven Descents of Myrtle (b). New York: Ethel Barrymore Theatre, 27 March-20 April 1968 (29 performances). José Quintero, director. Jo Mielziner, Jane Greenwood, designers. With Estelle Parsons (Myrtle), Harry Guardino (Chicken), Brian Bedford (Lot).

Production notes:

"New Williams Play Embroiled in Fight over Shifting Title." New York Times, 21 February 1968, p. 61.
Zolotow, Sam. "Quintero Leaves Williams Comedy." New York Times, 28 February 1968, p. 39.
_______. "Quintero Returns." New York Times, 29 February 1968, p. 30.

Reviews:

Commonweal, 88 (3 May 1968), 208-209: John Simon.
Life, 64 (26 April 1968), 18: Wilfred Sheed.
Nation, 206 (15 April 1968), 516-517: Harold Clurman.
New York Theatre Critics' Reviews, 29 (1968), 313-316:
Daily News, 28 March 1968: John Chapman.
Post, 28 March 1968: Richard Watts, Jr.
Wall Street Journal, 29 March 1968: Richard F. Cooke.
Women's Wear Daily, 28 March 1968: Chauncey Howell.
New York Times, 28 March 1968, p. 54 (NYTTR 8): Clive Barnes.
_______, 7 April 1968, sec. 2, p. 1 (NYTTR 8): Walter Kerr.
Reprint: Thirty (L 20), pp. 224-230.
New Yorker, 44 (6 April 1968), 109-110: Brendan Gill.
Newsweek, 71 (8 April 1968), 131: Jack Kroll.
Saturday Review, 51 (13 April 1968), 30: Henry Hewes.
Time, 91 (5 April 1968), 77.

Königreich auf Erden (adaptation by Jan Lustig). Hamburg:

Thalia-Theater, 1969. Detlef Sierek, director. Günther Walbeck, designer. With Gisela Peltzer (Myrtle), Siefried Wischnewski (Chicken), Joachim Ansorge (Lot).

Last of the Mobile Hot Shots/Blood Kin (Screenplay by Gore Vidal). Warner Brothers/Seven Arts film, 17 December 1964. Sidney Lumet, director. James Wong Howe, cameraman. Music by Quincy Jones. With Lynn Redgrave (Myrtle), Robert Hooks (Chicken), James Coburn (Jeb).

Production notes:

"Screen Rights Are Sold to a New Williams Play." New York Times, 8 December 1967, p. 60.

Reviews:

Holiday, 47 (March 1970), 37: Rex Reed.

New York Times, 15 January 1970, p. 38: Vincent Canby.

Newsweek, 75 (26 January 1970), 75: S. K. Oberbeck.

Time, 95 (19 January 1970), 67.

Kingdom of Earth (c). McCarter Theatre Company. Princeton, N.J.: 6 March 1975 (10 performances). Garland Wright, director. Paul Zalon, David James, Marc B. Weiss, designers. With Marilyn Chris (Myrtle), David Pendleton (Chicken), Courtney Burr (Lot).

Review:

New York Times, 12 March 1975, p. 28: Clive Barnes.

Kingdom of Earth. Bristol Old Vic Company. London: New Vic, 14 February 1978. Mike Newell, director. John Elvery, designer. With Gillian Borge (Myrtle), Peter Postlethwaite (Chicken), Jonathan Kent (Lot).

Review:

Plays and Players, 25 (April 1978), 39: Michael Anderson.

31. "THE LADY OF LARKSPUR LOTION."

"The Lady of Larkspur Lotion." American Club Theatre. Paris: Monceau Théâtre, 8 July 1949. George Voskovec, director.

Review:

New York Times, 9 July 1949, p. 9 (NYTTR 5).

Four by Tennessee. Play of the Week. PBS-TV, 6 February 1961. With Jo Van Fleet (Mrs. Harwicke-Moore).

Review:

New York Times, 7 February 1961, p. 67: John P. Shanley.

Three by Tennessee. New York: Lolly's Theater Club, 6 December 1973. Dick Garfield, Cindy Kaplana, directors.

32. "THE LAST OF MY SOLID GOLD WATCHES."

"The Last of My Solid Gold Watches." Las Palmas (Los Angeles): Actor's Laboratory Theater, 1947.

Three Short Plays. Dallas: Theatre '48, 1948. Margo Jones, director. With Vaughan Gloser (Charlie Colton), Tod Andrews (Bob Harper).

Production notes:

Jones, Margo. Theatre-in-the-Round. New York: McGraw-Hill, 1965. Pp. 149-150.

Three by Tennessee. Kraft Television Theater. NBC-TV, 16 April 1958. Sidney Lumet, director. With Thomas Chambers (Charlie Colton), Gene Saks (Bob Harper).

Review:

New York Times, 17 April 1958, p. 63: Jack Gould.

33. LAST OF THE MOBILE HOT-SHOTS see Kingdom of Earth

34. THE LATTER DAYS OF A CELEBRATED SOUBRETTE see "The Gnädiges Fräulein"

35. "THE LONG GOODBYE."

"The Long Goodbye." New York: New School for Social Research, 14 February 1940.

Two One-Act Plays. Nantucket: Straight Wharf Theatre, summer 1946. Albert Penalosa, director.

36. "THE LONG STAY CUT SHORT."

The play was produced in London during the 1970-1971 season, but I have found no other record of a professional production.

37. "LORD BYRON'S LOVE LETTER."

I can find no record of any production of the play. There have been at least two productions of the opera:

"Lord Byron's Love Letter" (b). New Orleans Opera Guild. New Orleans: Tulane University, 18 January 1955. Nicola Rescigno, conductor. With Patricia Neway (Grandmother), Gertrude Ribla (Spinster).

Reviews:

Musical America, 75 (1 February 1955), 33: Harry B. Loëb.

New York Times, 19 January 1955, p. 23 (NYTTR 6): Brooks Atkinson & Ewing Poteet.

Newsweek, 45 (31 January 1955), 81.

"Lord Byron's Love Letter" (b). Chicago: Lyric Theater, 21 November 1955. Nicola Rescigno, conductor. Gerald Ritholz, designer. With Astrid Varney (Grandmother), Gertrude Ribla (Spinster).

Review:

Musical America, 75 (15 Dec. 1955), 7: Howard Talley.

38. A LOVELY SUNDAY FOR CREVE COEUR see Creve Coeur

39. "THE MAGIC TOWER."
"The Magic Tower." Webster Groves Theatre Guild. Webster Groves, Mo.: October 1936. David Gibson, director.

40. "THE MIGRANTS."
"Tennessee Williams' 'The Migrants'" (television script by Lanford Wilson). Playhouse 90. CBS-TV, 3 February 1974. Tom Gries, director. With Cloris Leachman (mother), Ron Howard (son), Sissy Spacek (daughter).
Reviews:
New York Times, 1 February 1974, p. 61: John J. O'Connor.
_______, 3 February 1974, sec. 2, p. 19.

41. THE MILK TRAIN DOESN'T STOP HERE ANYMORE/BOOM!
The Milk Train Doesn't Stop Here Anymore (a). Spoleto, Italy: Festival of Two Worlds, 11 July 1962. With Hermione Baddeley (Goforth), Paul Roebling (Chris), Mildred Dunnock (Witch of Capri), Ann Williams (Blackie).
Reviews:
New York Times, 12 July 1962, p. 19 (NYTTR 7).
Paris Herald Tribune, 12 July 1962: Nino Lo Bello.
Time, 40 (20 July 1962), 40.

The Milk Train Doesn't Stop Here Anymore (b). New York: Morosco Theatre, 16 January-16 March 1963 (65 performances). Herbert Machiz, director. Jo Mielziner, Fred Voelpel, Peter Hall, designers. Music by Paul Bowles. With Hermione Baddeley (Goforth), Paul Roebling (Chris), Mildred Dunnock (Witch of Capri), Ann Williams (Blackie).
Reviews:
America, 108 (30 March 1963), 449: Theophilus Lewis.
Commonweal, 77 (8 February 1963), 515-517: Richard Gillman.
Reprint: Common and Uncommon Modes (L 13), pp. 144-147.
Educational Theatre Journal, 15 (May 1963), 186-187: John Gassner.
Reprint: Dramatic Soundings (L 12), pp. 588-589.
Encore, 10 (May-June 1963), 8-13: Lee Baxandall.
Hudson Review, 16 (Spring 1963), 87-89: John Simon.
Reprint: Uneasy Stages (L 30), pp. 6-8.
Nation, 196 (2 February 1963), 106: Harold Clurman.
National Review, 14 (9 April 1963), 291-293: W. H. Von Dreele.
New Republic, 148 (2 February 1963), 27: Robert Brustein.
Reprint: Seasons (L 8), p. 129.
New York Theatre Critics' Reviews, 24 (1963), 391-394:
Daily News: John Chapman.
Herald Tribune: Walter Kerr
Reprint: Thirty Plays (L 20), pp. 222-223.
Journal-American: John McClain.
Mirror: Robert Coleman.

Post: Richard Watts, Jr.
World-Telegram & Sun: Norman Nadel.
New York Times, 18 January 1963, p. 7 (NYTTR 7): Howard Taubman.
New Yorker, 38 (26 January 1963), 72: John McCarten.
Newsweek, 61 (28 January 1963), 79.
Reporter, 28 (25 April 1963), 48: Marya Mannes.
Saturday Review, 46 (2 February 1963), 20-21: Henry Hewes.
Theatre Arts, 47 (February 1963), 66: Alan Pryce-Jones.
Time, 81 (25 January 1963), 53.

The Milk Train Doesn't Stop Here Anymore (c). Abingdon, Va.: Barter Theater, 16 September 1963. Adrian Hall, Director. Bobby Soule, designer. With Claire Luce (Goforth), Donald Madden (Chris), Mary Finnery (Witch), Nancy Wilder (Blackie).

Review:
New York Times, 18 September 1963, p. 32 (NYTTR 7).

The Milk Train Doesn't Stop Here Anymore (c). New York: Brooks Atkinson Theatre, 1 January 1964 (4 performances). Tony Richardson, director. Rouben Ter-Artunian, Martin Aronstein, designers. Music by Ned Rorem. With Tallulah Bankhead (Goforth), Tab Hunter (Chris), Ruth Ford (Witch), Marian Seldes (Blackie).

Reviews:
Educational Theatre Journal, 16 (March 1964), 76-77: John Gassner.
Reprint: Dramatic Soundings (L 12), p. 590.
New York Theatre Critics' Reviews, 25 (1964), 397-400:
Daily News, 2 January 1964: John Chapman.
Herald Tribune, 2 January 1964: Walter Kerr.
Reprint: Thirty Plays (L 20), pp. 222-223.
Journal-American, 2 January 1964: John McClain.
Post, 2 January 1964: Richard Watts, Jr.
World-Telegram & Sun, 2 January 1964: Norman Nadel.
New York Times, 2 January 1964, p. 33 (NYTTR 7): Howard Taubman.
Newsweek, 63 (13 January 1964), 70.
Saturday Review, 47 (18 January 1964), 22: Henry Hewes.
Time, 83 (10 January 1964), 52.

The Milk Train Doesn't Stop Here Anymore (d). Actors Workshop Guild. San Francisco: Encore Theatre, 23 July 1965 (47 performances). John Hancock, director. Warren Travis, Ken Margolis, J. Thompson Poynter, designers. Music by Morton Subotnik. With Winifred Mann (Goforth), Robert Benson (Chris), Joyce Lancaster (Witch), Sally Kemp (Blackie).

Review:
New York Times, 27 July 1965, p. 25 (NYTTR 7): Howard Taubman.

Boom! (e). Limites/World Film Services. Universal film, May 1968. Joseph Losey, director. Douglas Slocombe, cameraman. Richard MacDonald, art director. Music by John Barry, Nazirali Jairazbhoy, Viram Jasani. With Elizabeth Taylor (Goforth), Richard Burton (Chris), Noel Coward (Witch), Joanna Shimkus (Blackie), Michael Dunn (Rudy).

Production notes:

"Burtons Taking 'Milk Train' for a 3d Run." New York Times, 3 October 1967, p. 55.

Shivas, Mark. "Was It Like This with Louis XIV?" New York Times, 15 October 1967, sec. 2, p. 15.

Reviews:

America, 118 (8 June 1968), 760-761: Moira Walsh.

Commonweal, 88 (14 June 1968), 385: Philip T. Hartung.

Life, 64 (21 June 1968), 12: Richard Schickel.

New Republic, 158 (8 June 1968), 26: Stanley Kauffmann.

New York Times, 27 May 1968, p. 56 (NYTFR): Vincent Canby.

Newsweek, 71 (3 June 1968), 104: Paul D. Zimmerman.

Saturday Review, 51 (1 June 1968), 19: Arthur Knight.

Time, 91 (31 May 1968), 56.

The Milk Train Doesn't Stop Here Anymore. London: Tower Theatre, fall 1968. Edgar Davies, director. Sue Plummer, designer. With Sara Randall (Goforth).

Review:

Times, 2 December 1968, p. 16: Irving Waddle.

Le train de l'aube ne s'arrête plus ici (adaptation by Michel Arnaud). Paris: Théâtre Edouard VII, 3 February 1971. Jean-Pierre Laruy, director. Pace, designer. With Claude Génia (Goforth), Claude Titre (Chris), Denis Grey (Witch), Dominique Arden (Blackie).

A production was begun in London at the Royal Court Theatre under the direction of George Devine, with Ruth Gordon (Goforth) and Donald Madden (Chris), at some date; but it never opened.

42. "MOONY'S KID DON'T CRY."

Two One-Act Plays. Nantucket: Straight Wharf Theatre, summer 1946. Albert Penalosa, director.

Three by Tennessee. Kraft Television Theater. NBC-TV, 16 April 1958. Sidney Lumet, director. With Ben Gazzara (Moony), Lee Grant (Jane).

Review:

New York Times, 17 April 1958, p. 63: Jack Gould.

"La goose de Moony ne pleure pas" (adaptation by Robert Postec). Un spectacle Tennessee Williams. La Compagnie Robert Postec. Paris: Théâtre de l'Alliance Française, 1962.

The play was also presented in London during the 1971-1972 season.

43. "THE MUTILATED."
Slapstick Tragedy. New York: Longacre Theatre, 22-26 February 1966 (7 performances). Alan Schneider, director. Ming Cho Lee, Noel Taylor, Martin Aronstein, designers. Music by Lee Hoiby. With Margaret Leighton (Trinket), Kate Reid (Celeste).
Reviews: see "The Gnädiges Fräulein" (K 24)

44. THE NIGHT OF THE IGUANA.
"The Night of the Iguana" (a). Spoleto, Italy: Festival of Two Worlds, 2 July 1959. Frank Corsaro, director. Paul Sylbert, designer. Music by Werner Torkanowsky. With Patrick O'Neal (Shannon), Rosemary Murphy (Hannah).
Review:
Saturday Review, 42 (1 August 1959), 30: Henry Hewes.

The Night of the Iguana (b). Miami: Coconut Grove Playhouse, 1960. Frank Corsaro, director.

The Night of the Iguana (c). New York: Royale Theater, 28 December 1961-29 September 1962 (316 performances). Frank Corsaro, director. Oliver Smith, Jean Rosenthal, Noel Taylor, Edward Beyer, designers. With Patrick O'Neal (Shannon), Bette Davis, later Shelley Winters (Maxine), Margaret Leighton, later Patricia Roe (Hannah), Alan Webb, later Leo Lucker (Nonno). Winner of the New York Drama Critics' Circle Award.
Production notes:
Peck, Seymour. "Rehearsal Time, Rehearsal Problems." New York Times Magazine, 29 October 1961, pp. 34-35.
"'Iguana' Is Cited by Critics Circle." New York Times, 11 April 1962, p. 46.
Davis, Bette. The Lonely Life: An Autobiography. New York: G. P. Putnam's Sons, 1962.
Reviews:
America, 106 (3 February 1962), 604: Theophilus Lewis.
Catholic World, 194 (March 1962), 380-381: Hilary Griffin.
Christian Century, 79 (7 February 1962), 169: Tom F. Driver.
Cresset, 25 (March 1962), 21: Walter Sorell.
Commonweal, 75 (26 January 1962), 460: Richard Gilman.
Reprint: Common and Uncommon Modes (L 13), pp. 140-143.
Educational Theatre Journal, 14 (March 1962), 69: John Gassner.
Reprint: Dramatic Soundings (L 12), p. 588.
Hudson Review, 14 (Spring 1961), 83-92: John Simon.
Life, 52 (13 April 1962), 67-70.

Mainstream, 15 (August 1962), 62-63: Robert Forrey.
Nation, 194 (27 January 1962), 86: Harold Clurman.
Reprint: Naked Savage (L 11), pp. 126-128.
New Republic, 146 (22 January 1962), 20-23: Robert Brustein.
Reprint: Seasons (L 8), pp. 126-129.
New York Theatre Critics' Reviews, 22 (1961), 131-134:
Daily News, 29 December 1961: John Chapman.
Herald Tribune, 29 December 1961: Walter Kerr.
Journal-American, 29 December 1961: John McClain.
Mirror, 29 December 1961: Robert Coleman.
Post, 29 December 1961: Richard Watts, Jr.
World-Telegram & Sun, 29 December 1961: Norman Nadel.
New York Times, 29 December 1961, p. 10 (NYTTR 7): Howard Taubman.
________, 7 January 1962, sec. 2, p. 1 (NYTTR 7): Howard Taubman.
New Yorker, 37 (13 January 1962), 61: Edith Oliver.
Newsweek, 59 (8 January 1962), 44.
Reporter, 26 (1 February 1962), 45: Marya Mannes.
Saturday Review, 45 (20 January 1962), 36: Henry Hewes.
Theatre Arts, 46 (March 1962), 57: John Simon.
Time, 79 (5 January 1962), 53.
Toneel (Leiden), 83 (January-February 1962), 15-19: Benjamin Hunningher.

Nacht des Leguan (adaptation by Franz Höllering). Berlin: Renaissance-Theater, 1963. Willi Maertens, director. Erich Crandeit, designer. With Peter Mosbacher (Shannon), Tilly Lauenstein (Maxine), Grete Mosheim (Hannah), Walter Janssen (Nonno).

The Night of the Iguana (screenplay by Tony Veiler). John Huston/Ray Stark Production. MGM/Seven Arts film, July 1964. John Huston, director. Gabriel Figueroa, cameraman. Stephen Grimes, art director. Music by Benjamin Frankel. With Richard Burton (Shannon), Ava Gardner (Maxine), Deborah Kerr (Hannah), Cyril Delevanti (Nonno), Sue Lyon (Charlotte).

Production notes:
Oulahan, Richard. "Stars Fell on Mismaloya." Life, 55 (20 December 1963), 69-74.
Haedens, Kleber. "De splendides Mexicains, des ivrognes, des acteurs fous." Candide, 159 (13-20 May 1964), 10 ff.
Victor, Thelda. "The Drama the Cameras Missed." Saturday Evening Post, 237 (11 July 1964), 27-32.
Kaminsky, Stuart. John Huston: Maker of Magic. Boston: Houghton, Mifflin, 1978. Pp. 155-160.
Reviews:
America, 111 (15 August 1964), 161: Moira Walsh.
Commonweal, 80 (21 August 1964), 580: Philip T. Hartung.

Illustrated London News, 245 (26 September 1964), 480:
Life, 57 (10 July 1964), 11: Richard Oulahan.
New Statesman, 68 (11 September 1964), 370: Penelope Houston.
New York Times, 1 July 1964, p. 42 (NYTFR): Bosley Crowther.
New Yorker, 40 (15 August 1964), 84-85: Edith Oliver.
Newsweek, 64 (13 July 1964), 85.
Reporter, 31 (8 October 1964), 49-50: Gerald Weales.
Saturday Review, 47 (18 July 1964), 22: Arthur Knight.
Spectator, 213 (11 September 1964), 340.
Time, 84 (17 July 1964), 86.
Vogue, 144 (1 September 1964), 106: Joan Didion.

The Night of the Iguana. London: Savoy Theatre, spring 1965. Philip Wiseman, director. Peter Farmer, designer. With Mark Eden (Shannon), Vanda Godsell (Maxine), Sian Phillips (Hannah), Donald Eccles (Nonno). Winner of London Critics' Poll for Best Foreign Play.

Review:
New Statesman, 19 (2 April 1965), 546: Ronald Bryden.

The Night of the Iguana. Equity Theater. New York: Masters Theater, fall 1966 (9 performances). Tom Brennan, director.

The Night of the Iguana. New York: Circle-in-the-Square Theater, 16 December 1976-20 February 1977 (77 performances). Joseph Hardy, director. H. R. Poindexter, Noel Taylor, designers. With Richard Chamberlain (Shannon), Sylvia Miles (Maxine), Dorothy McGuire (Hannah), William Roerick (Nonno).

Reviews:
America, 136 (8 January 1977), 20: Catherine Hughes.
Nation, 224 (1 January 1977), 28-29: Harold Clurman.
New York Theatre Critics' Reviews, 37 (1976), 62-65:
NBC, 16 December 1976: Leonard Probst.
Christian Science Monitor, 17 December 1976: John Beaufort.
Daily News, 17 December 1976: Douglas Watt.
Post, 17 December 1976: Martin Gottfried.
Wall Street Journal, 20 December 1976: Edwin Wilson.
Women's Wear Daily, 17 December 1976: Howard Kissel.
New York Times, 17 December 1976, sec. C, p. 2: Clive Barnes.
________, 19 December 1976, sec. 2, p. 3: Walter Kerr.
New Yorker, 52 (27 December 1976), 52: Brendan Gill.
Time, 108 (27 December 1976), 39: T. E. Kalem.

La nuit de l'iguane (adaptation by Sophie Becker). Paris: Bouffes du Nord, winter 1977. Andreas Voutsinas, director.

Hubert Monloup, Luc Perini, designers. With Pierre Vaneck (Shannon), Catherine Savage (Maxine), Natasha Parry (Hannah), Donald Eccles (Nonno).

Review:

International Herald Tribune, 18 February 1977: Thomas Quinn Curtis.

45. ORPHEUS DESCENDING see Battle of Angels

46. OUT CRY see The Two-Character Play

47. "A PERFECT ANALYSIS GIVEN BY A PARROT" see The Rose Tattoo

48. PERIOD OF ADJUSTMENT.

Period of Adjustment (a). Miami: Coconut Grove Playhouse, 29 December 1958-3 January 1959. Tennessee Williams, Owen Phillips, directors.

Review:

Time, 73 (12 January 1959), 54.

Period of Adjustment. New York: Helen Hayes Theatre, 10 November 1960-4 March 1961 (132 performances). George Roy Hill, director. Jo Mielziner, Patricia Zipprodt, designers. With James Daly (Ralph), Robert Webber (George), Barbara Baxley (Isabel), Rosemary Murphy (Dorothea).

Production notes:

Zolotow, Sam. "Kazan Bows Out of Williams Play." New York Times, 28 April 1960, p. 29.

Gelb, Arthur. "Williams and Kazan and the Big Walk-Out." New York Times, 1 May 1960, sec. 2, pp. 1, 3.

Reviews:

America, 104 (17 December 1960), 410-411: Theophilus Lewis.

Catholic World, 192 (January 1961), 255-256: Richard A. Duprey.

Christian Century, 77 (28 December 1960), 1536: Tom F. Driver.

Commonweal, 74 (2 June 1961), 255: Richard Hayes.

Educational Theatre Journal, 13 (March 1961), 51-53: John Gassner.

Reprint: Dramatic Soundings (L 12), pp. 586-587.

Horizon, 3 (March 1961), 102-103: Robert Hatch.

Hudson Review, 14 (Spring 1961), 83-84: John Simon.

Nation, 191 (3 December 1960), 443-444: Harold Clurman.

New Republic, 143 (28 November 1960), 38-39: Robert Brustein.

Reprint: Seasons (L 8), pp. 117-119.

New York Theatre Critics' Reviews, 21 (1960), 176-179:

Daily News, 11 November 1960: John Chapman.

Herald Tribune, 11 November 1960: Walter Kerr.

Journal-American, 11 November 1960: John McClain.
Mirror, 11 November 1960: Robert Coleman.
Post, 11 November 1960: Richard Watts, Jr.
World-Telegram & Sun, 11 November 1960: Frank Aston.
New York Times, 11 November 1960, p. 34 (NYTTR 7): Howard Taubman.
_______, 20 November 1960, sec. 2, p. 1 (NYTTR 7): Howard Taubman.
New Yorker, 36 (19 November 1960), 93-94: John McCarten.
Newsweek, 56 (21 November 1960), 79.
Reporter, 23 (22 December 1960), 35: Marya Mannes.
Saturday Review, 43 (26 November 1960), 28: Henry Hewes.
Theatre Arts, 45 (January 1961), 57-58: Alan Pryce-Jones.
Time, 76 (21 November 1960), 75.

Zeit der Anpassung (adaptation by Frank Höllering). Hamburg: 2 January 1962.
Review:
New York Times, 3 January 1962, p. 25 (NYTTR 7).

Period of Adjustment. London: Royal Court Theatre, 13 June 1962; Wyndham Theatre, 10 July 1962. Roger Graef, director. With Bernard Braden (Ralph), Neill McGallum (George), Collin Wincox (Isabel), Betty McDowall (Dorothea).
Reviews:
Nation, 195 (11 August 1962), 59: Harold Clurman.
New Statesman, 63 (22 June 1962), 917: Carl Foreman.
New York Times, 14 June 1962, p. 24 (NYTTR 7).
Spectator, 208 (22 June 1962), 823, 826: Bamber Cascoigne.

Period of Adjustment (screenplay by Isobel Lennart). MGM film, 31 October 1962. George Roy Hill, director. Paul C. Vogel, cameraman. George W. Davis, Edward Carfagne, art directors. Music by Lyn Murray. With Tony Franciosa (Ralph), Jim Hutton (George), Jane Fonda (Isabel), Lois Nettleton (Dorothea).
Reviews:
America, 108 (19 January 1963), 119-120: Moira Walsh.
Commonweal, 77 (14 December 1962), 315: Philip T. Hartung.
New Statesman, 65 (25 January 1963), 134: John Coleman.
New York Times, 1 November 1962, p. 34 (NYTFR): Bosley Crowther.
New Yorker, 38 (a0 November 1962), 234: Brendan Gill.
Newsweek, 60 (12 November 1962), 96.
Saturday Review, 45 (10 November 1962), 77: Arthur Knight.
Time, 80 (16 November 1962), 97.

The play was also offered in London during the 1974-1975 season.

49. "PORTRAIT OF A MADONNA."

"Portrait of a Madonna." Las Palmas (Los Angeles): Actors Laboratory Theatre, 1946-1947. Hume Cronyn, director. With Jessica Tandy (Miss Collins).

Three Short Plays. Dallas: Theatre '48, 1948. Margo Jones, director. With Katherine Squire (Miss Collins).
Production notes:
Jones, Margo. Theatre-in-the-Round. New York: McGraw-Hill, 1965. P. 151.

"Portrait of a Madonna." Berlin: Congress Hall, 20 September 1957.

Three One-Act Plays. Washington: Arena Stage, March 1957. John O'Shaughnessy, director. Robert Conley, Leo Gallenstein, Jane Stanhope, designers. With Dorothea Hammond (Miss Collins).
Review:
New York Times, 1 April 1957, p. 21 (NYTTR 6): Brooks Atkinson.

Triple Play. Theatre Guild. New York: Playhouse Theater, 15 April 1959. Hume Cronyn, director. David Hayes, Anna Hill Johnstone, designers. With Jessica Tandy (Miss Collins), Hume Cronyn (Doctor).
Reviews:
New York Theatre Critics' Reviews, 20 (1959), 320-323:
Daily Mirror, 16 April 1959: Robert Coleman.
Daily News, 16 April 1959: John Chapman.
Herald Tribune, 16 April 1959: Walter Kerr.
Journal-American, 16 April 1959: John McClain.
Post, 16 April 1959: Richard Watts, Jr.
World-Telegram & Sun, 16 April 1959: Frank Aston.
New York Times, 16 April 1959, p. 28 (NYTTR 6): Brooks Atkinson.
________, 26 April 1959, sec. 2, p. 1 (NYTTR 6): Brooks Atkinson.
Theatre Arts, 43 (June 1959), 9.

"Portrait d'une madone" (adaptation by Jacques Guicharnaud). Quatre pièces en un acte. Paris: Théatre des Champs-Elysées, 20 April 1960. Robert Postec, director. André Acquart, designer. With Reine Courtois (Miss Collins), Robert Postec (Doctor).

50. "THE PURIFICATION."

"The Purification." Pasadena, Calif.: Pasadena Laboratory Theatre, July 1944. Margo Jones, director.

"The Purification." Dallas: Theatre '54, May 1954. Margo Jones, director. Sarah Cabell Massey, designer.
Reviews:
New York Times, 29 May 1954, p. 12 (NYTTR 6): Brooks Atkinson.
______, 6 June 1954, sec. 2, p. 1 (NYTTR 6): Brooks Atkinson.

"The Purification." ANTA Matinee Theatre Series. New York: Theatre de Lys, 8 November 1959. Tom Brennan, director. Music and choreography by Sharon Young, Michael Childs. With Ted Von Briethaysen (Son), John Cunningham (Judge), Mary Hara (Mother), Stan Kahn (Father), Eva Stern (Elena).
Review:
New York Times, 9 December 1959, p. 57 (NYTTR 7): Arthur Gelb.

Four by Tennessee. Play of the Week. PBS-TV, 6 February 1961. With Mike Kellin, Thomas Chambers, Eileen Heckart, Salome Jens, Anne Revere.
Review:
New York Times, 7 February 1961, p. 67: John P. Shanley.

"The Purification." New York: Mama Gails, December 1975. Paul Kielar, director. Robert Soule, designer. Music by Bruce Pomahac. With Peter Kingsley (Son), Douglas Popper (Judge), Cara de Silva (Mother), George Riddle (Father), Marie Puma (Elena).
Review:
New York Times, 10 December 1975, p. 56: Mel Gussow.

51. THE RED DEVIL BATTERY SIGN.
The Red Devil Battery Sign (a). Boston: Schubert Theater, 18-28 June 1975. Edwin Sherin, director. Robin Wagner, Ruth Wagner, Marilyn Rennagel, designers. Music by Sidney Lippman. With Anthony Quinn (King Del Rey), Claire Bloom (Woman Downtown), Katy Jurado (Perla), Annette Cardona (Niña).
Production notes:
Calta, Louis. "News of the Stage." New York Times, 7 October 1973, p. 79.
Buckley, Tom. "About New York." New York Times, 16 June 1975, p. 19.

The Red Devil Battery Sign (b). Vienna: English Theatre, 17 January 1976. Franz Schafranek, director. With Keith Baxter (King Del Rey), Ruth Brinkmann (Woman Downtown), Maria Britneva (Perla), Lois Baxter (Niña).
Reviews:
International Herald Tribune, 21 January 1976: Thomas Quinn Curtiss.

Stanton (P 366), pp. 175-178: Sy Kahn.
Tharpe (P 375), pp. 362-371: Sy Kahn.

The Red Devil Battery Sign (b). London: Round House, 8 June 1977; Phoenix Theatre, 7-23 July 1977. Keith Baxter, David Leland, directors. Bob Ringwood, Kate Owen, David Hersey, designers. Music by Mario Ramos. With Keith Baxter (King Del Rey), Estelle Kohler (Woman Downtown), Maria Britneva (Perla), Nitzu Saul (Niña), Ken Shorter (Wolf).

Review:

Plays and Players, 24 (September 1977), 26-27: Charles Marowitz.

52. THE ROMAN SPRING OF MRS. STONE.

The Roman Spring of Mrs. Stone (screenplay by Gavin Lambert). Seven Arts Production. Warner Brothers film, 24 November 1961. José Quintero, director. Harry Warman, cameraman. Herbert Smith, art director. Music by Richard Addinsell, Paddy Roberts. With Vivien Leigh (Karen), Warren Beatty (Paolo), Lotte Lenya (Contessa).

Production notes:

Watts, Stephen. "'Roman Spring' Season in a London Studio." New York Times, 15 January 1961, sec. 2, p. 7.

Quintero, José. If You Don't Dance They Beat You. Boston: Little, Brown, 1974. Pp. 266-276.

Edwards, Anne. Vivien Leigh: A Biography. New York: Simon & Schuster, 1977. Pp. 241-246.

Reviews:

America, 106 (13 January 1962), 481: Moira Walsh.

Commonweal, 75 (29 December 1961), 365-366: Philip T. Hartung.

Illustrated London News, 240 (3 March 1962), 346.

New Statesman, 63 (23 February 1962), 273: John Coleman.

New York Times, 29 December 1961, p. 11 (NYTFR): Bosley Crowther.

New Yorker, 37 (13 January 1962), 97-98: Brendan Gill.

Newsweek, 59 (1 January 1962), 53.

Saturday Review, 44 (9 December 1961), 28: Arthur Knight.

Spectator, 208 (23 February 1962), 242.

Time, 78 (29 December 1961), 57.

53. THE ROSE TATTOO/"A PERFECT ANALYSIS GIVEN BY A PARROT."

The Rose Tattoo (b). Chicago: Erlanger Theatre, 29 December 1950; New York: Martin Beck Theatre, 3 February-27 October 1951 (306 performances). Daniel Mann, director. Boris Aronson, designer. Music by David Diamond. With Maureen Stapleton (Serafina), Eli Wallach (Alvaro), Phyllis Love (Rosa), Don Murray (Jack), Sal Mineo (Salvatore). Winner of Antoinette Perry (Tony) Award.

Production notes:
"'Dolls,' 'Tattoo' Get Perry Prize." New York Times, 26 March 1951, p. 20.
Reviews:
Catholic World, 172 (March 1951), 467-468: Euphemia Van Rennsselaer Wyatt.
Commonweal, 53 (23 February 1951), 492-494: Walter Kerr.
Life, 30 (26 February 1951), 80-84.
Nation, 172 (17 February 1951), 161-162: Margaret Marshall.
New Republic, 124 (19 February 1951), 22: Harold Clurman.
New York Theatre Critics' Reviews, 12 (1951), 363-366:
Daily Mirror, 5 February 1951: Robert Coleman.
Daily News, 5 February 1951: John Chapman.
Herald Tribune, 5 February 1951: Otis L. Guernsey, Jr.
Journal-American, 5 February 1951: John McClain.
Post, 5 February 1951: Richard Watts, Jr.
World-Telegram, 5 February 1951: William Hawkins.
New York Times, 5 February 1951, p. 19 (NYTTR 5): Brooks Atkinson.
________, 11 February 1951, sec. 2, p. 1 (NYTTR 5): Brooks Atkinson.
Response: 25 March 1951, sec. 2, p. 3; 1 April 1951, sec. 2, p. 3.
________, 3 June 1951, sec. 2, p. 1: Brooks Atkinson.
New Yorker, 26 (10 February 1951), 54: Wolcott Gibbs.
Newsweek, 37 (12 February 1951), 72.
Partisan Review, 18 (March-June 1951), 333-334: F. W. Dupee.
Saturday Review, 34 (10 March 1951), 22-24: John Mason Brown.
Reprint: As They Appear (L 4), pp. 161-166.
School and Society, 73 (24 March 1951), 181-183: William H. Beyer.
Theatre Arts, 35 (April 1951), 16.
Theatre Book of the Year 1950-1951 (New York: Alfred A Knopf, 1951), pp. 209-212: George Jean Nathan.
Time, 57 (12 February 1951), 53-54.

La rose tatouée (adaptation by Raymond Gerome). Brussels: Rideau de Bruxelles, 7-20 January 1952. Maurice Vaneau, director.

Die Tätowierte Rose (adaptation by Berthold Viertel). Hamburg: Thalia Theater, 30 September 1952. Leo Mittler, director. With Inge Meysel (Serafina), Wolfgang Wahl (Alvaro), Ingrid Andrée (Roma), Klaus Kammer (Jack).

Die Tätowierte Rose (adaptation by Berthold Viertel). Munich: Kammerspiels, 1953. Fritz Kortner, director. Caspar Neher, designer. With Maria Wimmer (Serafina).

La rose tatouée (adaptation by Paule de Beaumont). Paris: Théâtre Gramont, 21 March 1953. Pierre Valde, director. Annenkof, designer. With Lila Kedrova (Serafina), René Havard (Alvaro), Jane Lysa (Rosa), Gilbert Eduard (Jack).

The Rose Tattoo (c). Paramont film, 12 December 1955. Daniel Mann, director. James Wong Howe, cameraman. Hal Pereira, Tambia Larsen, art directors. Music by Alex North. With Anna Magnani (Serafina), Burt Lancaster (Alvaro), Marisa Pavan (Rosa), Ben Cooper (Jack), Jo Van Fleet (Bessie), Virginia Grey (Estelle).

Production notes:

Johnson, Grady. "Key West, Playwright Get into 'Tatoo' Act." New York Times, 5 December 1954, sec. 2, p. 9.

"The Rose Tattoo in Key West." Harper's Bazaar, 89 (February 1955), 124-125.

Reviews:

America, 94 (24 December 1955), 362;

Catholic World, 182 (December 1955), 218.

Commonweal, 63 (23 December 1955), 305-306: Philip T. Hartung.

Film Culture 5/6 (Winter 1955): Andrew Sarris. Reprint: Confessions (L 29), pp. 19-20.

Library Journal, 80 (1 November 1955), 2478: Herbert Cahoon.

Life, 39 (28 November 1955), 139-144.

Look, 19 (27 December 1955), 90.

Nation, 182 (7 January 1955), 18: Robert Hatch.

National Parent-Teacher, 50 (December 1955), 40.

New Statesman, 51 (3 March 1956), 192-193: William Whitebait.

New York Times, 13 December 1955, p. 55 (NYTFR): Bosley Crowther.

________, 18 December 1955, sec. 2, p. 3: Bosley Crowther.

New York Times Magazine, 10 April 1955, p. 47.

New Yorker, 31 (24 December 1955), 52: John McCarten.

Newsweek, 46 (26 December 1955), 65-66.

Reporter, 13 (29 December 1955), 36-37: Robert Bingham.

Saturday Review, 38 (10 December 1955), 25-26: Arthur Knight.

Spectator, 198 (21 June 1956), 814.

Time, 66 (19 December 1955), 94.

The Rose Tattoo (b). Dublin: Dublin Theatre Festival, 13-27 May 1957. Alan Simpson, director. With Anna Manahan (Serafina), Pat Nolan (Alvaro), Kate Binchy (Rosa).

Production notes:

"Theatre Director Arrested." Times, 24 May 1957, p. 10.

"Play Continues in Dublin." Times, 25 May 1957, p. 4.

"Run of 'The Rose Tattoo' Ends." Times, 27 May 1957, p. 6.

"The Rose Tattoo Judgment." Times, 10 June 1958, p. 6.
Review:
Times, 14 May 1957, p. 3.

Planned production in Salisbury, Southern Rhodesia:
Production notes:
"'Rose Tattoo' Play Canceled." New York Times, 22 July 1958, p. 21.

The Rose Tattoo (b). Liverpool: New Shakespeare Theatrical Club, fall 1958; London: New Theatre, 15 January 1959. Sam Wanamaker, director. With Lea Padovani (Serafina), Wanamaker (Alvaro).
Production notes:
"License Sought for 'Rose Tattoo.'" Times, 3 November 1958, p. 7.
"'The Rose Tattoo.'" Times, 21 November 1958, p. 16.
"The Rose Tattoo for London." Times, 18 December 1958, p. 14.
Reviews:
New Statesman, 57 (24 January 1959), 104: T. C. Worsley.
Theatre World, 55 (March 1959), 13-18: David Sim.

The Rose Tattoo (b). New York: City Center Theatre, 20 October 1966; Billy Rose Theatre, 9 November-31 December 1966 (76 performances). Milton Katselas, director. With Maureen Stapleton (Serafina), Harry Guardino (Alvaro), Maria Tucci (Rosa), Christopher Walker (Jack). Caedmon records, 1967 (D 5).
Reviews:
America, 115 (10 December 1966), 786: Theophilus Lewis.
Nation, 203 (7 November 1966), 493: Harold Clurman.
National Review, 19 (24 January 1967), 99: Arlene Croce.
New York Times, 21 October 1966, p. 36 (NYTTR 7): Dan Sullivan.
_______, 20 November 1966, sec. 2, p. 1 (NYTTR 7): Walter Kerr.
Saturday Review, 49 (26 November 1966), 60: Henry Hewes.
Time, 88 (18 November 1966), 80.

"A Perfect Analysis Given by a Parrot" (d). Key West Players. Key West: Waterfront Playhouse, 1 May 1970. Tenessee Williams, director.

"A Perfect Analysis Given by a Parrot" (d). New York: Quiagh Lunchtime Theater, 7 June 1976.

54. SENSO.
Senso/The Wanton Countess. Lux film, 1954. Luchino

Visconti, director. G. R. Aldo, B. Krasker, cameramen. Ottavio Scotti, Marcel Escoffier, Pietro Tosi, art directors. With Alida Valli (Countess Serpieri), Farley Granger (Lieutenant Mahler), Massimo Girotti (Marquis Ussoni), Heinz Moog (Count Serpieri).

Review:

New York Times, 9 July 1968, p. 31 (NYTFR): Bosley Crowther.

55. THE SEVEN DESCENTS OF MYRTLE see Kingdom of Earth

56. SLAPSTICK TRAGEDY see "The Gnädiges Fräulein" and "The Mutilated"

57. SMALL CRAFT WARNINGS/"CONFESSIONAL."

"Confessional" (a). Bar Harbour, Me.: Maine Theater Arts Festival, summer 1970. William E. Hunt, director.

Small Craft Warnings (b). New York: Truck and Warehouse Theatre, 2 April 1972; New Theatre, 6 June-17 September 1972 (200 performances). Richard Altman, director. Fred Voelpel, John Gleason, designers. With Helena Carroll, later Peg Murray (Leona), Gene Fanning (Monk), David Hooks, and sometimes Tennessee Williams (Doc), Cherry Davis, later Candy Darling (Violet), Alan Mixon (Quentin), William Hickey (Steve), Brad Sullivan (Bill).

Production notes:

Funke, Lewis. "One from Tennessee [...]." New York Times, 19 December 1971, sec. 2, pp. 3, 43.

Bell, Arthur. "'I've Never Faked It.'" Village Voice, 24 February 1972, p. 58.
Reprint: Leavitt (N 49), p. 154.

Calta, Louis. "Williams to Take Role." New York Times, 6 June 1972, p. 48.

Reviews:

America, 126 (29 April 1972), 462: Catherine Hughes.
Commonweal, 96 (5 May 1972), 214-216: Gerald Weales.
Nation, 214 (24 April 1972), 540-541: Harold Clurman.
New Republic, 166 (29 April 1972), 24: Stanley Kauffmann.
________, 168 (17 March 1973), 23: Robert Brustein.
New York Theatre Critics' Reviews, 33 (1972), 271-274:
CBS-TV, 2 April 1972: Leonard Harris.
NBC, 2 April 1972: Betty Rollin.
Daily News, 3 April 1972: Douglas Watt.
Post, 3 April 1972: Richard Watts.
Women's Wear Daily, 4 April 1972: Martin Gottfried.
New York Times, 3 April 1972, p. 50: Clive Barnes.
________, 6 April 1972, sec. 2, p. 8: Walter Kerr.
New Yorker, 48 (15 April 1972), 110: Edith Oliver.
Saturday Review, 55 (22 April 1972), 22-24: Henry Hewes.
Time, 99 (17 April 1972), 72: T. E. Kalem.
Times, 6 April 1972, p. 10. Response: 13 May 1972, p. 10.

Small Craft Warnings (b). London: Hampstead Theater Club, winter 1973; Comedy Theatre, late winter 1973. Vivian Matalon, director. Saul Rodomsky, designer. With Elaine Strich (Leona), Peter Jones (Monk), George Pravda (Doc), Frances de la Tour (Violet), Tony Beckley (Quentin), James Berwick (Steve), Edward Judd (Bill).

Reviews:

New Statesman, 85 (9 February 1973), 208-209: Benedict Nightingale.

International Herald Tribune, 3 February 1973: John Walker.

______, 30 March 1973: John Walker.

Sunday Times, 10 March 1973, p. 11.

Times, 30 January 1973, p. 9.

58. "SOMETHING UNSPOKEN."

"Something Unspoken." Lake Hopatcong, N. J.: Lakeside Summer Theatre, 22 June 1955. Herbert Machiz, director. Paul Georges, Jack Haupman, designers. With Patricia Ripley (Cornelia), Hortense Alden (Grace).

Garden District. New York: York Theatre, 7 January 1958. Herbert Machiz, director. Robert Soule, Stanley Simmons, Lee Watson, designers. Music by Ned Rorem. With Eleanor Phelps (Cornelia), Hortense Alden (Grace).

Reviews: see Suddenly Last Summer (K 62).

Garden District. London: Arts Theatre, 16 September 1958. Herbert Machiz, director. With Beryl Measor (Cornelia), Beatrix Lehmann (Grace).

Reviews: see Suddenly Last Summer (K 62).

Three by Tennessee. New York: Lolly's Theater Club, 6 December 1973. Dick Garfield, Cindy Kaplans, directors.

59. STAIRS TO THE ROOF.

Stairs to the Roof. Pasadena, Calif.: Pasadena Playhouse, 26 February 1947. Rita Glover, producer.

Reviews:

New York Times, 26 February 1947, p. 35 (NYTTR 5).

Theatre Arts, 31 (July 1947), 12.

60. "THE STRANGEST KIND OF ROMANCE."

I have found no record of an American or British production of any kind.

"La plus étrange des idylles" (adaptation by Jacques Guicharnaud). Quatre pièces en un acte. Paris: Théâtre des Champs-Elysées, 20 April 1960. Robert Postec, director. André Acquart, designer. With Paul Chevalier (Little Man), Madeleine Parion (Landlady).

"La plus étrange des idylles" (adaptation by Jacques

Guicharnaud). Paris: Café-Théâtre de l'Ile Saint-Louis, February 1968. With Jean Menaud (Little Man), Yvette Petit (Landlady).

61. A STREETCAR NAMED DESIRE.

A Streetcar Named Desire. New York: Barrymore Theatre, 3 December 1947-17 December 1949 (855 performances); City Center, 23 May 1950. Elia Kazan, director. Jo Mielziner, Lucinda Ballard, designers. With Jessica Tandy, later Uta Hagen (Blanche), Marlon Brando, later Anthony Quinn (Stan), Kim Hunter, later Jorja Cartright (Stella), Karl Malden, later George Matthews (Mitch). Winner of Pulitzer Prize for Drama, New York Drama Critics' Circle Award, and Donaldson Award.

Production notes:

Calta, Louis. "John Garfield Out of 'Streetcar' Cast." New York Times, 18 August 1947, p. 13.

"'Streetcar Named Desire' Captures Top Prize of Drama Critics Circle." New York Times, 1 April 1948, p. 29.

Adams, Frank S. "Pulitzer Prizes Go to 'Streetcar' and Michener's Stories of Pacific." New York Times, 4 May 1948, pp. 1, 22.

Tandy, Jessica. "One Year of Blanche du Bois." New York Times, 28 November 1948, sec. 2, pp. 1, 3.

"Thomas Benton Paints the Rough Side of 'Streetcar' and Playwright Tennessee Williams Likes It." Look, 13 (1 February 1949), 79.

Atkinson, Brooks. "Streetcar Passenger" [interview with Karl Malden]. New York Times, 12 June 1949, sec. 2, p. 1.

Downing, Robert. "Streetcar Conducter: Some Notes from Backstage." Theatre Annual, 9 (1950), 25-33.

Kazan, Elia. "Notebook for A Streetcar Named Desire." Directing the Play, ed. Toby Cole & Helen Krich Chinoy. Indianapolis: Bobbs, Merrill, 1953. Pp. 296-310.
Reprints: Oppenheimer (L 28), pp. 342-356; Miller (P 282), pp. 21-29;
Directors on Directing, ed. Toby Cole & Helen Chinoy (Indianapolis: Bobbs-Merrill, 1963), pp. 364-379.

Reviews:

Boston Herald, 4 November 1947: Elinor Hughes.
Reprint: Miller (P 282), pp. 27-29.

Catholic World, 166 (January 1948, 558: Euphemia Van Rensselaer Wyatt.

Commonweal, 47 (19 December 1947), 254-255: Kappo Phelan.

Forum, 109 (February 1948), 86-88: John Gassner.

Life, 23 (15 December 1947), 101-104.

Masses and Mainstream, 1 (April 1948), 51-56: Harry Taylor.

Reprint: Hurrell (P 194), pp. 96-99.
Nation, 165 (20 December 1947), 686-687: Joseph Wood Krutch.
Reprint: Miller (P 282), pp. 38-40.
New Republic, 117 (22 December 1947), 34-35: Irwin Shaw.
Reprint: Miller (P 282), pp. 45-47.
New York Theatre Critics' Reviews, 8 (1947), 249-252:
Daily Mirror, 4 December 1947: Robert Coleman.
Daily News, 4 December 1947: John Chapman.
Reprint: Miller (P 282), pp. 29-30.
Herald Tribune, 4 December 1947: Howard Barnes.
Reprint: Miller (P 282), pp. 34-36.
Journal-American, 4 December 1947: Robert Garland.
Reprint: Miller (P 282), pp. 36-38.
PM, 5 December 1947: Louis Kronenberger.
Post, 4 December 1947: Richard Watts, Jr.
Reprint: Miller (P 282), pp. 20-31.
Sun, 4 December 1947: Ward Morehouse.
World-Telegram, 4 December 1947: William Hawkins.
New York Times, 4 December 1947, p. 42 (NYTTR 5): Brooks Atkinson.
________, 14 December 1947, sec. 2, p. 3 (NYTTR 5): Brooks Atkinson.
Reprint: Miller (P 282), pp. 32-34.
________, 12 June 1949, sec. 2, p. 1 (NYTTR 5): Brooks Atkinson.
________, 24 May 1950, p. 36 (NYTTR 5): Brooks Atkinson.
New York Times Magazine, 23 November 1947, p. 14.
New Yorker, 23 (13 December 1947), 50-54: Wolcott Gibbs.
Newsweek, 30 (15 December 1947), 82-83.
Partisan Review, 25 (March 1948), 357-360: Mary McCarthy.
Reprints: Sights (L 21), Theatre Chronicles (L 22), pp. 131-135.
Saturday Review, 30 (27 December 1947), 22-24: John Mason Brown.
Reprints: Seeing More Things (L 6), pp. 266-278; Dramatic Personae (L 5), pp. 89-94; Miller (P 282), pp. 41-45.
School and Society, 67 (27 March 1948), 241-243: William Beyer.
Theatre Arts, 31 (December 1947), 18.
________, 32 (January 1948), 10-13: Rosamund Gilder.
________, 32 (February 1948), 35.
________, 32 (April-May 1948), 30: Gilbert W. Gabriel.
________, 32 (October 1948), 21: William Saroyan.
________, 33 (November 1949), 14: Eric Bentley.
Reprint: In Search (L 2), pp. 87-89.
Theatre Book of the Year 1947-1948 (New York: Alfred Knopf, 1948), pp. 163-166: George Jean Nathan.

Reprints: Magic Mirror (L 23), pp. 238-242; Hurrell (P 194), pp. 89-91.
Time, 50 (14 December 1947), 85.

Un travia llamado Deseo. Mexico City: 1949. Seki Sano, producer.
Review:
Theatre Arts, 33 (June 1949), 44.

Linje lusta. Goteborg, Sweden: 1949. With Kairn Koali (Blanche).

Un tram che se chiama Desiderio. Rome: Teatre Eliseo, 21 January 1949. Luchino Visconti, director. Franco Zeffirelli, designer. With Rina Morelli (Blanche), Vittorio Gassman (Stan), Vivi Gioi (Stella), Marcello Mastroianni (Mitch).

Endstation Sehnsucht. Zurich: 1949.

A Streetcar Named Desire (a). Manchester: 27 September 1949: London: Aldwych Theatre, 12 October 1949. Laurence Olivier, director. Jo Meilziner, Beatrice Dawson, designers. With Vivien Leigh (Blanche), Bonnard Colleano (Stan), Renée Asherson (Stella), Bernard Braden (Mitch).
Production notes:
"Ranks Lashes Out at Tax on Films," New York Times, 1 December 1949, p. 42.
"Muni to Quit 'Salesman.'" New York Times, 11 December 1949, p. 84.
Edwards, Anne. Vivien Leigh: A Biography. New York: Simon & Schuster, 1977. Pp. 170-172.
Reviews:
Illustrated London News, 215 (5 November 1949), 712: J. C. Trewin.
New Statesman, 38 (22 October 1949), 451: R. D. Smith.
________, 38 (17 December 1949), 723-724: T. C. Worsley.
New York Times, 29 September 1949, p. 38 (NYTTR 5).
________, 13 October 1949, p. 33 (NYTTR 5).
________, 11 December 1949, sec. 2, p. 3 (NYTTR 5): Brooks Atkinson.
Spectator, 183 (21 October 1949): Peter Fleming.
Theatre World, December 1949, pp. 9-10: Eric Johns.
Time, 54 (31 October 1949), 54.
Times, 13 November 1949: Harold Hobson.
Reprint: Miller (P 282), pp. 47-49.

Un tramway nommé Desir (translation by Paule de Beaumont; adaptation by Jean Cocteau). Paris: Théâtre Edouard VII, 15 October 1949. Raymond Rouleau, director. Lila de Nobili, designer. With Arletty (Blanche), Yves Vincent (Stan), Hélèna Bossis (Stella), Daniel Ivernel (Mitch).

Reviews:
Atlantic, 186 (July 1950), 94-95: René MacColl.
Reprint: Miller (P 282), pp. 49-52.
France Illustration, 5 (12 November 1949), 545.
Life, 27 (19 December 1949), 66.
New York Times, 19 October 1949, p. 36 (NYTTR 5).
Paris Herald Tribune, 19 October 1949: Frank Dorsey.
Theatre Arts, 34 (January 1950), 35.
Time, 54 (31 October 1949), 54.

Proposed production in Madrid, 1949.
Production notes:
"Williams' Snub Stirs Playgoers in Spain." New York Times, 12 December 1949, p. 28.
"Denies Madrid Story." New York Times, 23 December 1949, p. 16.

Endstation Sehnsucht (adaptation by Berthold Viertel). Berlin: Komödie, 1950. Berthold Viertel, director. With Marianne Hoppe (Blanche), Peter Mosbacher (Stan).

Endstation Sehnsucht (adaptation by Berthold Viertel). Pforzheim: Theater der Stadt, 17 March 1950. Hanskarl Zeiser, director. With Giesela Hagenua (Blanche), Heinz Kiefer (Stan), Giesela Leininger (Stella).

Proposed production in Namur, France, 1950.
Production notes:
"Namur, France, Bars 'Streetcar.'" New York Times, 27 December 1950, p. 51.

A Streetcar Named Desire (c). Group Production. Warner Brothers film, 19 September 1951. Elia Kazan, director. Harold Stradling, cameraman. Richard Day, art director. Music by Alex North. With Vivien Leigh (Blanche), Marlon Brando (Stan), Kim Hunter (Stella), Karl Malden (Mitch). Winner of New York Film Critics' Circle Award.
Production notes:
Brady, Thomas H. "'Streetcar.'" New York Times, 27 August 1950, sec. 2, p. 5.
Mitgang, Herbert. "A Familiar 'Streetcar' Passenger." New York Times, 9 September 1951, sec. 2, p. 5.
Kazan, Elia. "Pressure Problem." New York Times, 21 October 1951, p. 28.
Ciment, Michel, ed. Kazan on Kazan. London: Secker & Warburg, 1973. Pp. 66-71.
Edwards, Anne. Vivien Leigh: A Biography. New York: Simon & Schuster, 1977. Pp. 172, 176-181.
Reviews:
Christian Century, 68 (28 November 1951), 1397.
Commonweal, 54 (28 September 1951), 596-597: Philip T. Hartung.

Holiday, 10 (October 1951), 25-28: Al Hine.
Illustrated London News, 220 (22 March 1952), 502.
Library Journal, 76 (15 October 1951), 1722-1723: Gerald B. McDonald.
Life, 31 (24 September 1951), 91-95.
Mercure de France, 315 (June 1952), 329-331.
Nation, 173 (20 October 1951), 334: Manny Farber.
New Republic, 125 (8 October 1951), 21: Robert Hatch.
New Statesman, 43 (8 March 1952), 274: William Whitebait.
New York Times, 20 September 1951, p. 37 (NYTFR): Bosley Crowther.
_______, 23 September 1951, sec. 2, p. 1: Bosley Crowther.
New York Times Magazine, 22 July 1951, pp. 34-35.
New Yorker, 27 (29 September 1951), 111-112: John McCarten.
Newsweek, 38 (10 October 1951), 87.
Saturday Review, 34 (1 September 1951), 30-31: Hollis Alpert.
Theatre Arts, 35 (July 1951), 35, 88: Leda Bauer.
Time, 58 (17 September 1951), 105-106.

A Streetcar Named Desire (ballet choreographed by Vallerie Bettis; music by Alex North). Slavenska-Franklin Ballet Company. Montreal: Her Majesty's Theatre, 9 October 1952; New York: Century Theatre, 8 December 1952. Otto Frolich, conductor. Peter Larkin, Saul Bolasni, designers. With Mia Slavenska (Blanche), Frederic Franklin (Stan), Lois Ellyn (Stella), Marvin Kauter (Mitch).

Reviews:
New York Times, 9 December 1952, p. 42: John Martin.
New York Times Magazine, 7 December 1952, p. 63.
New Yorker, 28 (20 December 1952), 103-104: Douglas Watt.
Newsweek, 40 (22 December 1952), 71.
Time, 60 (22 December 1952), 43.

A Streetcar Named Desire. New York: Originals Only Playhouse, 3 March 1955. Joanna Albus, director. Niona Carlson, Larry Parker, designers. Music by Frances Ziffer. With Maria Britneva or Jean LeBouvier (Blanche), Richard W. White (Stan), Ann Paine or Kim Fisher (Stella), Eric Lindstrom or Donald Stuart (Mitch).

Review:
New York Times, 4 March 1955, p. 18 (NYTTR 6): Brooks Atkinson.

A Streetcar Named Desire. Miami: Coconut Grove Playhouse, 16 January-4 February 1956; New York: City Center Theatre, 15 February 1956. Herbert Machiz, director. Watson Barrett, designer. With Tallulah Bankhead (Blanche), Gerald O'Laughlin (Stan), Frances Heflin (Stella), Rudy Bond (Mitch).

Reviews:
Catholic World, 183 (April 1956), 67: Euphemia Van Rensselaer Wyatt.
New York Theatre Critics' Reviews, 17 (156), 362-365:
Daily Mirror, 16 February 1956: Robert Coleman.
Daily News, 16 February 1956: John Chapman.
Herald Tribune, 16 February 1956: Walter F. Kerr.
Journal-American, 16 February 1956: John McClain.
Post, 16 February 1956: Richard Watts, Jr.
World-Telegram, 16 February 1956: William Hawkins.
New York Times, 16 February 1956, p. 24 (NYTTR 6): Brooks Atkinson.
Response: 11 March 1956, sec. 2, p. 3.
Saturday Review, 39 (3 March 1956), 22: Henry Hewes.
Theatre Arts, 40 (April 1956), 24.
Time, 67 (13 February 1956), 32.
_______, 67 (27 February 1956), 61.

Planned Off-Broadway Production, September 1958.
Production notes:
Gelb, Arthur. "Negroes Slated for 'Streetcar.'" New York Times, 14 July 1958, p. 16.
Calta, Louis. "'Streetcar' Postponed." New York Times, 25 September 1958, p. 30.

A Streetcar Named Desire. Princeton, N. J.: McCarter Theater, 13 November 1964. Tom Brennan, director.

Un travia llamado Deseo. Havana: El Sotano, 17 February 1965.
Reviews:
New York Times, 19 February 1965, p. 27 (NYTTR 7).

Endstation Sehnsucht. Hamburg: Deutsches Schauspielhaus, 1967. Heinrich Koch, director. With Joana Maria Gorvin (Blanche), Rolf Boysen (Stan).

A Streetcar Named Desire. Los Angeles: Ahmanson Theater, March 28-April 1973. James Bridges director. With Faye Dunaway (Blanche), Jon Voight (Stan), Lee McCain (Stella), Earl Holliman (Mitch).
Review:
New York Times, 1 April 1973, sec. 2, pp. 1, 15: Stephen Farber.

A Streetcar Named Desire. Lincoln Center Repertory Company. New York: Vivian Beaumont Theatre, 26 April-29 July 1973 (110 performances). Elias Rabb, director. Douglas W. Schmidt, John Gleason, Nancy Potts, designers. Music by Cathy McDonald. With Rosemary Harris (Blanche), James Farentino (Stan), Patricia Connally (Stella), Philip Bosco (Mitch). Caedmon records, 1973 (D 6).

Production notes:
Klemesrud, Judy. "Stanley Kowalski Loves Gittel Mosca" [interview with James Farentino]. New York Times, 10 June 1973, sec. 2, pp. 1, 3.
Reviews:
America, 128 (26 May 1973), 495: Catherine Hughes.
Nation, 216 (14 May 1973), 635-636: Harold Clurman.
New York Theatre Critics' Reviews, 34 (1973), 281-284:
ABC-TV, 26 April 1973: Kevin Sanders.
CBS-TV, 26 April 1973: Leonard Harris.
Daily News, 27 April 1973: Douglas Watt.
Post, 27 April 1973: Richard Watts.
Wall Street Journal, 14 May 1973: Edwin Wilson.
Women's Wear Daily, 30 April 1973: Martin Gottfried.
New York Times, 27 April 1973, p. 31: Clive Barnes.
_______, 6 May 1973, sec. 2, pp. 1, 10: Walter Kerr.
New Yorker, 49 (5 May 1973), 81: Brendan Gill.
Newsweek, 81 (7 May 1973), 109-110: Jack Kroll.
Time, 101 (7 May 1973), 88: T. E. Kalem.

A Streetcar Named Desire. New York: St. James Theater, 4 October-18 November 1973. Jules Irving, director. Douglas W. Schmidt, John Gleason, Nancy Potts, designers. Music by Cathy McDonald. With Lois Nettleton (Blanche), Alan Feinstein (Stan), Barbara Eda-Young (Stella), Biff McGuire (Mitch).
Production notes:
Calta, Louis. "News of the Stage." New York Times, 29 July 1973, p. 40.
Reviews:
New York Theatre Critics' Reviews, 34 (1973), 224-225:
NBC, 4 October 1973: Leonard Probst.
Daily News, 5 October 1973: Douglas Watt.
Post, 5 October 1973: Richard Watts.
Women's Wear Daily, 8 October 1973.
New York Times, 5 October 1973, p. 19: Clive Barnes.

A Streetcar Named Desire (a). London: Piccadilly Theatre, 14 March 1974 (more than 90 performances). Edwin Sherin, director. Patrick Robertson, Beatrice Dawson, Richard Pilbrow, Molly Friedel, designers. With Claire Bloom (Blanche), Martin Shaw (Stan), Morag Hood (Stella), Joss Ackland (Mitch).
Production notes:
"'Streetcar' to Mark 25th in London." New York Times, 27 June 1973, p. 37.
Reviews:
Drama, 113 (Summer 1974), 45-46: J. W. Lambert.
New York Times, 17 August 1974, p. 16: Clive Barnes.
Plays and Players, 21 (May 1974), 28-31: H. Dawson.

Un tramway nommé Dèsir (adaptation by Paule de Beaumont). Paris: Théâtre de l'Atelier, February 1975. Michel Fagadau, director. With Andrée Lachapelle (Blanche), Jean-Claude Drouot (Stan), Colette Castel (Stella), Claude Brosset (Mitch).

Review:

International Herald Tribune, 14 February 1975: Thomas Quinn Curtiss.

A Streetcar Named Desire. Minneapolis: Guthrie Theater, 16 June 1975. Ken Ruta, director.

Review:

Educational Theatre Journal, 27 (December 1975), 552-553: Richard L. Homan.

A Streetcar Named Desire. Academy Festival Theater. Lake Forest (Chicago): Drake Theater, 8 June 1976. Jack Gelber, director. With Geraldine Page (Blanche), Rip Torn (Stan), Flora Elkins (Stella), Jack Hollander (Mitch).

A Streetcar Named Desire. Princeton, N.J.: McCarter Theater, 7 October 1976 (15 performances). Michael Kahn, director. Michael H. Yeargen, Lawrence King, Jane Greenwood, John McLain, designers. With Shirley Knight (Blanche), Kenneth Welsh (Stan), Glenn Close (Stella), George Dzundza (Mitch).

Review:

New York Times, 11 October 1976, p. 34: Mel Gussow.

62. SUDDENLY LAST SUMMER

Garden District (a). New York: York Theatre, 7 January 1958. Herbert Machiz, director. Robert Soule, Stanley Simmons, Lee Watson, designers. Music by Ned Rorem. With Anne Meacham (Catherine), Hortense Alden (Mrs. Venable), Robert Lansing (Dr. Cukrowicz).

Reviews:

Catholic World, 186 (March 1958), 469-470: Euphemia Van Rensselaer Wyatt.

Christian Century, 75 (29 January 1958), 136: Tom F. Driver.

Commonweal, 68 (30 May 1958), 232-233: Richard Hayes.

Nation, 186 (25 January 1958), 86-87: Harold Clurman.

New Republic, 138 (27 January 1958), 20: Patrick Dennis.

New York Times, 8 January 1958, p. 23 (NYTTR 6): Brooks Atkinson.

________, 19 January 1958, sec. 2, p. 1 (NYTTR 6): Brooks Atkinson.

New Yorker, 33 (18 January 1958), 64-66: Wolcott Gibbs.

Newsweek, 51 (20 January 1958), 84.

Partisan Review, 25 (Spring 1958), 283-284: Elizabeth Hardwick.

Reporter, 18 (6 February 1958), 42-43: Marya Mannes.

Saturday Review, 41 (25 January 1958), 26: Henry Hewes.

Theatre Arts, 42 (March 1958), 13.

Time, 71 (20 January 1958), 42.

Garden District (a). London: Arts Theatre, 16 September 1958. Herbert Machiz, director. With Patricia Neal (Catherine), Beatrix Lehmann (Mrs. Venable), David Cameron (Dr. Cukrowicz).

Reviews:

New Statesman, 56 (27 September 1958), 407-408: Robert Robinson.

New York Times, 17 September 1958, p. 44 (NYTTR 6).

Suddenly Last Summer (b). Columbia film, 11 December 1959. Joseph Mankiewicz, director. Jack Hildyard, cameraman. William Keller, art director. Music by Burton Orr, Malcolm Arnold. With Elizabeth Taylor (Catherine), Katharine Hepburn (Mrs. Venable), Montgomery Clift (Dr. Cukrowicz).

Production notes:

LaGuardia, Robert. Monty: A Biography of Montgomery Clift. New York: Arbor House, 1977. Pp. 198-204.

Bosworth, Patricia. Montgomery Clift: A Biography. New York: Harcourt, Brace, Jovanovich, 1978. Pp. 306-307.

Reviews:

America, 102 (9 January 1960), 428-429: Moira Walsh.

Commonweal, 71 (1 January 1960), 396: Philip T. Hartung.

Film Quarterly, 13 (Spring 1960), 40-42: Albert Johnson.

McCalls, 87 (February 1960), 8: Richard Marek.

Nation, 190 (16 January 1960), 59: Robert Hatch.

New Republic, 142 (18 January 1960), 20: Stanley Kauffmann.

Reprint: World on Film (L 17), pp. 81-82.

New Statesman, 59 (21 May 1960), 753: William Whitebait.

New York Times, 23 December 1959, p. 22 (NYTFR): Bosley Crowther.

New Yorker, 35 (9 January 196), 74-75: John McCarten.

Newsweek, 54 (28 December 1959), 64.

Reporter, 22 (4 February 1960), 37-38: Jay Jacobs.

Saturday Review, 43 (2 January 1960), 31: Arthur Knight.

Spectator, 204 (20 May 1960), 736-738.

Time, 75 (11 January 1960), 64.

Suddenly Last Summer (a). Equity Library Theatre. New York: Master Theater, 30 October 1964 (9 performances). Pirie MacDonald, director.

Soudain l'été dernier (adaptation by Jacques Guicharnaud). Paris: Théâtre des Mathurins, 12 November 1965. Jean Danet, director. With Silvia Monfort (Catherine), Jeanine Crispin (Mrs. Venable), Jean Danet (Dr. Cuckrowicz).

Review:

Le Figaro Littéraire, 29 April-5 May 1965, p. 12: Jacques Lemarchand.

Soudain l'été dernier (adaptation by Jacques Guicharnaud). Les Tréteaux de France. French tour, 1967.

Suddenly Last Summer (c). Key West: Greene Street Theatre, April 1976. William Prosser, director. With Roxana Stuart (Catherine), Janice White (Mrs. Venable), Jay Drury (Dr. Cukrowicz).

Review:

New York Times, 27 April 1976, p. 28.

The play was also performed in New York during the 1974-1975 season.

63. SUMMER AND SMOKE/THE ECCENTRICITES OF A NIGHTINGALE

Summer and Smoke (a). Theatre '47. Dallas: Gulf Oil Playhouse, 8 July 1947. Margo Jones, director. With Katherine Balfour (Alma), Tod Andrews (John).

Production notes:

Jones, Margo. Theatre-in-the-Round. New York: McGraw-Hill, 1965. Pp. 142-146.

Reviews:

New York Times, 9 July 1947, p. 18 (NYTTR 5): John Rosenfield.

________, 10 August 1947, sec. 2, p. 1 (NYTTR 5): Brooks Atkinson.

Theatre Arts, 31 (September 1947), 11.

Summer and Smoke (a). New York: Music Box Theatre, 6 October 1948-1 January 1949 (100 performances). Margo Jones, director. Jo Mielziner, designer. Music by Paul Bowles. With Margaret Philipps (Alma), Tod Andrews (John).

Production notes:

"Lighting Up for 'Summer and Smoke.'" New York Times, 5 December 1948, sec. 2, p. 7.

Reviews:

Catholic World, 168 (November 1948), 161: Euphemia Van Rensselaer Wyatt.

Commonweal, 49 (29 October 1948), 68-69: Kappo Phelan.

Forum, 110 (December 1948), 352-353: John Gassner.

Life, 25 (25 October 1948), 102-103.

Nation, 167 (23 October 1948), 473-474: Joseph Wood Krutch.

New Republic, 119 (25 October 1948), 25-26: Harold Clurman.

Reprints: Lies (L 10), 80-83: Divine Pastime (L 9), 18-20.

________, 119 (15 November 1948), 28: Harold Clurman.

New York Theatre Critics' Reviews, 9 (1948), 205-209:

Daily Mirror, 7 October 1948: Robert Coleman.

Daily News, 7 October 1948: John Chapman.

Herald Tribune, 7 October 1948: Howard Barnes.

Journal-American, 7 October 1948: Robert Garland.
Post, 7 October 1948: Richard Watts, Jr.
Star, 8 October 1948: John Lardner.
Sun, 7 October 1948: Ward Morehouse.
World-Telegram, 7 October 1948: William Hawkins.
New York Times, 7 October 1948, p. 33 (NYTTR 5): Brooks Atkinson.
_______, 17 October 1948, sec. 2, p. 1 (NYTTR 5): Brooks Atkinson.
New York Times Magazine, 26 September 1948, pp. 66-67.
New Yorker, 24 (16 October 1948), 51-52: Wolcott Gibbs.
Newsweek, 32 (18 October 1948), 88.
Saturday Review, 31 (30 October 1948), 31-33: John Mason Brown.
School and Society, 68 (30 October 1948), 303-304: William Beyer.
Theatre Arts, 33 (January 1949), 10-11: Gilbert W. Gabriel.
Theatre Book of the Year 1948-1949 (New York: Alfred Knopf, 1949), pp. 114-121: George Jean Nathan.
Theatre Time, 1 (Spring 1949), 5-11: John Gassner.
Time, 52 (18 October 1948), 82-83.

Summer and Smoke. Actors Company. La Jolla, Calif.: Playhouse, October 1950; tour of Western United States, fall 1950. With Dorothy McGuire (Alma), John Ireland (John), Una Merkel (Mrs. Winemiller).

Review:
New York Times, 29 October 1950, sec. 2, p. 3 (NYTTR 5): John Goodman.

Der steinerne Engel. Stuttgart: Jungen Theater, 22 November 1951. Franz Essel, director. With Rosemarie Kilian (Alma), Horst Otto Reiner (John).

Summer and Smoke. London: Lyric Theatre, Hammersmith, 22 November 1951: Duchess Theatre, 24 January 1952. Peter Glenville, director. Reece Pemberton, William Chappell, designers. Music by Paul Bowles. With Margaret Johnston (Alma), William Sylvester (John), Maria Britneva (Rosemary).

Reviews:
New Statesman, 42 (8 December 1951), 664: T. C. Worsley.
New York Times, 23 November 1951, p. 32.
_______, 25 January 1952, p. 13 (NYTTR 6).
_______, 10 February 1952, p. 3 (NYTTR 6): W. A. Darlington.
Spectator, 187 (7 December 1951), 772: Kenneth Tynan.
Times, 23 November 1951, p. 2.

Summer and Smoke (b). New York: Circle-in-the-Square

Theater, 24 April 1952. José Quintero, director. Keith Cuerden, designer. With Geraldine Page (Alma), Lee Richard (John).

Production notes:

Little, Stuart W. Off-Broadway: The Prophetic Theater. New York: Coward, McCann & Geoghegan, 1972. Pp. 13-27.

Quintero, José. If You Don't Dance They Beat You. Boston: Little, Brown, 1974. Pp. 111-122.

Reviews:

Catholic World, 176 (November 1952), 148-149: Euphemia Van Rennselaer Wyatt.

New York Times, 25 April 1952, p. 19 (NYTTR 6): Brooks Atkinson.

________, 4 May 1952, sec. 2, p. 1 (NYTTR 6): Brooks Atkinson.

Saturday Review, 35 (10 May 1952), 28: Henry Hewes.

Eté et fumées (adaptation by Paule de Beaumont). Paris: Théâtre de l'Oeuvre, 16 December 1953. Michel le Pulain, director. Léonor Fini, designer. With Silvia Monfort (Alma), Gilbert Edard (John).

Review:

Paris Herald Tribune, 25 December 1953: Thomas Quinn Curtiss.

Summer and Smoke (screenplay by James Poe and Meade Roberts). Paramount film, 15 November 1961. Peter Glenville, director. Charles Lange, Jr., cameraman. Walter Tyler, Hal Pereira, art directors. Music by Elmer Berstein. With Geraldine Page (Alma), Laurence Harvey (John), Rita Moreno (Rosa), Una Merkel (Mrs. Winemiller).

Production notes:

Schumach, Murray. "Hollywood Trial." New York Times, 29 January 1961, sec. 2, p. 7.

Reviews:

America, 106 (25 November 1961), 308-310: Moira Walsh.

Commonweal, 75 (1 December 1961), 259: Philip T. Hartung.

Illustrated London News, 240 (28 April 1962), 676:

Mainstream, 15 (May 1962), 59-60: Sidney Finkelstein.

New Republic, 145 (27 November 1961), 18-20: Stanley Kauffmann.

New Statesman, 63 (20 April 1962), 570-571: John Coleman.

New York Times, 17 November 1961, p. 41 (NYTFR): Bosley Crowther.

________, 19 November 1961, sec. 2, p. 1: Bosley Crowther.

New Yorker, 37 (25 November 1961), 205-206: Brendan Gill.

Newsweek, 58 (20 November 1961), 106.

Redbook, 118 (December 1961), 16.
Saturday Review, 44 (11 November 1961), 32: Arthur Knight.
Time, 32 (1 December 1961), 76.

The Eccentricities of a Nightingale (c). Nyack, N. Y.: Tappan Zee Playhouse, 25 June 1964.

The Eccentricities of a Nightingale (c). Washington: Theater Club, 20 April 1966 (31 performances). Darey Marlin-Jones, director.

The Eccentricities of a Nightingale (c). Guildford, Eng.: Yvonne Arnaud Theatre, October 1967. With Sian Phillips (Alma).

Review:
International Herald Tribune, 14 October 1967: Thomas Quinn Curtiss.

Summer and Smoke (opera: libretto by Lanford Wilson; music by Lee Hoiby). St. Paul: St. Paul Opera, 19 June 1971. Frank Coraro, director. Julius Nudel, conductor. Lloyd Evans, Hans Sandheimer, designers. With Mary Beth Pell (Alma), John Heardan (John).

Production notes:
Hoiby, Lee. "Making Tennessee Williams Sing." New York Times, 13 June 1971, sec. 2, pp. 17, 20.
Reviews:
High Fidelity & Musical America, 21 (September 1971), MA 20: Judith Gerstel.
New York Times, 25 June 1971, p. 18: Raymond Ericson.
Opera News, 36 (September 1971), 18-20: Mary Ann Feldman.

Summer and Smoke. British Broadcasting Cooperation, 23 January 1972. With Lee Remick (Alma), David Hedison (John), Betsy Blair (Mrs. Winemiller).

Review:
Times, 24 January 1972.

Summer and Smoke (opera by Lanford Wilson & Lee Hoiby). New York City Opera Company. New York: State Theater, 19 March 1972. Frank Corsaro, director. Julius Rudel, conductor. Lloyd Evans, Hans Sandheimer, designers. With Mary Beth Pell (Alma), John Reardon (John).

Reviews:
High Fidelity & Musical America, 22 (July 1972), MA 10: Martin Mayer.
New Republic, 166 (8 April 1972), 19: Ned Rorem.
New York Times, 21 March 1972, p. 34: Harold G. Schonberg.
New Yorker, 48 (8 April 1972), 121-125: Winthrop Sargeant.

Saturday Review, 55 (8 April 1972), 18: Irving Kolodin.

Summer and Smoke. New York: Roundabout Stage One, 16 September-19 November 1975 (64 performances). Gene Feist, director. Holmes Easley, Christina Giannini, Ian Calderon, designers. Music by Philip Campanella. With Debra Mooney (Alma), Michael Storm (John).

Review:

New York Times, 19 October 1975, sec. 2, pp. 1, 5: Walter Kerr.

The Eccentricities of a Nightingale. Theater in America. PBS-TV, 16 June 1976. With Blythe Danner (Alma), Frank Langella (John).

Review:

New York Times, 16 June 1976, p. 79: John Leonard.

The Eccentricities of a Nightingale (d). Buffalo: Studio Arena Theatre, 8 October-6 November 1976 (39 performances): New York: Morosco Theatre, 23 November-12 December 1976 (24 performances). Edwin Sherwin, director. William Ritman, Theoni V. Aldredge, Marc Weiss, designers. Music by Charles Cross. With Betsy Palmer (Alma), David Selby (John).

Reviews:

New York Theatre Critics' Reviews, 37 (1976), 383-385:
- NBC, 23 November 1976: Leonard Probst.
- Christian Science Monitor, 26 November 1976: John Beaufort.
- Daily News, 24 November 1976: Douglas Watt.
- Post, 24 November 1976: Martin Gottfried.
- Wall Street Journal, 13 October 1976: Edwin Wilson.
- Women's Wear Daily, 24 November 1976: Howard Kissel.

New York Times, 24 November 1976, p. 23: Clive Barnes.

_______, 5 December 1976, sec. 2, pp. 3, 26: Walter Kerr.

New Yorker, 52 (6 December 1976), 134-135: Brendan Gill.

The Eccentricities of a Nightingale. Long Beach, Calif.: Long Beach Theatre Festival, 14 February-11 March 1979. Michael Flanagan, director. Gerry Hariton, Vicki Baral, Diana Eden, designers. With Sandy Dennis (Alma), Perry King (John), Nan Martin (Mrs. Buchanan).

64. SWEET BIRD OF YOUTH/"THE ENEMY: TIME."

So far as I know "The Enemy: Time" has never been produced.

Sweet Bird of Youth (b). Coral Gables, Fla.: Studio M Playhouse, 16 April 1956. George Keathley, director &

designer. With Alan Mixon (Phil), Margrit Wyler (Princess), Ruth Martin (Valerie), James Reese (Boss Finley), Blanche Kelly (Aunt Nonnie), Eleanor Sherman (Miss Lucy), Robert Choromokos (Fred Finley).

Reviews:

New York Times, 17 April 1956, p. 27 (NYTTR 6).

Theatre Arts, 40 (August 1956), 66-67.

Sweet Bird of Youth (c). New York: Martin Beck Theatre, 10 March 1959-30 January 1960 (383 performances). Elia Kazan, director. Jo Mielziner, Anna Hill Johnstone, designers. Music by Paul Bowles. With Paul Newman (Chance), Geraldine Page (Princess), Sidney Blackmer (Boss Finley), Madeleine Sherwood (Miss Lucy), Rip Torn (Tom).

Production notes:

Zolotov, Sam. "Williams' Drama Attracts Throng." New York Times, 12 March 1959, p. 26.

"Sweet Bird of Youth: In Unmeditated Flight." Esquire, 51 (April 1959), 24.

Reviews:

America, 101 (4 April 1959), 55-56: Theophilus Lewis.

Catholic World, 189 (May 1959), 158-159: Euphemia Van Rensselaer Wyatt.

________, 189 (June 1959), 191-194: Richard Duprey.

Christian Century, 76 (15 April 1959), 455: Tom F. Driver.

________, 76 (17 June 1959), 726: Tom F. Driver. Response: 76 (22 July 1959), 854-855.

Commonweal, 70 (24 April 1959), 102: Richard Hayes.

Educational Theatre Journal, 11 (May 1959), 122-124: John Gassner.

Encounter, 12 (June 1959), 59-60: Robert Brustein.

Hudson Review, 12 (Summer 1959), 255-260: Robert Brustein.

Life, 46 (20 April 1959), 71-73.

Nation, 188 (28 March 1959), 281-283: Harold Clurman. Reprint: Naked Savage (L 11), pp. 123-126.

New Republic, 140 (20 April 1959), 21-22: Tom F. Driver.

New York Theatre Critics' Reviews, 20 (1959), 347-350:

Daily Mirror, 11 March 1959: Robert Coleman.

Daily News, 11 March 1959: John Chapman.

Herald Tribune, 11 March 1959: Walter Kerr.

Reprint: Theatre (L 20), pp. 247-255.

Journal-American, 11 March 1959: John McClain.

Post, 11 March 1959: Richard Watts, Jr.

World-Telegram & Sun, 11 March 1959: Frank Aston.

New York Times, 11 March 1959, p. 39 (NYTTR 6): Brooks Atkinson.

________, 22 March 1959, sec. 2, p. 1 (NYTTR 6): Brooks Atkinson.

New Yorker, 35 (21 March 1959), 98-100: Kenneth Tynan. Reprint: Curtains (L 32), pp. 306-307.

Newsweek, 53 (23 March 1959), 75.
Reporter, 20 (16 April 1959), 34: Marya Mannes.
Saturday Review, 42 (28 March 1959), 26: Henry Hewes.
Response: 42 (18 April 1959), 29.
Theatre Arts, 43 (May 1959), 21-22.
Time, 73 (23 March 1959), 58.

Süssen Vogel Jugend (adaptation by Hans Sahl). Berlin: Schillertheater, 1959. Hans Lietzau, director. A. M. Vargas, designer. With Klaus Kammer (Chance), Marianne Hoppe (Princess).

Sweet Bird of Youth (d). Hollywood (Los Angeles): Civic Playhouse, 1 November 1961. Edward Ludlom, director.
Production notes:
Schumach, Murray. "Author Changes 'Sweet Bird' Play." New York Times, 27 October 1961, p. 27.

Sweet Bird of Youth (screenplay by Richard Brooks). MGM film, 20 February 1962. Richard Brooks, director. Milton Krasner, cameraman. George W. Davis, Urie McCleary, art directors. Music by Harold Gelman. With Paul Newman (Chance), Geraldine Page (Princess), Shirley Knight (Heavenly), Ed Begley (Boss Finley), Madeleine Sherwood (Miss Lucy), Rip Torn (Tom).
Production notes:
Schumach, Murray. "Muted Hollywood." New York Times, 27 August 1961, sec. 2, p. 7.
Reviews:
Commonweal, 76 (30 March 1962), 18: Philip T. Hartung.
Esquire, 57 (June 1962), 56-58: Dwight MacDonald.
Illustrated London News, 240 (12 May 1962), 770.
National Review, 12 (27 February 1962), 137-138: Morton Cronin.
New Republic, 146 (16 April 1962), 28: Stanley Kauffman.
Reprint: World (L 17), pp. 85-87.
New Statesman, 63 (11 May 1962), 688: John Coleman.
New York Times, 29 March 1962, p. 28 (NYTFR): Bosley Crowther.
New Yorker, 38 (7 April 1962), 148: Brendan Gill.
Newsweek, 59 (2 April 1962), 86.
Saturday Review, 45 (30 March 1962), 26: Hollis Alpert.
Time, 75 (30 March 1962), 83.

Sweet Bird of Youth. Manchester: Experimental Club, February 1964. With Ron Skinner (Chance), Irene Rostron (Princess).

Sweet Bird of Youth. Watford, Eng.: Palace Theatre, 19 November 1968. Giles Havergal, director. With Christopher Gable (Chance), Vivien Merchant (Princess), John Savident (Boss).
Review:
Times, 19 November 1968, p. 9: Irving Waddle.

Le doux oiseau de la jeunesse (adaptation by Françoise Sagan). Paris: Théâtre de l'Atelier, 1 October 1971. André Barsacq, director. Jacques Dupont, designer. Music by Frédéric Botton. With Bernard Fresson (Chance), Edwige Feullère (Princess), Jacques Monod (Boss Finley).

Sweet Bird of Youth (c). Washington: Kennedy Center, 9 October 1975 (97 performances); New York: Brooklyn Academy of Music, 3-14 December 1975 (15 performances); Harkness Theater, 29 December 1975-7 February 1976 (48 performances). Edwin Sherin, director. Karl Eigst, Ken Billington, Laura Cross, designers. With Christopher Walker (Chance), Irene Worth (Princess), Pat Corley (Boss Finley).

Reviews:

America, 134 (31 January 1976), 75: Catherine Hughes.

Nation, 221 (27 December 1975), 700: Harold Clurman.

New Republic, 174 (17 January 1976), 28-29: Stanley Kauffmann.

New York Theatre Critics' Reviews, 36 (1975), 113-117:

Christian Science Monitor, 10 December 1975: John Beaufort.

Daily News, 4 December 1975: Douglas Watt.

Post, 4 December 1975: Martin Gottfried.

Wall Street Journal, 8 December 1975: Edwin Wilson.

New York Times, 4 December 1975, p. 53: Clive Barnes.

______, 21 December 1975, sec. 2, p. 5: Walter Kerr.

Time, 106 (15 December 1975), 71: Gina Mallet.

65. "TALK TO ME LIKE THE RAIN AND LET ME LISTEN...."

"Talk to Me Like the Rain and Let Me Listen." Westport, Conn.: White Barn Theatre, 26 July 1958.

"Parle-moi comme la pluie et laisse-moi écouter" (adaptation by Jacques Guicharnaud). Quatre pièces en un acte. Paris: Théâtre des Champs-Elysées, 20 April 1960. Robert Postec, director. André Acquart, designer. With Reine Courtois (Woman), Robert Postec (Man).

"Parle-moi comme la pluie et laisse-moi écouter" (adaptation by Jacques Guicharnaud). Un spectacle Tennessee Williams. La Compagnie Robert Postec. Paris: Théâtre de l'Alliance Française, 1962. Robert Postec, director.

"Parle-moi comme la pluie et laisse-moi écouter" (adaptation by Jacques Guicharnaud). Paris: Café Théâtre "Le Tripot," 1969, 1970. With Valéry Quincy (Woman), Stephen Meldegg (Man).

"Talk to Me Like the Rain and Let Me Listen." PBS-TV, 3 December 1970. Glenn Jordan, director. With Lois Smith (Woman), William Mixon (Man).

Review:
New York Times, 4 December 1970, p. 95: Jack Gould.

"Talk to Me Like the Rain and Let Me Listen." Hamm and Clov Stage Company. Paris: Café-Théâtre "Arlequin-Parnasse," July 1972. With Hollin Hood (Woman), David Villaire (Man).

Three by Tennessee. New York: Lolly's Theater Club, 6 December 1973. Dick Garfield, Cindy Kaplans, directors.

66. TENNESSEE WILLIAMS'S SOUTH.
"Tennessee Williams's South" (script by Harry Rasky). Canadian Broadcasting Corporation, 1973; PBS-TV, 8 December 1976. Harry Rasky, director. With Tennessee Williams, Burl Ives, Maureen Stapleton, Colleen Dewhurst, Jessica Tandy.
Review:
New York Times, 8 December 1976, sec. C, p. 24: John J. O'Connor.

67. THIS IS (AN ENTERTAINMENT).
This Is (An Entertainment). American Conservatory Theater. San Francisco: Geary Theater, 20 January 1976 (21 performances). Allen Fletcher, director. John Jensen, F. Mitchell Dana, Robert Morgan, designers. Music by Conrad Susa. With Elizabeth Huddle (Countess), Ray Reinhardt (Count), Nicholas Cortland.
Reviews:
Educational Theatre Journal, 28 (October 1976), 406-407: Ruby Cohn.
New York Times, 12 February 1976, sec. 2, p. 5: Stanley Eichelbaum.
Stanton (P 366), pp. 179-181: Judith Hersh Clark.

68. "THIS PROPERTY IS CONDEMNED."
"This Property Is Condemned." New York: New School for Social Research, May 1942.

Three Short Plays. Dallas: Theatre '48, 1948. Margo Jones, director. With Rebecca Hargis (Willie), Charles Taliaferro (Tom).
Production notes:
Jones, Margo. Theatre-in-the-Round. New York: McGraw-Hill, 1965. Pp. 150-151.

Three Premieres. New York: Cherry Lane Theatre, 28 October 1956. Charles Olsen, director. With Sandra Kolb (Willie), Billy James (Tom).
Review:
New York Times, 29 October 1956, p. 34 (NYTTR 6): Lewis Funke.

"This Property Is Condemned." Berlin: Congress Hall, 20 September 1957.

Three by Tennessee. Kraft Television Theater, NBC-TV, 16 April 1958. Sidney Lumet, director. With Zina Bethune (Willie), Martin Huston (Tom).

Review:

New York Times, 17 April 1958, p. 63: Jack Gould.

"Propriété Condamnée" (adaptation by Jacques Guicharnaud). Quatre pièces en un acte. Paris: Théâtre des Champs-Elysées, 20 April 1960. Robert Postec, director. André Acquart, designer. With Rosette Zuchelli (Willie), François Perez (Tom).

"This Property Is Condemned." London: Arts Theatre, 25 August 1960.

This Property Is Condemned (screenplay by Francis Ford Coppola, Fred Coe, Edith Sommer). Seven Arts/Ray Stark film, June 1966. Sydney Pollack, director. James Wong Howe, cameraman. Hal Pereira, Stephen Grimes, Phil Jeffries, art directors. With Natalie Wood (Alva), Robert Redford (Owen), Mary Badham (Willie), Jon Provost (Tom), Kate Reid (Hazel), Charles Bronson (Nichols).

Production notes:

Reed, Rex. "Tennessee Williams Took His Name Off It." New York Times, 16 January 1966, sec. 2, p. 13.

Reprint: Conversations in the Raw: Dialogues, Monologues, and Selected Short Subjects. New York: World, 1969. Pp. 235-240.

Reviews:

Commonweal, 84 (19 August 1966), 533-534: Philip T. Hartung.

New York Times, 4 August 1966, p. 24 (NYTFR): Bosley Crowther.

New Yorker, 42 (27 August 1966), 88-90: Renata Adler

Newsweek, 68 (1 August 1966), 83.

Saturday Review, 49 (25 June 1966), 40: Hollis Alpert.

Time, 88 (22 July 1966), 62.

"Propriété condamnée" (adaptation by Jacques Guicharnaud). Paris: Café-Théâtre"Le Tripot," 1969, 1970. With Valéry Quincy (Willie), Stephen Meldegg (Tom).

69. "THREE PLAYERS OF A SUMMER GAME" see Cat on a Hot Tin Roof

70. TIGER TAIL see "27 Wagons Full of Cotton"

71. "27 WAGONS FULL OF COTTON"/BABY DOLL/TIGER TAIL.
"27 Wagons Full of Cotton" (a). New Orleans: Tulane

University, 18 January 1955. Edward Ludlam, director. George Hendrickson, Homer Pouport, designers. With Maureen Stapleton (Flora), Felice Orlandi (Silva), Paul Ballentyne (Jake).

Review:

New York Times, 19 January 1955, p. 23 (NYTTR 6): Brooks Atkinson.

All in One (a). New York: Playhouse Theatre, 19 April 1955. Vincent J. Donehue, director. Eldon Elder, Pat Campbell, designers. With Maureen Stapleton (Flora), Felice Orlandi (Silva), Myron McCormick (Jake).

Reviews:

America, 93 (15 May 1955), 193: Theophilus Lewis.
Catholic World, 181 (June 1955), 227: Euphemia Van Rensselaer Wyatt.
Commonweal, 62 (10 June 1955), 255: Richard Hayes.
New Republic, 132 (2 May 1955), 22: Eric Bentley.
New York Theatre Critics' Reviews, 16 (1955), 325-328:
Daily Mirror, 20 April 1955: Robert Coleman.
Daily News, 20 April 1955: John Chapman.
Herald Tribune, 20 April 1955: Walter F. Kerr.
Journal-American, 20 April 1955: John McClain.
Post, 20 April 1955: Richard Watts, Jr.
World-Telegram, 20 April 1955: William Hawkins.
New York Times, 20 April 1955, p. 40 (NYTTR 6): Brooks Atkinson.
________, 24 April 1955, sec. 2, p. 1 (NYTTR 6): Brooks Atkinson.
New Yorker, 31 (30 April 1955), 69-71: Wolcott Gibbs.
Saturday Review, 38 (14 May 1955), 26: Henry Hewes.
Theatre Arts, 39 (July 1955), 17.
________, 39 (July 1955), 23: Maurice Zolotow.
Time, 65 (2 May 1955), 78.

Baby Doll (b). Newtown Production. Warner Brothers film, 18 December 1956. Elia Kazan, director. Boris Kaufman, cameraman. Richard Sylbert, art director. Music by Kenyon Hopkins. With Carroll Baker (Baby Doll), Eli Wallach (Silva), Karl Malden (Archie), Mildred Dunnock (Aunt Rose).

Production notes:

Esterow, Milton. "'Baby Doll' in Dixie and Flatbush." New York Times, 26 February 1956, sec. 2, p. 5.
Berger, Meyer. "About New York." New York Times, 22 October 1956, p. 23.
"New Kazan Movie Put on Black List." New York Times, 28 November 1956, p. 32.
"Crowther, Bosley. "Spotlight Events." New York Times, 9 December 1956, sec. 2, p. 5.
"Cardinal Scores 'Baby Doll' Film." New York Times, 17 December 1956, p. 28.
"Mayor Not Backing 'Baby Doll' Group." New York Times, 18 December 1956, p. 39.

"'Baby Doll' Is Approved by British Priest for Showing to Adult Roman Catholics." New York Times, 21 December 1956, p. 18.
Ciment, Michel, ed. Kazan on Kazan. London: Secker & Warburg, 1973. Pp. 73-81.
Reviews and notes on resulting controversy:
America, 96 (15 December 1956), 320.
_______, 96 (29 December 1956), 367.
_______, 96 (5 January 1957), 386.
Catholic World, 184 (January 1957), 302: James Fenlon Finley.
_______, 184 (April 1957), 62-63: James Fenlon Finley.
Christian Century, 74 (23 January 1957), 110-112: Nathan A. Scott, Jr.
Commonweal, 65 (28 December 1956), 335: Philip T. Hartung.
_______, 65 (11 January 1957), 371-372.
_______, 65 (11 January 1957), 381: John Cogley.
_______, 65 (1 February 1957), 465: John Cogley.
_______, 67 (22 November 1957), 202-204: Maryvonne Butcher.
Cosmopolitan, 142 (January 1957), 23.
Holiday, 21 (February 1957), 93, 103: Harry Kurnitz.
Illustrated London News, 230 (12 January 1957), 80: Alan Dent.
Library Journal, 81 (1 December 1956), 2838: Charlotte Bilkey Speicher.
Life, 40 (11 June 1956), 111-112.
_______, 42 (7 January 1957), 60-65.
Look, 20 (25 December 1956), 95.
Nation, 183 (29 December 1956), 567: Robert Hatch.
National Parent-Teacher, 41 (January 1957), 36.
New Republic, 136 (21 January 1957), 21: Janet Winn.
New Statesman, 53 (5 January 1957), 14: Lindsay Anderson.
New York Times, 19 December 1956, p. 40 (NYTFR): Bosley Crowther.
_______, 23 December 1956, sec. 1, p. 17.
_______, 23 December 1956, sec. 4, p. 8: Thomas Pryor.
_______, 24 December 1956, p. 14.
_______, 27 December 1956, p. 21.
_______, 28 December 1956, p. 17.
_______, 30 December 1956, sec. 1, p. 24.
_______, 1 January 1957, p. 19.
_______, 3 January 1957, p. 28.
_______, 4 January 1957, p. 19.
_______, 5 January 1957, p. 11.
_______, 6 January 1957, sec. 1, p. 86.
_______, 6 January 1957, sec. 2, p. 1: Bosley Crowther.
_______, 7 January 1957, p. 20.
_______, 8 January 1957, p. 26.

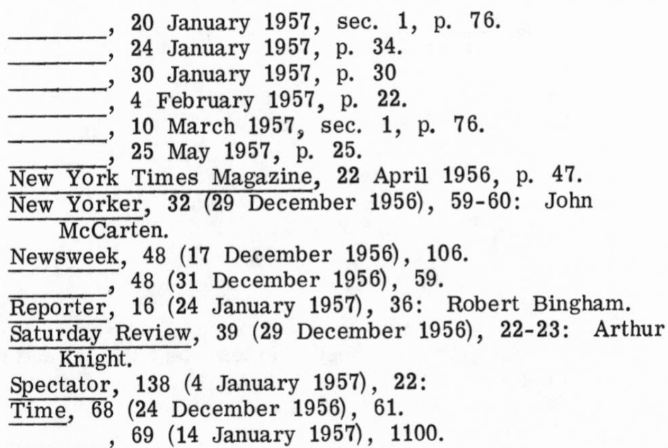

________, 20 January 1957, sec. 1, p. 76.
________, 24 January 1957, p. 34.
________, 30 January 1957, p. 30
________, 4 February 1957, p. 22.
________, 10 March 1957, sec. 1, p. 76.
________, 25 May 1957, p. 25.
New York Times Magazine, 22 April 1956, p. 47.
New Yorker, 32 (29 December 1956), 59-60: John McCarten.
Newsweek, 48 (17 December 1956), 106.
________, 48 (31 December 1956), 59.
Reporter, 16 (24 January 1957), 36: Robert Bingham.
Saturday Review, 39 (29 December 1956), 22-23: Arthur Knight.
Spectator, 138 (4 January 1957), 22:
Time, 68 (24 December 1956), 61.
________, 69 (14 January 1957), 1100.

"27 Wagons Full of Cotton" (a). New York: Phoenix Theater, 26 January 1976 (33 performances). Arvin Brown, director. James Tilton, Albert Wolsky, designers. With Meryl Streep (Flora), Tony Musante (Silva), Roy Pople (Jake).

Reviews:
Nation, 222 (14 February 1976), 189-190: Harold Clurman.
New York Theatre Critics' Reviews, 37 (1976), 382-385:
NBC, 27 January 1976: Leonard Probst.
Christian Science Monitor, 4 February 1976: John Beaufort.
Daily News, 27 January 1976: Douglas Watt.
Post, 27 January 1976: Martin Gottfried.
Wall Street Journal, 2 February 1976: Edwin Wilson.
Women's Wear Daily, 28 January 1976: Christopher Sharp.
New York Times, 27 January 1976, p. 26: Clive Barnes.
________, 8 February 1976, sec. 2, p. 5: Walter Kerr.
New Yorker, 51 (9 February 1976), 78: Brendan Gill.

Tiger Tail (c). Atlanta: Alliance Theatre, winter 1978. Harry Rasky, director. With Elizabeth Kemp (Baby Doll), Nick Mancuso (Silva), Thomas Toner (Archie Lee), Mary Nell Santacroce (Aunt Rose).

Review:
Advocate, 22 March 1978, p. 30: Steve Warren.

72. THE TWO-CHARACTER PLAY/OUT CRY.

The Two-Character Play (a). London: Hampstead Theatre Club, 12 December 1967. James Rosse-Evans, director. With Peter Wyngarde (Felice), Mary Ure (Claire).

Reviews:
London Times, 13 December 1967: David Wade.
New Statesman, 74 (22 December 1967), 886-887: Philip French.

New York Times, 13 December 1967, p. 54 (NYTTR 8).
Time, 90 (22 December 1967), 63.

Out Cry (b). Chicago: Ivanhoe Theatre, 8 July 1971. George Keathley, director. With Donald Madden (Felice), Eileen Herlie (Claire).

Production notes:

"New Williams Play Due to Open July 8." New York Times, 10 March 1971, p. 33.

Funke, Lewis. "Tennessee's 'Two.'" New York Times, 2 May 1971, sec. 2, pp. 1, 24.

Out Cry (c). New York: Lyceum Theatre, 1-10 March 1973 (12 performances). Peter Glenville, director. Jo Mielziner, Sandy Cole, designers. With Michael York (Felice), Cara Duff-MacCormick (Claire).

Reviews:

America, 128 (17 March 1973), 242: Catherine Hughes.
Nation, 216 (19 March 1973), 380: Harold Clurman.
New York Theatre Critics' Reviews, 34 (1973), 343-346:
ABC-TV, 1 March 1973: Melba Tolliver.
CBS-TV, 1 March 1973: Leonard Harris.
NBC, 1 March 1973: Leonard Probst.
Daily News, 2 March 1973: Douglas Watt.
Post, 2 March 1973: Richard Watts.
Wall Street Journal, 6 March 1973: Edwin Wilson.
Women's Wear Daily, 5 March 1973: Martin Gottfried.
New York Times, 2 March 1973, p. 18: Clive Barnes.
________, 11 March 1973, sec. 2, pp. 1, 5: Mel Gussow.
Response: 8 April 1973, sec. 2, p. 6.
Newsweek, 81 (12 March 1973), 88: Jack Kroll.
Time, 101 (12 March 1973), 89: T. E. Kalem.
Village Voice, 8 March 1973, p. 58: Julius Novick.

Out Cry (c). New York: Thirteen Street Repertory Company, June 1974. Laura Zucker, director.

The Two-Character Play (d). New York: Quaigh Theatre, 14 August 1975. Bill Lentsch, director. Greg Huskinko, Isabelle Harris, designers. With Robert Stattel (Felice), Mayellen Flynn (Claire).

Review:

New York Times, 22 August 1975, p. 16: Lawrence Van Gelder.

The Two-Character Play (d). Los Angeles: Callboard Theater, 22 February 1977 (24 performances). John Hancock, director. Stephen Roberts, Robert LaVigne, Alan Blacher, designers. Music by Fred Karlin. With Scott Wilson (Felice), Dorothy Tristan (Claire).

73. "THE UNSATISFACTORY SUPPER" see "The Long Stay Cut Short"

74. VIEUX CARRE.

Vieux Carré (a). New York: St. James Theater, 11-15 May 1977 (5 performances). Arthur Allan Seidelman, director. James Tilton, Jane Greenwood, designers. Music by Galt MacDermott. With Sylvia Sidney (Mrs. Wire), Richard Alfieri (Writer), Tom Aldredge (Painter), John William Reilly (Tye), Diane Kagan (Jane).

Reviews:

Nation, 224 (28 May 1977), 669: Harold Clurman.

New York Theatre Critics' Reviews, 38 (1977), 244-247:

NBC, 11 May 1977: Leonard Probst.

Christian Science Monitor, 23 May 1977: John Beaufort.

Daily News, 12 May 1977: Douglas Watt.

Post, 12 May 1977: Martin Gottfried.

Women's Wear Daily, 12 May 1977: Howard Kissel.

New York Times, 12 May 1977, sec. C, p. 22: Clive Barnes.

________, 22 May 1977, sec. 2, pp. 5, 30: Walter Kerr.

New Yorker, 53 (23 May 1977), 83: Brendan Gill.

Time, 109 (23 May 1977), 108: T. E. Kalem.

Vieux Carré (b). Nottingham, Eng.: Playhouse Theatre, 16 May 1978; London: Picadilly Theatre, 9 August 1978. With Sylvia Miles (Mrs. Wire), Karl Johnson (Writer), Richard Kane (Nightingale), Jonathan Kent (Tye), Di Trevis, later Sheila Gish (Jane).

Production note:

Robson, David. "Sylvia Miles Talks...." Sunday Times, 20 August 1978, p. 41.

Reviews:

Drama, 129 (Summer 1978), 68-69: E. Shorter.

New Statesman, 96 (25 August 1978), 251-252: Ian Hamilton.

Plays and Players, 25 (July 1978), 20-21: S. Aire.

Spectator, 241 (26 August 1978), 20-21: Peter Jenkins.

75. THE WANTON COUNTESS see Senso

76. YOU TOUCHED ME.

You Touched Me. Cleveland: Playhouse, 13 October 1943. Margo Jones, director. With Carl Benton Reid.

You Touched Me. Pasadena, Calif.: Playbox, 29 November-5 December 1943. Margo Jones, director. With Onsolow Stevens.

Review:

New York Times, 17 October 1943, sec. 2, p. 2 (NYTTR 5).

You Touched Me! New York: Booth Theatre, 25 September

1945-5 January 1946 (109 performances). Guthrie McClintie, Lee Schubert, directors. With Montgomery Clift (Hadrian), Harianne Stewart (Matilda), Edmund Gwenn (Captain).

Production notes:

Bosworth, Patricia. Montgomery Clift: A Biography. New York: Harcourt, Brace, Jovanovich, 1978. Pp. 101-103.

Reviews:

Catholic World, 162 (November 1945), 166-167: Euphemia Van Rensselaer Wyatt.

Commonweal, 42 (12 October 1945), 623-624: Kappo Phelan.

Free World, 10 (November 1945), 87-88: Norris Houghton.

Nation, 161 (6 October 1945), 349-350: Joseph Wood Krutch.

New York Theatre Critics' Reviews, 6 (1945), 164-167:
- Daily News, 26 September 1945: John Chapman.
- Herald Tribune, 26 September 1945: Howard Barnes.
- Journal-American, 26 September 1945: Robert Garland.
- PM, 26 September 1945: Louis Kronenberger.
- Post, 26 September 1945: Wilella Wardorf.
- Sun, 26 September 1945: Ward Morehouse.
- World-Telegram, 26 September 1945: Burton Rascoe.
  Reprint: Leavitt (N 49), p. 68.

New York Times, 26 September 1945, p. 27 (NYTTR 5): Lewis Nichols.

________, 30 September 1945, sec. 2, p. 1 (NYTTR 5): Lewis Nichols.

New York Times Magazine, 23 September 1945, pp. 28-29.

New Yorker, 21 (6 October 1945), 48: Wolcott Gibbs.

Theatre Arts, 29 (November 1945), 618-621: Rosamond Gilder.

________, 29 (December 1945), 680.

Theatre Book of the Year 1945-1946 (New York: Alfred A. Knopf, 1946), pp. 87-96: George Jean Nathan.

Time, 46 (8 October 1945), 77.

Proposed film version (screenplay by Montgomery Clift), 1950.

Production notes:

Bosworth, Patricia. Montgomery Clift: A Biography. New York: Harcourt, Brace, Jovanovich, 1978. Pp. 151-152.

L. COLLECTED REVIEWS

1. Bentley, Eric. *The Dramatic Event: An American Chronicle.* New York: Horizon Press, 1954; Boston: Beacon Press, 1956. Pp. 197-110.

2. ______. *In Search of Theatre.* New York: Alfred A. Knopf, 1953. Pp. 31-34.

3. ______. *What Is Theatre? Incorporating the Dramatic Event and Other Reviews 1949-1967.* New York: Atheneum, 1968. Pp. 74-78, 224-231.

4. Brown, John Mason. *As They Appear.* New York: McGraw-Hill, 1952. Pp. 161-166.

5. ______. *Dramatic Personae: A Retrospective Show.* New York: Viking Press, 1963. Pp. 89-94.

6. ______. *Seeing More Things.* New York: McGraw-Hill, 1948. Pp. 266-272.

7. ______. *Seeing Things.* New York: McGraw-Hill, 1946. Pp. 224-230.

8. Brustein, Robert. *Seasons of Discontent: Dramatic Opinions 1959-1965.* New York: Simon & Schuster, 1965. Pp. 117-129.

9. Clurman, Harold. *The Divine Pastime: Theatre Essays.* New York: Macmillan, 1974. Pp. 11-23.

10. ______. *Lies Like Truth: Theatre Reviews and Essays.* New York: Macmillan, 1958. Pp. 72-86.

11. ______. *The Naked Savage: Observations on the Modern Theatre.* New York: MacMillan, 1966. Pp. 123-143.

12. Gassner, John. *Dramatic Soundings: Evaluations and Retractions Culled from 30 Years of Dramatic Criticism.* Edited by Glenn Loncy. New York: Crown, 1968. Pp. 585-590.

13. Gilman, Richard. *Common and Uncommon Modes: Writings on the Theatre 1961-1970.* New York: Random House, 1971. Pp. 140-151.

14. Kael, Pauline. *I Lost It at the Movies.* Boston: Little, Brown, 1965. Pp. 139-140.

15. _______. Kiss Kiss Bang Bang. Boston: Little, Brown, 1968. Pp. 232, 352-353.

16. _______. Reeling. Boston: Little, Brown, 1976. Pp. 246-247.

17. Kauffmann, Stanley. A World on Film: Criticism and Comment. New York: Harper & Row, 1966. Pp. 79-87.

18. Kerr, Walter. God on the Gymnasium Floor and Other Theatrical Adventures. New York: Simon & Schuster, 1969. Pp. 172-176.

19. _______. The Theater in Spite of Itself. New York: Simon & Schuster, 1963. Pp. 247-255.

20. _______. Thirty Plays Hath November: Pain and Pleasure in the Contemporary Theatre. New York: Simon & Schuster, 1968. Pp. 224-230.

21. McCarthy, Mary. Sights and Spectacles 1937-1956. New York: Farrar, Straus, & Cudahy, 1956. Pp. 131-135.

22. _______. Theatre Chronicles 1937-1962. New York: Farrar, Straus, 1963. Pp. 131-135.

23. Nathan, George Jean. The Magic Mirror: Selected Writings on the Theatre. Edited by Thomas Quinn Curtiss. New York: Alfred A. Knopf, 1960. Pp. 238-242.

24. _______. The Theatre in the Fifties. New York: Alfred A. Knopf, 1953. Pp. 109-112.

25. New York Critics' Theatre Reviews. Volumes 6-38. New York: Critics' Theatre Reviews, 1945-1977.

26. The New York Times Film Reviews 1913-1968. Volumes 4-5. New York: Arno Press, 1970.

27. The New York Times Theatre Reviews 1920-1970. Volumes 4-8. New York: Arno Press, 1971.

28. Oppenheimer, George, ed. The Passionate Playgoer: A Personal Scrapbook. New York: Viking Press, 1958.

29. Sarris, Andrew. Confessions of a Cultist: On the Cinema 1955-1969. New York: Simon & Schuster, 1970. Pp. 19-20.

30. Simon, John. Uneasy Stages: A Chronicle of the New York Theater 1963-1973. New York: Random House, 1975. Pp. 6-8, 197-199, 392-393.

31. Theatre Arts Anthology. New York: Robert M. MacGregor, 1950.

32. Tynan, Kenneth. Curtains: Selections from the Drama Criticism and Other Writings. New York: Atheneum, 1961. Pp. 173-176, 302-304, 306-309.

33. Young, Stark. Immortal Shadows. New York: Charles Scribner's Sons, 1948. Pp. 249-253.

PART 5

BIOGRAPHICAL INFORMATION

Introduction

As we watch the playwright continue to work, we can be glad that it is too early to write his biography. But it would be nice if someone would arrange the abundance of material that is already available into an interim biography. (Prentice-Hall has announced one by Catherine Hughes, but as I write this, it has not yet appeared. Meanwhile, Dakin Williams is working on his memoirs.) We need someone, moreover, to separate the fact from the fiction: Williams, like his fellow Mississippian Faulkner, has a tendency to make his autobiography into a work of art. Donald Windham (N 81, p. x) has written: "There is probably not an episode described in the 'Memoirs' that did not happen at some time, to some one, in some way, but more likely than not to a different person, at a different time, with different details"; Gore Vidal (N 75, pp. 133, 141) agrees. Even a definite chronology of Williams's life has yet to be established.

Vidal also says (N 75, p. 145) that Williams "does not develop; he simply continues," that no "new information (or feeling?) has got through to him in the twenty-eight years" they had then known each other. The statement is somewhat doubtful: Williams's essays and interviews show him to be far more astute about contemporary culture--and even, though in a more muddled fashion, politics--than most critics will admit. Williams has been friends with many a notable in the world of art and letters, has read more widely than Vidal says, and has been influenced by contemporaries as well as older writers and painters.

He has been quite generous with interviews. I have listed all that I have found some degree of definite information about. (Letters, A 157, indicates some others which I have not recorded as the information is too vague.) There are undoubtedly many others in newspapers, large and small, throughout the world in places where Williams has lived--especially New York, New Orleans, Key West, and St. Louis--and has visited.

M. INTERVIEWS

1. Anonymous. "Celluloid Brassière." New Yorker, 21 (14 April 1945), 18-19.

2. _______. "E' proprio vero quello che dice Williams?" Ultima, 25 March 1948.

3. _______. "The Life and Ideas of Tennessee Williams." New York PM Magazine, 6 May 1945, pp. 6 ff.

4. _______. "The Playwright: Man Named Tennessee." Newsweek, 49 (1 April 1957), 81.

5. _______. "Talk with the Playwright." Newsweek, 53 (23 March 1959), 75-76.

6. _______. "Tennessee Williams May Depart 'Southern Belle' for Mysticism." New York Times, 2 August 1962, p. 16.

7. "Tennessee Williams Reflects on Fragility of Friendship." New York Times, 15 March 1979, sec. C, p. 16.

8. _______. "Unbeastly Williams." Newsweek, 55 (27 June 1960), 96.

9. _______. "Way Down Yonder in Tennessee." Time, 71 (3 March 1958), 72-74.

10. _______. "Writing and the Theatre." Folio (University of Miami), 3 (Spring 1958), 6-9.

11. Berkvist, Robert. "Broadway Discovers Tennessee Williams." New York Times, 21 December 1975, sec. 2, pp. 1, 4-5.

12. Braggiotti, Mary. "Away from It All." New York Post, 12 December 1947.

13. Brown, Cecil. "Interview with Tennessee Williams." Partisan Review, 45 (1978), 276-305.

14. Buchwald, Art. "'Baby Doll' Wasn't Good for Him." Paris Herald Tribune, 19 April 1957.

15. Clarity, James F. "Williams Finds Cannes Festival a Crass Menagerie." New York Times, 24 May 1976, p. 36.

16. Fayard, Jeanne. "Rencontre avec Tennessee Williams" [Paris, 3 October 1971]. Tennessee Williams. Paris: Seghers, 1972. Pp. 130-135.

16a. Feineman, Neil. "Talking with Tennessee: A Playwright in Reticence." Advocate, 270 (28 June 1979), 31.

17. Fleming, Shirley. "Lee Hoiby--Tennessee Williams." High Fidelity & Musical America, 21 (July 1971), MA 16, 32.

18. Frost, David. The Americans. New York: Stein & Day, 1970; Avon, 1970; London: Heinemann, 1971. Pp. 33-40 (S&D).

19. Funke, Lewis. "News and Gossip Gathered on the Rialto." New York Times, 6 December 1959, sec. 2, p. 5.

20. _______. "Tennessee's 'Cry.'" New York Times, 3 December 1972, sec. 2, pp. 1, 27.

21. _______. "Williams Revival? Ask the Playwright." New York Times, 8 January 1970, p. 45.

22. _______, and John E. Booth. "Williams on Williams." Theatre Arts, 46 (January 1962), 16-19, 72-73.

23. Gaines, Jim. "A Talk about Life and Style with Tennessee Williams." Saturday Review, 44 (29 April 1972), 25-29.

24. Gelb, Arthur. "Williams and Kazan and the Big Walkout." New York Times, 1 May 1960, sec. 2, pp. 1, 3.

25. Gilroy, Harry. "Mr. Williams Turns to Comedy." New York Times, 28 January 1951, sec. 2, pp. 1, 3.

26. Glover, William. "Outraged Puritan." International Herald Tribune, 10 May 1972.

27. Goldman, William. The Season: A Candid Look at Broadway. New York: Harcourt, Brace & World, 1969. Pp. 94-96.

28. Goth, Trudy. "Tutto va bene per Williams." Fiera Litteraria, 12 (22 March 1953), 2.

29. Gruen, John. "The Inward Journey of Tennessee Williams." New York Herald Tribune Magazine, 2 May 1965, p. 29.
Reprint: Close-Up. New York: Viking, 1968. Pp. 86-98.

29a. Grunwald, Beverly. "Williams Longs for Togetherness." Houston Post, 22 July 1979 (from Women's Wear Daily).

30. Gussow, Mel. "Tennessee Williams on Art and Sex." New York Times, 3 November 1975, p. 49.

31. ______. "Williams Looking to Play's Opening" [Small Craft Warnings]. New York Times, 31 March 1972, p. 10.

32. ______. "Williams Still Hopes to Bring 'The Red Devil' to Broadway Despite Boston Closing." New York Times, 15 July 1975, p. 39.

33. Heinrich, Ludwig. [Title unknown.] Frankfurt Abendpost-Nachtausgabe, 27 December 1975.

34. Hewes, Henry. "Tennessee Williams--Last of Our Solid Gold Bohemians." Saturday Review, 36 (28 March 1953), 25-27.

35. Highwater, Jamake. "Lifestyles: Tennessee Williams Is Alive and Well at the Plaza Hotel." Playgirl, 2 (July 1974), 35-36.

36. Jennings, C. Robert. "Playboy Interview: Tennessee Williams." Playboy, 20 (April 1973), 69-84.

37. Klemesrud, Judy. "Tennessee Williams Is a Reluctant Performer for an Audience of High School Students." New York Times, 13 March 1977, p. 51.

38. Lewis, R. C. "A Playwright Named Tennessee." New York Times Magazine, 7 December 1947, pp. 19, 67-70.

39. Mattia, E. G. "Intervista con Williams." Fiera Litteraria, 27 (February 1948).

39a. Oakes, Philip. "Return Ticket." Sunday Times, 17 March 1974, p. 35.

39b. ______ "Strictly in Character" [interview with Williams and Maria Britneva]. Sunday Times, 24 July 1977, p. 35.

40. Peck, Seymour. "Williams and 'The Iguana.'" New York Times, 24 December 1961, sec. 2, p. 5.

41. Probst, Leonard. "The Shirley Temple of Modern Letters." Village Voice, 13 April 1972, pp. 64, 84.

42. Radin, Victoria. "Fighting Off the Furies." London Observer, 22 May 1977, p. 22.

42a. Raynor, Henry. "Intimate Conversation." Times, 16 July 1970, p. 9.

43. Reed, Rex. "Tennessee Williams Turns Sixty." Esquire, 76 (September 1971), 105-108, 216-223.

44. Ross, Don. "Williams on Art and Morals." New York Herald Tribune, 3 March 1957, sec. 4, pp. 1-2.

45. Schmidt-Mulisch, Lothar. [Title unknown.] Welt (West Berlin), 29 December 1975.

46. Shanley, John P. "Tennessee Williams on Television." New York Times, 13 April 1958, sec. 2, p. 13.

47. Singer, Kurt. [Title unknown.] Tribune de Genève, 15 July 1959.

48. Stang, Joanne. "Williams: 20 Years After 'Glass Menagerie.'" New York Times, 28 March 1965, sec. 2, pp. 1, 3.

48a. Stein, Harry. "A Day in the Life: Tennessee Williams." Esquire, 91 (5 June 1979), 79-80.

49. Van Gelder, Robert. "Playwright with 'A Good Conceit.'" New York Times, 22 April 1945, sec. 2, p. 1.

50. Wagner, Walter. "Playwright as Individual: A Conversation with Tennessee Williams." Playbill, 3 (March 1966), 13-15, 42-45. Expanded version: The Playwrights Speak. New York: Delacorte Press, 1967. Pp. 213-237.

51. Wallace, Mike. Mike Wallace Asks: Highlights from 46 Controversial Interviews New York: Simon & Schuster, 1958. Pp. 20-23.

52. Weatherby, W. J. "Lonely in Uptown New York." Manchester Guardian Weekly, 23 July 1959, p. 14.

53. Whitmore, George. "Interview: Tennessee Williams." Gay Sunshine, 33/34 (Summer-Fall 1977), 1-4.
Reprint: Gay Sunshine Interviews, Volume I. Edited by Winston Leyland. San Francisco: Gay Sunshine Press, 1978. Pp. 309-325.

54. Zolotow, Sam. "Tennessee Williams Gives Play to Actors Studio." New York Times, 12 April 1962, p. 43.

N. BIOGRAPHIES

1. Acton, Harold. More Memoirs of an Aesthete. London: Methuen, 1970. Memoirs of an Aesthete 1939-1969, Volume 2. New York: Viking Press, 1970. Pp. 212-215.

2. Anonymous. "Brandeis Presents Awards in the Arts." New York Times, 29 March 1965, p. 43.

3. _______. "A Desire Named Tennessee." Palm (Alpha Tau Omega), May 1962, p. 35.

4. _______. "Donates Pulitzer Cash." New York Times, 9 June 1955, p. 33.

5. _______. "14 Win Admission to Arts Institute." New York Times, 8 February 1952, p. 18.

6. _______. "The Life and Ideas of Tennessee Williams." New York PM Magazine, 6 May 1945, pp. 6 ff.

7. _______. McGraw-Hill Encyclopedia of World Drama. Volume 4. New York: McGraw-Hill, 1972. Pp. 410-420.

7a. _______. "Mr. Tennessee Williams at the Crossroads." Times, 19 June 1957, p. 3.

8. _______. Proceedings of the American Academy of Arts and Letters and the National Institute of Arts and Letters, 20 (1970), 27-28.

9. _______. "Suddenly by Stages; State of Tennessee." Theatre Arts, 42 (May 1958), 10-11.

10. _______. "Tennessee Williams Ailing." New York Times, 22 February 1969, p. 20.

11. _______. "Tennessee Williams Ill." New York Times, 4 October 1969, p. 24.

11a. _______. "Tennessee Williams Reflects on Fragility of Friendship." New York Times, 15 March 1979, sec. C, p. 16.

12. _______. "Tennessee Williams Turns to Roman Catholic Faith." New York Times, 12 January 1969, sec. 1, p. 86.

13. _______. "That Sweet Bird." Time, 75 (11 April 1960), 76-78.

14. _______. "The Watched and the Watchers." Look, 27 (26 March 1963), 54.

15. _______. "Williams Gets Theater Award." New York Times, 8 December 1972, p. 33.

16. _______. "Williams to Get Literature Medal." New York Times, 15 February 1975, p. 35.

17. _______. "Williams to Give Papers to Texas U." New York Times, 23 January 1963, p. 5.

17a. Baker, Joe. "Key West Thugs Mug Tennessee Williams." Advocate, 5 April 1979, p. 10.

18. Balch, Jack S. "A Profile of Tennessee Williams." Theatre, 1 (April 1958), 15, 36, 40.

19. Barnett, Lincoln. "Tennessee Williams." Life, 24 (16 February 1948), 113-127.
Reprint: Writings on Life: Sixteen Close-Ups. New York: William Sloane, 1951. Pp. 243-261.

20. Bowles, Paul. Without Stopping: An Autobiography. New York: G. P. Putnam's Sons, 1972. Pp. 229, 256, 288-290, 321-323, 332, 342, 348, 351-354.

21. Buckley, Tom. "Tennessee Williams Survives." Atlantic, 226 (November 1970), 98-108.

22. Burgess, Charles E. "An American Experience: William Inge in St. Louis, 1943-1949." Papers in Language and Literature, 12 (1976), 438-468.

23. Canby, Vincent. "'I Never Depended on the Kindness of Strangers'" [interview with Audrey Wood]. New York Times, 8 May 1966, sec. 2, pp. 1, 3.

24. Carr, Virginia Spenser. The Lonely Hunter: A Biography of Carson McCullers. Garden City, N.Y.: Doubleday, 1975. Pp. 271-277 and passim.

25. Carroll, Sidney. "A Streetcar Named Tennessee." Esquire, 29 (May 1948), 46.

26. Crawford, Cheryl. One Naked Individual: My Fifty Years in the Theatre. Indianapolis: Bobbs-Merrill, 1977. Pp. 183-201.

27. Da Ponte, Durant. "Tennessee's Tennessee Williams." University of Tennessee Studies in the Humanities, 1 (1956), 11-17.

28. Davis, Bette. The Lonely Life: An Autobiography. New York: G. P. Putnam's Sons, 1962.

29. Davis, Louise. "That Baby Doll Man." Nashville Tennessean Magazine, 3 March 1957, pp. 12-13, 30-31.

29a. Demaret, Kent. "In His Beloved Key West, Tennessee Williams Is Center Stage in a Furor over Gays." People Weekly, 11 (7 May 1979), 32-35.

30. Donahue, Francis. The Dramatic World of Tennessee Williams. New York: Frederick Ungar, 1964. 243 p.

31. Evans, Oliver. The Ballad of Carson McCullers. New York: Coward-McCann, 1966.

32. ________. "A Pleasant Evening with Yukio Mishima." Esquire, 77 (May 1972), 126-130, 174-180.

33. Fosburgh, Lacey. "Art and Literary People Urged to Look Inward." New York Times, 22 May 1969, p. 52.

34. Fraser, C. Gerald. "Miss Woodward, Newman Feted." New York Times, 6 May 1975, p. 48.

35. Gassner, John and Edward Quinn. The Reader's Encyclopedia of Drama. New York: Thomas Y. Crowell, 1969.

36. Gill, Brendan. Tallulah. New York: Holt, Rinehart & Winston, 1972. Pp. 55, 79-80, 83-84.

37. Groueff, Stephane. "Un 'condamné' nommé Tennessee." Paris Match, 409 (9 February 1957), 10-15.

38. Harte, Barbara and Carolyn Riley, eds. 200 Contemporary Authors: Bio-Bibliographies of Selected Leading Writers of Today with Critical and Personal Sidelights. Detroit: Gale Research, 1969. Pp. 296-301.

39. Hewes, Henry. "Broadway Postscript." Saturday Review, 35 (21 June 1952), 32.

40. Hofmann, Paul. "Williams Tells Brother He's Fine." New York Times, 30 June 1968, p. 54.
Reprint: Leavitt, p. 149.

41. Houghton, Norris. "Tomorrow Arrives Today: Young Talent on Broadway." Theatre Arts, 30 (February 1946), 85-86.

42. Hughes, Catherine. "Tennessee Williams at 65." America, 134 (1 May 1976), 382-383.

43. Israel, Lee. Miss Tallulah Bankhead. New York: G. P. Putnam's Sons, 1972. Pp. 300-304, 340-344.

44. Johnston, Laurie. "Tennessee Williams Receives Centennial Medal of Cathedral Church of St. John the Divine." *New York Times*, 10 December 1973, p. 13.

45. Kalem, T. E. "Angel of the Odd." *Time*, 79 (9 March 1962), 53-60.

46. Karsh, Yousuf. "Tennessee Williams." *Coronet*, 48 (May 1960), 62-63.

47. Klebs, Albin. "Notes on People." *New York Times*, 4 December 1976, p. 30.

48. Kunitz, Stanley J., ed. *Twentieth Century Authors.* First Supplement: *A Biographical Dictionary of Modern Literature*, New York: H. W. Wilson, 1955. Pp. 1087-1089.

49. Leavitt, Richard F., ed. *The World of Tennessee Williams.* New York: G. P. Putnam's Sons, 1978; London: W. H. Allen, 1978. 169 p.
Reviews: *Advocate*, 22 February 1979; Karl Maves; *Best Seller*, 38 (January 1979), 317; *Choice*, 15 (December 1978), 1369; *Christian Century*, 95 (4 October 1978), 932; *Critic*, 37 (15 October 1978), 8; *Library Journal*, 103 (15 November 1978), 2330: Larry Earl Bone; *West Coast Review of Books*, (4 November 1978), 52.

50. Lewis, R. C. "A Playwright Named Tennessee." *New York Times Magazine*, 7 December 1947, pp. 19, 67-70.

51. Ludwig, Richard M. "T. Williams." *McGraw-Hill Encyclopedia of World Biography*, Volume 2. New York: McGraw-Hill, 1973. Pp. 392-393.

52. McCullers, Carson. "The Flowering Dream: Notes on Writing." *Esquire*, 42 (December 1959), 164.
Reprint: *The Mortgaged Heart*, ed. Margarita G. Smith. Boston: Houghton, Mifflin, 1971. Pp. 280-281.

53. Matlaw, Myron. *Modern World Drama: An Encyclopedia.* New York: E. P. Dutton, 1972. Pp. 820-832.

54. Maxwell, Gilbert. *Tennessee Williams and Friends.* Cleveland: World, 1965. 333 p.
Reviews: *Library Journal*, 90 (July 1965), 3024: George Freedley; *New York Times Book Review*, 7 November 1965, p. 83: Gene Baru.

55. Moor, Paul. "A Mississippian Named Tennessee." *Harper's* 197 (July 1948), 63-71.

56. Moritz, Charles, ed. Current Biography Yearbook 1972. New York: H. W. Wilson, 1973. Pp. 448-451.

57. Nelson, Benjamin. Tennessee Williams: The Man and His Work. New York: Ivan Obolensky, 1961. 304 p. Tennessee Williams: His Life and Work. London: Peter Owens, 1961. 262 p.
    Reviews: see Section P.

58. Newlove, Donald. "A Dream of Tennessee Williams." Esquire, 72 (November 1969), 172-178, 64-80.

59. Newman, David. "The Agent as Catalyst" [Audrey Wood]. Esquire, 58 (December 1962), 217-218, 261-264.

60. Nicklaus, Frederick. "Tangier: Three Poems for T. W." The Man Who Bit the Sun: Poems. New York: New Directions, 1964. Pp. 29-32.

61. Nin, Anaïs. The Diary of Anaïs Nin 1947-1955. Edited by Gunther Stuhlmann. New York: Harcourt, Brace, Jovanovich, 1974. Pp. 64-65, 77, 81, 88, 194.

62. O'Connor, John. "The Great God Gadg" [Elia Kazan]. Audience, 7 (Winter 1960), 25-31.

63. Phillips, Gene D. "Tennessee Williams and the Jesuits." America, 136 (25 June 1977), 564-565.

64. Reed, Rex. "Tennessee Williams Turns Sixty." Esquire, 76 (September 1971), 105-108, 216-223.

65. Rice, Robert. "A Man Named Tennessee." New York Post, 21 April-4 May 1958.

66. Schumach, Murray. "Tennessee Williams Expresses Fear for Life in Note to Brother." New York Times, 29 June 1969, p. 19.
    Reprint: Leavitt (N 49), p. 150.

67. Staton, Robert W. "Tennessee Williams: The Playwright as Painter." Advocate, 253 (1 November 1978), 40-41.

68. Steen, Mike. A Look at Tennessee Williams. New York: Hawthorn, 1969. Introduction by William S. Gray, xii-xvi; Interviews with Karl Malden, 1-15; Irving Rapper, 16-39; George Cukor, 40-55; Hal Wallis, 56-62; Margaret Leighton and Michael Wilding, 63-78; Hermione Baddeley, 79-92; William Inge, 93-123; Alice Ghostley and Felice Orlandi, 124-140; Paul Bowles, 141-156; Hume Cronyn, 157-166; Jessica Tandy, 167-178; Deborah Kerr and Peter Viertel, 182-192; Anaïs Nin, 193-207; Rip Torn, 208-221; Geraldine Page, 222-245; Shelley Winters, 246-260; Estelle Parsons, 261-281;

Maureen Stapleton, 282-287; Anne Jackson and Eli Wallach, 288-299; Mildred Dunnock, 300-309.

Reviews: Choice, 7 (November 1970), 1245; Library Journal, 94 (1 September 1969), 2913: Paul Myers.

69. Sturdevant, John. "Tennessee Williams." American Weekly, 21 June 1959, pp. 12-15.

70. Taft, Adon. "Tennessee Williams Converts." Christianity Today, 13 (31 January 1969), 75.

71. Tailleur, Roger. Elia Kazan (Cinema d'Aujourd'hui). Paris: Seghers, 1966. Second edition, 1971.

72. Thompson, Howard. "TV: Cavett and Williams." New York Times, 22 August 1974, p. 67.

73. Tynan, Kenneth. "Valentine to Tennessee Williams." Mademoiselle, 42 (February 1956), 130-131, 200-203.

74. Vidal, Gore. "Tennessee Williams." Double Exposure. Edited by Roddy McDowall. New York: Delacorte, 1966.

Reprint: McCalls, 94 (October 1966), 107.

75. ________. "Selected Memories of the Glorious Bird and the Golden Age." New York Review of Books, 5 February 1976, pp. 13-18.

Reprint: Matters of Fact and Fiction: Essays 1973-1976. New York: Random House, 1977. Pp. 129-147.

76. ________. Two Sisters: A Memoir in the Form of a Novel. Boston: Little, Brown, 1970; London: William Heinemann, 1970.

76a. Waters, Arthur B. "Tennessee Williams: Ten Years Later." Theatre Arts, 39 (July 1955), 72-73.

77. Webster, Margaret. Don't Put Your Daughter on the Stage. New York: Alfred A. Knopf, 1972. Pp. 68-74.

78. Williams, Edwina Dakin, as told to Lucy Freeman. Remember Me to Tom. New York: G. P. Putnam's Sons, 1963; London: Cassell, 1964. 255 p.

Excerpts: "My Son's Heroines." Cosmopolitan, 154 (June 1963), 46-53.

Reviews: America, 108 (23 March 1963), 416: Lois Hartley; Best Sellers, 22 (15 March 1963), 463: J. J. Quinn; Harper's, 226 (February 1963), 107: K. G. Jackson; Library Journal, 88 (1 February 1963), 558: Miriam Ylvisaker; New York Herald Tribune Books, 5 May 1963, p. 7: Joseph Morgenstern; New York Times Book Reviews, 7 April 1963, p. 6: Maurice Zolotow.

79. Windham, Donald. *The Hero Continues* [roman à clef with Dennis Freeman as Tennessee Williams]. New York: Thomas Y. Crowell, 1960. 191 p.

80. ________. Letters to the Editor: "Tennessee Williams--Donald Windham." *New York Times Book Review*, 15 January 1978, pp. 14, 18.

81. ________, ed. *Tennessee Williams's Letters to Donald Windham 1940-65*. Verona, Italy: Sandy M. Campbell, 1976; New York: Holt, Rinehart & Winston, 1977. 333 p.
Reviews: see A 157 & A 167.

PART 6

CRITICISM

Introduction

Though an appreciable body of criticism has grown up around Williams, not that much is really first-rate--a remark that could, of course, be made about any major writer. But Williams has suffered unduly from irrelevant polemics. As much hysteria has been generated by his plays and works of fiction as was ever endured by D. H. Lawrence. Several times Williams has appropriated Lawrence's metaphor of a fox in the henhouse: and that is exactly the situation he has often found himself in. Critics have drawn back in fascinated shock, sometimes real and sometimes feigned, and nervously catalogued any "deviations" which have appeared in his works too frequently for it to be amusing any longer. The fact that he has been popular has also irritated many. Signi Falk, in the first edition of her study for the Twayne series, implied that Williams's fame was the result of powerful actors, a good packaging job by New Directions, Williams's catering to the public's prurience, and only incidentally his genius. Perhaps it is a sign of the future that she cut these asides in her 1978 edition and now affirms that Williams is indeed one of the greatest dramatists of this century.

The critical field is still practically wide open: so far only certain repeated subjects have gained widespread attention. Williams's religious dimensions have often been explored, as well as his obsession with time and death. His sexual theories have been subjected to Freudian analyses, but much remains to be said. No one has yet confronted fully the question whether there is such a thing as a homosexual sensibility and, if so, how it influences a writer's development, his portrayal of characters and dramatic situations. Williams's social and political beliefs have been scarcely studied. In spite of the fact that so many of the plays are set in a political context, some critics have even denied that Williams is interested in politics. His use of theatrical elements has been pretty thoroughly investigated. The effect of the cinema on his writing (as well as his own considerable influence on cinema) has been the subject of several of the best critical articles. But little attention has been directed to Williams's several plays that strictly observe the unities. Much has been said concerning his style: the language he assigns his characters (here is where he is so superior to O'Neill) and his patterns of symbolism, including names. But more remains to be said; in particular, it would be well to see more Jungian analyses of his symbolism and dramatic structures than presently exist. Williams's mixture of comic and tragic modes has always drawn attention, and by now his enormous comic gifts, including his brilliant use of black humor, are fully acknowledged. Also, his character types, particularly his women, have been repeatedly examined.

Williams's use of literary and mythical allusions has been frequently noted. Some attention has been paid to the influence Strindberg, Chekhov, O'Neill, and Shaw have had on him, but much remains to be explored concerning his dramatic roots. Lawrence's influence has been overplayed. That of Hart Crane, who Williams has repeatedly said is his favorite author, has been ignored, as well as the influence that such writers as Faulkner, Eliot, and Proust have unquestionably had. The possibility of influences from his direct contemporaries (McCullers, Vidal, Bowles, Capote, Pinter, etc.) has likewise gone unstudied; and no one has examined Williams's knowledge of painters and sculptors. Except for his influence on McCullers, Albee, and Kopit, Williams's importance to the development of American literature has remained largely in the dark.

Above all, the reader should be struck with how little, comparatively, has been written on Williams, especially when one takes out all the dramatic histories and superficial gossip about his plays which are interspersed among the genuine criticism.

O. BIBLIOGRAPHIES

1. Adleman, Irving, and Rita Dworkin. *Modern Drama: A Checklist of Critical Literature on 20th Century Plays.* Metuchen, N. J.: Scarecrow Press, 1967. Pp. 324-332.

2. Brown, Andreas. "Tennessee Williams by Another Name." *Papers of the Bibliographical Society of America*, 57 (1963), 377-378.

3. Carpenter, Charles A., Jr., and Elizabeth Cook. "Addenda to Tennessee Williams: A Selected Bibliography." *Modern Drama*, 2 (December 1959), 220-223.

4. Coleman, Arthur, and Gary R. Tyler. *Drama Criticism*, Volume I: *A Checklist of Interpretation Since 1940 of English and American Plays.* Denver: Alan Swallow, 1966. Pp. 224-229.

5. Dony, Nadine. "Tennessee Williams: A Selected Bibliography." *Modern Drama*, 1 (December 1958), 181-191.

6. Eddleman, Floyd E. *American Drama Criticism*, Supplement 2. Hamden, Conn.: Shoe String Press, 1976. Pp. 178-183.

7. Fidell, Estelle A. *Play Index 1961-1967.* New York: H. W. Wilson, 1968. P. 376.

8. ________. *Play Index 1968-1972.* New York: H. W. Wilson, 1973. Pp. 327-328.

9. ________, and Dorothy Margaret Peale. *Play Index 1953-1960.* New York: H. W. Wilson, 1963. Pp. 327-328.

10. Gunn, Drewey Wayne. "The Various Texts of Tennessee Williams's Plays." *Educational Theatre Journal*, 30 (October 1978), 368-375.

11. Howard, Patsy C. *Theses in American Literature 1896-1971.* Ann Arbor: Pierian Press, 1973. Pp. 247-249.

12. Ishida, Akira. ["A Bibliography of Tennessee Williams in Japan." *Annual Report of Studies* (Doshisha Women's College), 22 (1971), 355-386.] In Japanese.

13. Keller, Dean H. *Index to Plays in Periodicals.* Metuchen, N. J.: Scarecrow, 1971. Pp. 442-443. Supplement. Metuchen, N. J.: Scarecrow, 1973. Pp. 211-212.

14. Litto, Frederic. American Dissertations on the Drama and the Theatre: A Bibliography. Kent, Ohio: Kent State University Press, 1969.

15. Ottemiller, John H. Index to Plays in Collections: An Author and Title Index to Plays Appearing in Collections Published between 1900 and 1962. New York: Scarecrow Press, 1964. P. 150.

16. Presley, Delma E. "Tennessee Williams: Twenty-Five Years of Criticism." Bulletin of Bibliography, 30 (January-March 1973), 21-29.

17. Salem, James M. A Guide to Critical Reviews, Part 1: American Drama 1909-1969, Second Edition. Metuchen, N. J.: Scarecrow Press, 1973. Pp. 520-532. Part 4: The Screenplay from "The Jazz Singer" to "Dr. Strangelove." 2 vols. Metuchen, N. J. Scarecrow Press, 1971.

18. Spiller, Robert E., et al. Literary History of the United States: Bibliography, Fourth Edition. New York: Macmillan, 1974. Pp. 1372-1375.

19. West, Dorothy Herbert, and Dorothy Margaret Peake. Play Index 1949-1952. New York: H. W. Wilson, 1953. P. 192.

20. Woodress, James, and Marian Koritz. Dissertations in American Literature 1891-1966. Durham: Duke University Press, 1968.

P. CRITICAL ARTICLES AND BOOKS

1. Adler, Jacob H. "Night of the Iguana: A New Tennessee Williams?" Ramparts, 1 (November 1962), 59-68.

2. ________. "The Rose and the Fox: Notes on the Southern Drama." South: Modern Southern Literature in Its Cultural Setting. Edited by Louis D. Rubin, Jr., and Robert D. Jacobs. Garden City, N.Y.: Doubleday, 1961. Pp. 347-375.
   Revision: "Tennessee Williams' South: The Culture and the Power." Tharpe, pp. 30-52.

3. Adler, Thomas P. "The Dialogue of Incompletion: Language in Tennessee Williams' Later Plays." Quarterly Journal of Speech, 61 (February 1975), 48-58.
   Excerpts: Stanton (P 366), pp. 74-85.

4. ________. "The Search for God in the Plays of Tennessee Williams." Renascence, 26 (Autumn 1973), 48-56.
   Reprint: Stanton (P 366), pp. 138-148.

5. Anonymous. "No Time Like the Present: Excerpts from Issues of Time Magazine." Esquire, 59 (April 1963), 58-59.

6. Antonini, Giacomo. "Assillo ed ortifizio in Tennessee Williams." Fiera Letteraria, 13 (29 June 1958), 8.

7. Armato, Philip M. "Tennessee Williams' Meditations of Life and Death in Suddenly Last Summer, The Night of the Iguana, and The Milk Train Doesn't Stop Here Anymore." Tharpe (P 375), pp. 558-570.

8. Asselineau, Roger. "Tennessee Williams, ou la Nostalgie de la pureté." Etudes Anglaises, 10 (October-December 1957), 431-443.

9. Atkinson, Brooks. Broadway. New York: Macmillan, 1970. Pp. 394-397, 399-402, 429-432.

10. ________. "Everything Is Poetic." New York Times, 6 June 1948, sec. 2, p. 1.

11. ________. "His Bizarre Images Can't Be Denied." New York Times, 26 November 1961, sec. 2, pp. 1, 36.

12. ________, and Albert Hirschfeld. The Lively Years, 1920-1973. New York: Association Press, 1973. Pp. 191-194, 227-231.

13. Aubriant, Michel. "Tennessee Williams a mis la femme en accusation." Paris Theatre, 11 (1958), 6-10.

14. Babuscio, Jack. "The Cinema of Camp." Gay Sunshine, 35 (Winter 1978), 21-22.

15. Barksdale, Richard K. "Social Background in the Plays of Miller and Williams." College Language Association Journal, 6 (March 1963), 161-169.

16. Barton, Lee. "Why Do Homosexual Playwrights Hide Their Homosexuality?" New York Times, 23 January 1972, sec. 2, pp. 1, 3.
Reply: Bentley, Eric. New York Times, 13 February 1972, sec. 2, p. 5.

17. Baumgart, Wolfgang. "Die Gegenwart des Barochtheaters." Archiv fur das Studium der neueren Sprachen und Literaturen, 1961, pp. 65-76.

18. Beaton, Cecil, and Kenneth Tynan. Persona Grata. New York: G. P. Putnam's Sons, 1954. Pp. 96-97.

19. Beaurline, Lester A. "The Glass Menagerie: From Story to Play." Modern Drama, 8 (September 1965), 142-149.

20. Bennett, Beate Hein. "Williams and European Drama: Infernalists and Forgers of Modern Myths." Tharpe (P 375), pp. 429-459.

21. Bentley, Eric. "Broadway Today." Sewanee Review, 54 (January-March 1946), 314-315.

22. Berkman, Leonard. "The Tragic Downfall of Blanche Dubois." Modern Drama, 10 (December 1967), 249-257.

23. Berkowitz, Gerald M. "The 'Other World' of The Glass Menagerie." Players, 48 (April-May 1973), 150-153.

24. ________. "Williams' 'Other Places'--A Theatrical Metaphor in the Plays." Tharpe (P 375), pp. 712-719.

25. Berlin, Normand. "Complementarity in A Streetcar Named Desire." Tharpe, pp. 97-103.

26. Bernard, Kenneth. "The Mercantile Mr. Kowalski." Discourse, 7 (Summer 1964), 337-340.

27. Bigsby, C. W. E. "Tennessee Williams' Streetcar to Glory." The Forties: Fiction, Poetry, Drama. Edited by Warren French. De Land, Fla.: Everett/Edwards, 1969.
Excerpts: J. Y. Miller (P 282), Interpretations, pp. 103-108.

28. Birney, Earle. "North American Drama Today: A Popular Art?" *Transactions of the Royal Society of Canada*, 51 (June 1957), 31-42.

29. Blackwell, Louise. "Tennessee Williams and the Predicament of Women." *South Atlantic Bulletin*, 35 (March 1970), 9-14.
Revision: Stanton (P 366), pp. 100-106.

30. Blanke, Gustav H. "Das Bild des Menschen in modernen amerikanischen Drama." *Neueren Sprachen*, 18 (March 1969), 117-129.

31. Blitgen, M. Carol. "Tennessee Williams: Modern Idolator." *Renascence*, 22 (Summer 1970), 192-197.

32. Bluefarb, Sam. "*The Glass Menagerie*: Three Visions of Time." *College English*, 24 (April 1963), 513-518.

33. Bradbury, John M. *Renaissance in the South: A Critical History of the Literature 1920-1960.* Chapel Hill: University of North Carolina Press, 1963. Pp. 192-195.

34. Brandon, Henry. "The State of the Theater: A Conversation with Arthur Miller." *Harper's*, 221 (November 1960), 63-69.

35. Brandt, George. "Cinematic Structure in the Work of Tennessee Williams." *American Theatre* (Stratford-upon-Avon Studies). London: Edward Arnold, 1967. Pp. 163-187.

36. Brockett, Oscar G., and Robert R. Findlay. *Century of Innovation: A History of European and American Theatre and Drama Since 1870.* Englewood Cliffs, N.J.: Prentice-Hall, 1973. Pp. 568-570.

37. Brooking, Jack. "Directing *Summer and Smoke*: An Existentialist Approach." *Modern Drama*, 2 (February 1960), 377-385.

38. Brooks, Charles B. "The Comic Tennessee Williams." *Quarterly Journal of Speech*, 44 (October 1958), 275-281.

39. ________. "The Multiple Set in American Drama." *Tulane Drama Review*, 3 (December 1958), 35-37.

40. ________. "Williams' Comedy." Tharpe, pp. 720-735.

41. Broussard, Louis. *American Drama: Contemporary Allegory from Eugene O'Neill to Tennessee Williams.* Norman, Okla.: University of Oklahoma Press, 1962. Pp. 111-116.

42. Brown, Ray C. B. "Tennessee Williams: The Poetry of Stagecraft." *Voices*, 138 (1949), 4.

43. Brustein, Robert. "America's New Culture Hero: Feelings Without Words." Commentary, 25 (February 1958), 123-129.

44. Bryer, Jackson R. The Glass Menagerie (Tennessee Williams). Phonotape-Cassette. De Land, Fla.: Everett/Edwards, 1971.

45. Buchloh, Paul G. "Gesellschaft, Individuum und Gemeinschaft bei Tennessee Williams." Studium Generale, 21 (1968), 49-73.

46. _______. "Tennessee Williams: Assoziationschriffren." Studien zur englischen und amerikanischen Sprache und Literatur: Festschrift für Helmut Papjewski. Neumünster: Wacholtz, 1974. Pp. 405-439.

47. _______. "Verweisende Zeichen in Tennessee Williams: Camino Real." Anglia, 77 (1959), 173-203.

48. Buell, John. "The Evil Imagery of Tennessee Williams." Thought, 38 (Summer 1963), 162-189.

49. Bukoski, Anthony. "The Lady and Her Business of Love in Selected Southern Fiction." Studies in the Humanities, 5, i (1976), 14-18.

49a. Bunsch, Iris. "Tennessee Williams: Orpheus Descending." Theater und Drama in Amerika: Aspekte und Interpretationen. Edited by Edgar Lohner and Rudolf Haas. Berlin: Schmidt, 1978. Pp. 278-294.

50. Cahalan, Thomas L., and Paul A. Doyle. Modern American Drama. Boston: Student Outlines Company, 1960. Pp. 133-143.

51. Callahan, Edward F. "Tennessee Williams' Two Worlds." North Dakota Quarterly, 25 (Summer 1957), 61-67.

52. Campbell, Michael L. "The Theme of Persecution in Tennessee Williams' Camino Real." Notes on Mississippi Writers, 6 (1973), 35-40.

53. Cardullo, Bert. "Drama of Intimacy and Tragedy of Incomprehension: A Streetcar Named Desire Reconsidered." Tharpe (P 375), pp. 137-153.

54. Carlisle, Olga, and Rose Styron. "Arthur Miller: An Interview." Paris Review, 10 (Summer 1966), 61-98.
Reprint: Writers at Work: The Paris Review Interviews, Third Series. New York: Viking Press, 1967. Pp. 197-230 (see especially pp. 206-207).

55. Carter, Hodding. "Yes, Tennessee, There Are Southern Belles." New York Times Magazine, 7 October 1962, pp. 32-33, 93.

56. Casper, Leonard. "Triangles of Transaction in Tennessee Williams." Tharpe (P 375), pp. 736-752.

57. Casty, Alan. "Tennessee Williams and the Small Hands of the Rain." Mad River Review, 1 (Fall-Winter 1965), 27-43.

58. Cate, Hollis C., and Delma E. Presley. "Beyond Stereotype: Ambiguity in Amanda Wingfield." Notes on Mississippi Writers, 3 (Winter 1971), 91-100.

59. Chesler, S. Alan. "Orpheus Descending." Players Magazine, 52 (October 1977), 10-13.

60. _______. "A Streetcar Named Desire: Twenty-Five Years of Criticism." Notes on Mississippi Writers, 7 (1974), 44-53.

61. _______. "Tennessee Williams: Reassessment and Assessment." Tharpe (P 375), pp. 848-880.

62. Ciment, Michel, ed. Kazan on Kazan (Cinema One Series). London: Secker & Warburg, 1973. Pp. 35, 45, 47, 66-82.

63. Clayton, John S. "The Sister Figure in the Works of Tennessee Williams." Carolina Quarterly, 11 (Summer 1960), 47-60.

64. Clurman, Harold. "Tennessee Williams: Poet and Puritan." New York Times, 29 March 1970, sec. 2, pp. 5, 11.
Reprint: The Divine Pastime: Theatre Essays. New York: Macmillan, 1974. Pp. 227-231.

65. Coakley, James. "Time and Tide on the Camino Real." Tharpe, pp. 232-236.

66. _______. "Williams in Ann Arbor." Drama Critique, 11 (Winter 1968), 52-56.

67. Coffey, Warren. "Tennessee Williams: The Playwright as Analysand." Ramparts, 1 (November 1962), 51-58.

68. Cohn, Ruby. Dialogue in American Drama. Bloomington: Indiana University Press, 1971. Pp. 97-129.
Excerpts: Stanton (P 366), pp. 45-60.

69. Cole, Charles W., and Carol I. Franco. "Critical Reaction to Tennessee Williams in the Mid-1960's." Players, 49 (Fall-Winter 1974), 18-23.

70. Conway, Mary L. "Williams in Cleveland." Drama Critique, 11 (Winter 1968), 58-60.

71. Corrigan, Mary Ann. "Beyond Verisimilitude: Echoes of Expressionism in Williams' Plays." Tharpe (P 375), pp. 375-412.

72. _______. "Memory, Dream and Myth in the Plays of Tennessee Williams." Renascence, 28 (Spring 1976), 155-167.

73. _______. "Realism and Theatricalism in A Streetcar Named Desire." Modern Drama, 19 (December 1976), 385-396.

74. Corrigan, Robert W. "The Soulscape of Contemporary American Drama." World Theatre, 11 (Winter 1962-1963), 316-328.

75. Costello, Donald P. "Tennessee Williams' Fugitive Kind." Modern Drama, 15 (May 1972), 26-43.
Abridgement: Stanton (P 366), pp. 107-122.

76. Cowser, R. L., Jr. "Symbolic Names in the Plays of Tennessee Williams." Of Edsels and Marauders. Edited by Fred Tarpley and Ann Moseley. Commerce, Texas: Names Institute Press, 1971. Pp. 89-93.

77. Crowther, Bosley. "Wronging, Writing." New York Times, 8 April 1962, sec. 2, p. 1.

78. Curley, Dorothy Nyren, et al. A Library of Literary Criticism: Modern American Literature. New York: Frederick Ungar, 1969. Volume 3, pp. 373-379.

79. Da Ponte, Durant. "Tennessee Williams' Gallery of Feminine Characters." Tennessee Studies in Literature, 10 (1965), 7-26.
Excerpts: J. Y. Miller (P 282), Interpretations, pp. 53-56.

80. Davis, Joseph K. "The American South as Mediating Image in the Plays of Tennessee Williams." Amerikanisches Drama und Theater im 20 Jahrhundert. Edited by Alfred Weber and Siegfried Neuweiler. Gottingen: Vandenhoeck, 1976. Pp. 171-189.

81. _______. "Landscapes of the Dislocated Mind in Williams' The Glass Menagerie." Tharpe (P 375), pp. 192-206.

82. Debusscher, Gilbert. "The Artistry of Tennessee Williams's Personal Nomenclature." Handelinger von het Tweeendertigste Nederlands Filologencongres. Amsterdam: University Press, 1974. Pp. 234-244.

83. _______. "Oedipus in New Orleans: Myth in Suddenly Last Summer." Revue des Langues Vivantes, Bicentennial Issue (1971), 53-63.

84. _______. "Tennessee Williams as Hagiographer: An Aspect of Obliquity in Drama." Revue des Langues Vivantes, 40 (1974), 44-56.
Reprint: Stanton (P 366), pp. 149-157.

85. _______. "Tennessee Williams's Unicorn Broken Again." Revue Belge de Philologie et d'Histoire, 49 (1971), 875-885.

86. Devi, K. Lakshmi. "The World of Tennessee Williams." Andhra University Magazine, 20 (1959-1960), 86-92.

87. Dickinson, Hugh. "Tennessee Williams: Orpheus as Savior." Myth on the Modern Stage. Urbana: University of Illinois, 1969. Pp. 278-309.

88. Dickinson, Vivienne. "A Streetcar Named Desire: Its Development through the Manuscripts." Tharpe (P 375), pp. 154-171.

89. Dietrich, Margret. "Der Dramitiker Tennessee Williams und sein Werk für das heutige Theatre." Universitas (Stuttgart), 23 (May 1968), 511-516.

90. Dommergues, Pierre. Les écrivains d'aujourd'hui (Que Sais-Je?). Paris: Presses Universitaires de France, 1967.

91. _______. Les U. S. A. à la recherche de leur identité: Rencontres avec quarante écrivains américains. Paris: Grasset, 1967.

92. Donahue, Francis. The Dramatic World of Tennessee Williams. New York: Frederick Ungar, 1964. 243 p.

93. Downer, Alan S. "Experience of Heroes: Notes on the New York Theatre 1961-1962." Quarterly Journal of Speech, 48 (October 1962), 261-270.

94. _______. Fifty Years of American Drama 1900-1950. Chicago: Henry Regnery, 1951. Pp. 102-105, 145-147.

95. _______. "Mr. Williams and Mr. Miller." Furioso, 4 (Summer 1949), 66-70.

96. _______. Recent American Drama (University of Minnesota Pamphlets on American Writers). Minneapolis: University of Minnesota Press, 1961. Pp. 28-33.

97. _______. "The Two Worlds of Arthur Miller and Tennessee Williams." Princeton Alumni Weekly, 72 (20 October 1961), 8-11, 17, 20.

98. Drake, Constance. "Blanche Dubois: A Re-evaluation." Theatre Annual, 24 (1969), 58-69.

99. Draya, Ren. "The Fiction of Tennessee Williams." Tharpe (P 375), pp. 647-662.

100. Driver, Tom F. Romantic Quest and Modern Query: A History of the Modern Theater. New York: Delacorte, 1970. Pp. 309-310, 313.

101. Dukore, Bernard F. "American Abelard: A Footnote to Sweet Bird of Youth." College English, 26 (May 1965), 630-634.

102. _______. "The Cat Has Nine Lives." Tulane Drama Review, 8 (Fall 1963), 95-100.

103. Duprey, Richard A. "The Battle for the American Stage." Catholic World, 197 (July 1963), 246-251.

104. _______. "Where Are Our Playwrights?" America, 108 (5 January 1963), 10-12.

105. Durham, Frank. "Tennessee Williams: Theatre Poet in Prose." South Atlantic Bulletin, 36 (March 1971), 3-16.

106. Dusenbury, Winifred. "Baby Doll and The Ponder Heart." Modern Drama, 3 (February 1961), 393-395.

107. _______. The Theme of Loneliness in Modern American Drama. Gainesville: University of Florida Press, 1960. Pp. 134-154.

108. Efstate, Ileana. "Tennessee Williams--A Few Considerations on A Streetcar Named Desire." Analele Universitatii Bueuresti, Limbi Germanice, 21 (1972), 107-113.

109. Ehrenpries, Irwin. "Readable Americans." Revue des Langues Vivantes, 25 (1959), 416-419.

110. Ehrlich, Alan. "A Streetcar Named Desire Under the Elms: A Study of Dramatic Space in A Streetcar Named Desire and Desire Under the Elms." Tharpe (P 375), pp. 126-136.

111. Ellis, Brobury Pearce. "'The True Originall Copies'" [The Glass Menagerie]. Tulane Drama Review, 5 (September 1960), 113-116.

112. Embrey, Glenn. "The Subterranean World of The Night of the Iguana." Tharpe (P 375), pp. 325-340.

113. Enck, John Jacob. "Memory and Desire and Tennessee Williams' Plays." Transactions of the Wisconsin Academy of Sciences, Arts, Letters, 42 (1953), 249-256.

114. Falk, Signi Lenea. "The Profitable World of Tennessee Williams." Modern Drama, 1 (December 1958), 172-180.
Reprint: Hurrell, pp. 117-123.

115. _______. Tennessee Williams (Twayne's United States Authors Series). New York: Twayne, 1962. 224 p. Second edition, 1978. 194 p.
Reprint: Chapter 3: J. Y. Miller, Interpretations, pp. 94-102.

Reviews: Booklist, 58 (15 March 1962), 471; Choice, 15 (December 1978), 1366; London Times Literary Supplement, 8 June 1962, p. 428; New York Herald Tribune Books, 4 March 1962, p. 12.

116. Farnsworth, T. A. "The Same Old Streetcar: Sex Plays Are Becoming as Stodgy as Puritanism." Forum (South Africa), 9 (February 1961), 23-24.

117. Fayard, Jeanne. Tennessee Williams (Théâtre de Tous les Temps). Paris: Seghers, 1972. 190 p.

118. Fedder, Norman J. The Influence of D. H. Lawrence on Tennessee Williams (Studies in American Literature). The Hague: Mouton, 1966. 131 p.

119. ______. "Tennessee Williams' Dramatic Technique." Tharpe (P 375), pp. 795-812.

120. Fitch, Robert E. "La Mystique de la Merde." New Republic, 135 (3 September 1956), 17-18.

121. Flaxman, Seymour L. "The Debt of Williams and Miller to Ibsen and Strindberg." Comparative Literature Studies, Special Advance Issue (1963), 51-60.

122. Free, William J. "Williams in the Seventies: Directions and Discontents." Tharpe (P 375), pp. 815-828.

123. Freedley, George. "Freudians Both." Players, 32 (March 1956), 235-249.

124. Frenz, Horst. "American Playwrights and the German Psyche." Neueren Sprachen, 10 (April 1961), 170-178.

125. ______, and Ulrich Weisstein. "Tennessee Williams and His German Critics." Symposium, 14 (Winter 1960), 258-275.

126. Fritscher, John J. "Popular Culture as Cyclic Phenomenon in the Evolution of Tennessee Williams." Challenges in American Culture. Edited by Ray B. Browne et al. Bowling Green, Ohio: Popular Press, 1970.

127. ______. "Some Attitudes and a Posture: Religious Metaphor and Ritual in Tennessee Williams' Query of the American God." Modern Drama, 13 (September 1970), 201-215.

128. Funatsu, Tatsumi. "Blanche's Loneliness in A Streetcar Named Desire." Kyushu American Literature (Fukuoka, Japan), 5 (April 1962), 36-41.

129. ______. "A Study of Cat on a Hot Tin Roof." Kyushu American Literature, 2 (May 1959), 33-39.

130. _______. "A Study of Suddenly Last Summer." Fukuoka University Review of Literature and Science, 7 (March 1963), 341-362.

131. Ganz, Arthur. "The Desperate Morality of the Plays of Tennessee Williams." American Scholar, 31 (Spring 1962), 278-294.
Reprint: American Drama and Its Critics: A Collection of Critical Essays. Chicago: University of Chicago Press, 1965. Pp. 203-217. Revision: Stanton (P 366), pp. 123-137.

132. Gardiner, Harold C. "Is Williams' Vision Myopic?" America, 103 (30 July 1960), 495-496.
Reply: Boyle, Robert. "Williams and Myopia." America, 104 (19 November 1960), 263-265.

133. Gardner, Peter. "An Essay on Tennessee Williams." Kyushu American Literature (Fukuoka, Japan), 1 (June 1958), 2-8.

134. Gardner, R. H. The Splintered Stage: The Decline of the American Theatre. New York: MacMillan, 1965. Pp. 111-12.

135. Gassner, John. "Anchors Aweigh: Maxwell Anderson and Tennessee Williams." Theatre Time, Spring 1949.
Reprint: Dramatic Soundings: Evaluations and Retractions Culled from 30 Years of Dramatic Criticism. Edited by Glenn Loncy. New York: Crown, 1968. Pp. 304-313.

136. _______. "The Influence of Strindberg in the United States." World Theatre, 11 (Spring 1962), 21-29.

137. _______. "Realism and Poetry in New American Playwrighting." World Theatre, 2 (Spring 1953), 19-20.

138. _______. "Tennessee Williams: Dramatist of Frustration." College English, 10 (October 1946), 1-7.

139. _______. Theatre at the Crossroads. New York: Holt, Rinehart & Winston, 1960. Pp. 77-91, 218-231.

140. _______. The Theatre in Our Times. New York: Crown, 1954. Pp. 342-354. Abridgement: On Contemporary Literature. Edited by Richard Kostelanetz. Freeport, N.Y.: Books for Libraries, 1964. Pp. 48-63.

141. Gellert, Roger. "A Survey of the Homosexual in Some Plays." Encore, 8 (January-February 1961), 34-35.

142. Gérard, Albert. "The Eagle and the Star: Symbolic Motifs in 'The Roman Spring of Mrs. Stone.'" English Studies, 36 (August 1955), 145-153.

143. Gerigk, H.-J. "Tennessee Williams und Anton Cechov." Zeitschrift fur Slavische Philogie, 39 (1976), 157-165.

144. Gillman, Richard. "The Drama Is Coming Now." Tulane Drama Review, 7 (Summer 1963), 27-42.

145. Glicksberg, Charles I. "Depersonalization in the Modern Drama." Personalist, 39 (Spring 1958), 158-169.

146. _______. "The Lost Self in Modern Literature." Personalist, 43 (Autumn 1962), 527-538.

147. _______. "The Modern Playwright and the Absolute." Queen's Quarterly, 65 (Autumn 1958), 459-471.

148. Golden, Joseph. The Death of Tinkerbell. Syracuse: Syracuse University Press, 1967. Pp. 123-131.

149. Goldfarb, Alvin. "Period of Adjustment and the New Tennessee Williams." Tharpe (P 375), pp. 310-317.

150. Goldstein, Malcolm. "Body and Soul on Broadway." Modern Drama, 7 (February 1965), 411-421.

151. Gorowara, Krishna. "The Fire Symbol in Tennessee Williams." Literary Half-Yearly, 8 (January-July 1967), 57-73.

152. Gottfried, Martin. A Theater Divided: The Postwar American Stage. Boston: Little, Brown, 1967. Pp. 248-257.

153. Gould, J. R. Modern American Playwrights. New York: Dodd, Mead, 1966. Pp. 225-246.

154. Grande, Luke M. "Metaphysics of Alienation in Tennessee Williams' Short Stories." Drama Critique, 4 (November 1961), 118-122.

155. _______. "Tennessee Williams' New Poet-Prophet." Drama Critique, 4 (Spring 1963), 60-64.

156. Gray, Paul. "The Theatre of the Marvelous." Tulane Drama Review, 7 (Summer 1963), 143-145.

157. Gray, Richard. The Literature of Memory: Modern Writers of the American South. Baltimore: Johns Hopkins University Press, 1977. Pp. 258-260.

158. Green, William. "Significant Trends in the Modern American Theatre." Manchester Review, 8 (1957), 65-78.

159. Gresset, Michel. "Orphée sous les tropiques, ou les Thèmes dans le théâtre recent de Tennessee Williams." Le Théâtre moderne, Volume 2. Edited by Jean Jacquot. Paris: Centre National de la Recherche Scientifique, 1967.

160. Groene, Horst. "Tennessee Williams im Zwiespalt der Meinungen: Ein Forschungsbericht über die englisch- und deutschsprachige Literatur zu Williams dramatischem Werk." Literatur in Wissenschaft und Unterright (Kiel), 5 (1971), 66-87.

161. Groff, Edward. "Point of View in Modern Drama." Modern Drama, 2 (December 1959), 268-282.

162. Guerrero Zamora, Juan. Historia del teatro contemporaneo, Volume 4. Barcelona: Juan Flores, 1967. Pp. 125-137.

163. Gunn, Drewey Wayne. American and British Writers in Mexico, 1556-1973. Austin: University of Texas Press, 1974. Pp. 208-215.

164. Gwynn, Frederick, and Joseph Blotner. Faulkner in the University: Class Conferences at the University of Virginia 1957-1958. Charlottesville: University of Virginia Press, 1959. P. 13.

165. Hafley, James. "Abstraction and Order in the Language of Tennessee Williams." Tharpe (P 375), pp. 753-762.

166. Hagopian, John V. "Cat on a Hot Tin Roof." Insight IV: Analyses of Modern British and American Drama. Edited by Hermann J. Weiand. Frankfurt: Hirschgraben, 1975. Pp. 269-275.

167. Hainsworth, J. D. "Tennessee Williams: Playwright on a Hot Tin Roof?" Etudes Anglaises, 20 (1968), 225-232.

168. Hall, Peter. "Tennessee Williams: Notes on the Moralist." Encore, 4 (September-October 1957), 16-19.

169. Harwood, Britton J. "Tragedy as Habit: A Streetcar Named Desire." Tharpe (P 375), pp. 104-115.

170. Haskell, Molly. From Reverence to Rape: The Treatment of Women in the Movies. New York: Holt, Rinehart & Winston, 1974; Penguin Books, 1974. Pp. 248-253.

171. Hays, Peter L. "Arthur Miller and Tennessee Williams." Essays in Literature, 4 (1977), 239-249.

172. ______. "Tennessee Williams' Use of Myth in Sweet Bird of Youth." Educational Theatre Journal, 18 (October 1966), 255-258.

173. Heal, Edith. "Words about Williams." Columbia University Forum, 10 (Spring 1967), 45-47.

174. Heilman, Robert B. "Tennessee Williams: Approaches to

Tragedy." Southern Review, 1 (August 1965), 770-790.
Reprint: The Iceman, the Arsonist, and the Troubled Agent: Tragedy and Melodrama on the Modern Stage. Seattle: University of Washington, 1973. Pp. 115-141.
Excerpts: Stanton (P 366), pp. 17-35.

175. _______. Tragedy and Melodrama: Versions of Experience. Seattle: University of Washington Press, 1968. Pp. 120-122.

176. Heiney, Donald. Recent American Literature. New York: Barron's Educational Series, 1961. Pp. 406-415.

177. Hendrick, George. "Jesus and the Osiris-Isis Myth: Lawrence's The Man Who Died and Williams' The Night of the Iguana." Anglia, 84 (4 March 1966), 398-406.

178. Hernlund, Bengt. "Tennessee Williams's enaktare." Röster i Radio, 20 (1953), 9, 36.

179. Hethmon, Robert. "The Foug Rag-and-Bone Shop of the Heart." Drama Critique, 7 (Fall 1965), 94-102.

180. Hewes, Henry. "The Boundaries of Tennessee." Saturday Review, 39 (29 December 1956), 23-24.
Reprint: Oppenheimer (L 28), pp. 250-254.

181. Highet, Gilbert. "A Memorandum." Horizon, 1 (May 1959), 54-55.

182. Hilfer, Anthony C., and R. Vance Ramsey. "Baby Doll: A Study in Comedy and Critical Awareness." Ohio University Review, 11 (1969), 75-88.

183. Hill, F. A. "The Disaster of Ideals in Camino Real by Tennessee Williams." Notes on Mississippi Writers, 1 (Winter 1969), 100-109.

183a. Hirsch, Foster. A Portrait of the Artist: The Plays of Tennessee Williams. Port Washington, N.Y.: Kennikat, 1978.

184. _______. "Sexual Imagery in Tennessee Williams' Kingdom of Earth." Notes on Contemporary Literature, 1, ii (1971), 10-13.

185. _______. "Tennessee Williams." Cinema, 8 (Spring 1973).

186. _______. "The World Still Desires 'A Streetcar.'" New York Times, 15 April 1973, sec. 2, pp. 1, 3.
Response: New York Times, 10 June 1973, sec. 2, p. 4.

187. Honors English 11-1 (1966-1967), Roy C. Ketcham Senior High School, Wappingers Falls, N.Y. "Through a Glass Starkly." English Journal, 57 (February 1968), 209-212, 220.

188. Howell, Elmo. "The Function of Gentlemen Callers: A Note on Tennessee Williams' *The Glass Menagerie.*" *Notes on Mississippi Writers*, 2 (Winter 1970), 83-90.

189. Hunningher, Benjamin. "Tennessee Williams tegenover de vijand Tijd." *Gids*, 123 (January 1960), 38-57.

190. Hurley, Paul J. "The Sad Fate of Tennessee Williams." *Shenandoah*, 15 (Winter 1964), 61-66.

191. ______. "*Suddenly Last Summer* as 'Morality Play.'" *Modern Drama*, 8 (February 1966), 392-398.

192. ______. "Tennessee Williams: The Playwright as Social Critic." *Theatre Annual*, 21 (1964), 40-56.

193. ______. "Williams's 'Desire and the Black Masseur': An Analysis." *Studies in Short Fiction*, 2 (Fall 1964), 51-55.

194. Hurrell, John D., ed. *Two Modern American Tragedies: Reviews and Criticism of Death of a Salesman and A Streetcar Named Desire.* New York: Charles Scribner's Sons, 1961.

195. Hurt, James R. "*Suddenly Last Summer*: Williams and Melville." *Modern Drama*, 3 (February 1961), 396-400.

196. Hyman, Stanley Edgar. "Some Notes on the Albertine Strategy." *Hudson Review*, 6 (Autumn 1953), 416-422.

197. ______. "Some Trends in the Novel." *College English*, 20 (October 1958), 2-9.

198. Isaac, Dan. "Big Daddy's Dramatic Word Strings." *American Speech*, 40 (December 1965), 272-278.

199. ______. "In Defense of Tennessee Williams." *Religious Education*, 53 (September-October 1958), 452-453.

200. ______. "A Streetcar Named Desire--or Death?" *New York Times*, 18 February 1968, sec. 2, pp. 1, 7.

201. Ishida, Akira. ["Some Ideas of Theatre in Tennessee Williams." *Annual Report of Studies* (Doshisha Women's College, Kyoto, Japan), 24 (1973), 138-162.] In Japanese.

202. ______. ["Tennessee Williams and Japan." *Annual Report of Studies*, 23 (1973), 217-238.] In Japanese.

203. ______. ["Tennessee Williams' 'Slapstick Tragedy.'" *Annual Report of Studies*, 20 (1969), 439-465.] In Japanese.

204. ______. ["Tennessee Williams' *The Two-Character Play.*" *Annual Report of Studies*, 21 (1970), 399-426.] In Japanese.

205. Ishizuka, Koji. "Two Memory Plays: Williams and Miller." American Literature in the 1940's (Annual Report). Tokyo: American Literary Society of Japan, 1975. Pp. 208-212.

206. Itschert, Hans. Das amerikanische Drama von den Anfängen zur Gegenwart. Darmstadt: Wissenschaftliche, 1972. Pp. 265-292.

207. Iwamoto, Iwao. ["Truth and Illusion in the Plays of Tennessee Williams." Studies in English Literature (Tokyo), 41 (August 1964), 73-86.] In Japanese.

208. Jackson, Esther Merle. The Broken World of Tennessee Williams. Madison: University of Wisconsin Press, 1965. 179 p.
Reviews: American Literature, 37 (November 1965), 362; Canadian Forum, 45 (December 1965), 208: D. A. Lee.

209. _______. "The Emergence of the Anti-Hero in the Contemporary Drama." Central States Speech Journal, 12 (1960-1961), 92-99.
Excerpts: Stanton (P 366), pp. 87-90.

210. _______. "Music and Dance as Elements of Form in the Drama of Tennessee Williams." Revue d'Histoire du Théâtre, 15 (1963), 294-301.

211. _______. "The Problem of Form in the Drama of Tennessee Williams." College Language Association Journal, 4 (September 1960), 8-12.

212. _______. "Tennessee Williams." The American Theater Today. Edited by Alan S. Downer. New York: Basic Books, 1967. Pp. 73-84.

213. _______. "Tennessee Williams: Poetic Consciousness in Crisis." Tharpe, pp. 53-72.

214. Jauslin, Christian. Tennessee Williams. Hannover: Friedrich, 1969. 154 p.

215. John, Mary. "Williams in Cincinnati." Drama Critique, 11 (Winter 1968), 56-58.

216. Johnson, Mary Lynn. "Williams's Suddenly Last Summer, Scene One." Explicator, 21 (April 1963), item 66.

217. Jones, Robert Emmet. "Sexual Roles in the Works of Tennessee Williams." Tharpe (P 375), pp. 545-557.

218. _______ "Tennessee Williams's Early Heroines." Modern Drama, 2 (December 1959), 211-219.
Reprint: Hurrell (P 194), pp. 111-116.

219. Josephson, Lennart. "Tennessee Williams, Dramatik." *Bonniers Litterära Magasin* (Stockholm), 18 (March 1949), 207-211.

220. Jotterand, Frank. *Le nouveau théâtre américain* (Collection Points). Paris: Seuil, 1970.

221. Joven, Nilda G. "Illusion and Reality in Tennessee Williams' *The Glass Menagerie.*" *Dillman Review*, 14 (January 1966), 81-89.

222. Justice, Donald. "The Unhappy Fate of the 'Poetic.'" *Poetry*, 93 (March 1959), 402-403.

223. Kahn, Sy. "*Baby Doll*: A Comic Fable." Tharpe (P 375), pp. 292-309.

224. _______. *The Night of the Iguana (Tennessee Williams)*. Phonotape-Cassette. De Land, Fla.: Everett/Edwards, 197-.

225. _______. *A Streetcar Named Desire (Tennessee Williams)*. Phonotape-Cassette. De Land, Fla.: Everett/Edwards, 197-.

226. _______. "Through a Glass Menagerie Darkly: The World of Tennessee Williams." *Modern American Drama: Essays in Criticism*. Edited by William E. Taylor. De Land, Fla.: Everett/Edwards, 1968.

227. Kalson, Albert E. "Tennessee Williams at the Delta Brilliant." Tharpe (P 375), pp. 774-794.

228. _______. "Tennessee Williams Enters *Dragon Country*." *Modern Drama*, 16 (June 1973), 61-67.

229. _______. "Tennessee Williams' *Kingdom of Earth*: A Sterile Promontory." *Drama and Theatre* (Purdue), 8 (Winter 1969-1970), 90-93.

230. Keating, Edward M. "Mildew on the Old Magnolia." *Ramparts*, 1 (November 1962), 69-74.

231. Kernan, Alvin B. "Truth and Dramatic Mode in the Modern Theatre: Chekhov, Pirandello and Williams." *Modern Drama*, 1 (September 1958), 111-114.

232. Kerr, Walter. "Failures of Williams." *Pieces at Eight*. New York: Simon & Schuster, 1957. Pp. 125-134.

233. Kesting, Marianne. "Tennessee Williams." *Hochland*, 50 (December 1957), 171-174.

234. King, Kimball. *The Works of Tennessee Williams*. Phonotape-Cassette. De Land, Fla.: Everett/Edwards, 197-.

235. King, Thomas L. "Irony and Distance in The Glass Menagerie." Educational Theater Journal, 25 (May 1973), 207-214.

236. Klinger, Kurt. "Zwischenruf zur Toleranz: Zun Werk von Tennessee Williams nach dessen 50. Geburtstag." Forum, 11 (1964), 266-268.

237. Koepsel, Jurgen. Der amerikanische Suden und seine Funktionen im dramatischen Werk von Tennessee Williams (Mainzer Studien zur Amerikanistik). Bern: Herbert Lang, 1974; Frankfurt: Peter Lang, 1974.

238. Kolin, Philip C. "'Sentiment and humor in equal measure': Comic Forms in The Rose Tattoo." Tharpe, pp. 214-231.

239. Kourilsky, Françoise. Le théâtre aux U.S.A. (Collection Dionysos). Paris: Renaissance du Livre, 1967.

240. Kramer, Victor A. "Memoirs of Self-Indictment: The Solitude of Tennessee Williams." Tharpe, pp. 663-675.

241. Kratch, Fritz Andre. "Rise and Decline of U. S. Theater on German Stages." American-German Review, 22 (June-July 1966), 13-15.

242. Krutch, Joseph Wood. The American Drama Since 1918: An Informal History. New York: George Braziller, 1957. Pp. 324-332.

243. ________. "Modernism" in Modern Drama. Ithaca: Cornell University Press, 1953. Pp. 126-130.

244. ________. "Why the O'Neill Star Is Rising." New York Times Magazine, 19 March 1961, pp. 36-37, 108.

245. Kunkel, Francis L. "Tennessee Williams and the Death of God." Commonweal, 87 (23 February 1968), 614-617.

246. Larsen, June Bennett. "Tennessee Williams: Optimistic Symbolist." Tharpe (P 375), pp. 413-428.

247. Laufe, Abe. Anatomy of a Hit. New York: Hawthorn Books, 1966. Pp. 169-172, 180-185, 308-313.

248. Law, Richard A. "'A Streetcar Named Desire' as Melodrama." English Record, 14 (February 1964), 2-8.

249. Lawrence, Elaine Louise. "Four Defeated Heroines: Tennessee Williams' Southern Gentlewomen." Lit, 7 (Spring 1966), 7-39.

250. Lawson, John Howard. "Modern U.S. Dramaturgy." Inostrannava Literatura, 8 (August 1962), 186-196.

251. Lee, M. Owen. "Orpheus and Eurydice: Some Modern Versions." Classical Journal, 56 (April 1961), 307-313.

252. Lees, Daniel E. "The Glass Menagerie: A Black Cinderella." Unisa English Studies, 11 (March 1973), 30-34.

253. Lemaire, Marcel. "Fiction in U. S. A. from the South." Revue des Langues Vivantes, 27 (1966), 244-253.

254. Leon, Ferdinard. "Time, Fantasy, and Reality in Night of the Iguana." Modern Drama, 11 (May 1968), 87-96.

255. Lewis, Allan. American Plays and Playwrights of the Contemporary Theatre. New York: Crown, 1965. Second edition, 1970. Pp. 53-65.

256. Lewis, Theophilus. "Freud and the Split-Level Drama." Catholic World, 187 (May 1958), 98-103.

257. Leyburn, Ellen Douglass. "Comedy and Tragedy Transposed." Yale Review, 53 (Summer 1964), 553-562.

258. Link, Franz H. Tennessee Williams' Dramen: Einsamkeit u. Liebe (Anglistik und Amerikanstik). Darmstadt: Thesen-Verlag, 1974. 144 p.

259. Lolli, Giorgio. "Alcoholism and Homosexuality in Tennessee Williams' Cat on a Hot Tin Roof." Quarterly Journal of Studies on Alcohol, 17 (1956), 543-553.

260. Lopez, C. J. "El teatro de Tennessee Williams." Cuadernos Hispanoamericanos (Madrid), 29 (May 1952), 208-212.

261. Lotersztein, S. Tennessee Williams: Poeta del naufragio. Buenos Aires: Instituto Amigos de Libro Argentino, 1965.

262. Lubbers, Klaus. "Tennessee Williams." Amerikanische Literatur der Gegenwart. Edited by Martin Christadler. Stuttgart: Alfred Kröner, 1973, pp. 425-449.

263. Lucignani, Luciano. "Lettera da Roman sull'annata teatrale." Comunita, 72 (1959), 78-89.

264. Lumley, Frederick. New Trends in 20th Century Drama: A Survey Since Ibsen and Shaw, Fourth Edition. New York: Oxford University Press, 1972. Pp. 182-199.

265. McBride, Mary. "Prisoners of Illusion: Surrealistic Escape in The Milk Train Doesn't Stop Here Anymore." Tharpe (P 375), pp. 341-348.

266. McCarthy, Mary. "American Realists, Playwrights." Encounter, 17 (July 1961), 24-31.

Reprint: Theatre Chronicles 1937-1962. New York: Farrar, Straus, 1963. Pp. 209-229.

267. ________. "'Realism' in the American Theater." Harper's, 223 (July 1961), 45-52.

268. Macey, Samuel L. "Nonheroic Tragedy: A Pedigree for American Tragic Drama." Comparative Literature Studies, 6 (March 1969), 1-19.

269. McGlinn, Jeanne M. "Tennessee Williams' Women: Illusion and Reality, Sexuality and Love." Tharpe (P 375), pp. 510-524.

270. Machts, Walter. "Das Menschenbild in den Dramen Tennessee Williams." Neueren Spachen, 10 (October 1961), 445-455.

271. MacMullan, Hugh. "Translating 'The Glass Menagerie' to Film." Hollywood Quarterly, 5 (Fall 1950), 14-32.

272. MacNicholas, John. "Williams' Power of the Keys." Tharpe (P 375), pp. 581-605.

273. Magid, Marion. "The Innocence of Tennessee Williams." Commentary, 35 (January 1963), 34-43.
Reprint: J. Y. Miller (P 282), Interpretations, pp. 73-79; Essays in the Modern Drama (Boston; D. C. Heath, 1964), pp. 280-293.

274. Mannes, Marya. "Plea for Fair Ladies." New York Times Magazine, 29 May 1960, pp. 16 ff.

275. Matthew, David C. C. "'Toward Bethlehem': Battle of Angels and Orpheus Descending." Tharpe (P 375), pp. 172-191.

276. May, Charles E. "Brick Pollitt as Homo Ludens: 'Three Players of a Summer Game' and Cat on a Hot Tin Roof." Tharpe (P 375), pp. 277-291.

277. Miller, Arthur. "Morality and Modern Drama." Educational Theater Journal, 10 (October 1958), 190-202.
Reprint: The Theater Essays of Arthur Miller. Edited by Robert A. Martin. New York: Viking Press, 1978. Pp. 195-214.

278. ________. "The Shadow of the Gods: A Critical View of the American Theater." Harper's, 217 (August 1958), 46-51.
Reprints: American Playwrights on Drama. Edited by Horst Frenz. New York: Hill & Wang, 1965. Pp. 147-150. Theater Essays (P 277), pp. 175-194.

279. Miller, J. William. Modern Playwrights at Work. Vol. 1. New York: Samuel French, 1968. Pp. 375-385.

280. Miller, Jordan Y. "Camino Real." The Fifties: Fiction, Poetry, Drama. Edited by Warren French. De Land, Fla.: Everett/Edwards, 1970. Pp. 241-248.

281. ________. "Myth and the American Dream: O'Neill to Albee." Modern Drama, 7 (September 1964), 190-198.

282. ________, ed. Twentieth Century Interpretations of A Streetcar Named Desire: A Collection of Critical Essays. Englewood Cliffs, N.J.: Prentice-Hall, 1971.

283. Millhauser, Milton. "Science, Literature, and the Image of Man." Humanist, 23 (May-June 1963), 85-88.

284. Milstead, John. "The Structure of Modern Tragedy." Western Humanities Review, 12 (August 1958), 365-369.

285. Mitchell, John D. "Applied Psychoanalysis in the Drama." American Image, 14 (Fall 1953), 272-273.

286. Mood, John J. "The Structure of A Streetcar Named Desire." Ball State University Forum, 14, iii (1973), 9-10.

287. Moody, R. Bruce, and Beckman H. Cottrell. "Two Views of Summer and Smoke." Contexts of the Drama. Edited by Richard Goldstone. New York: McGraw-Hill, 1968. Pp. 664-670.

288. Moorman, Charles. "The Night of the Iguana: A Long Introduction, a General Essay, and No Explication at All." Tharpe (P 375), pp. 318-324.

289. Mueller, W. R. "Tennessee Williams: A New Direction?" Christian Century, 81 (14 October 1964), 1271-1272.

290. Napieralski, Edmund A. "Tennessee Williams' The Glass Menagerie: The Dramatic Metaphor." Southern Quarterly, 16 (1977), 1-12.

291. Nardin, James T. "What Tennessee Williams Didn't Write." Essays in Honor of Esmond Linworth Marilla. Edited by Thomas A. Kirby and William J. Olive. Baton Rouge: Louisiana State University Press, 1970. Pp. 331-341.

292. Narumi, Hiroshi. ["Tennessee Williams's Black Plays." Rikkyo Review of Arts and Letters (Tokyo), 24 (March 1963), 26-51.] In Japanese.

293. Natanson, Wojciech. "American Plays on Polish Stages." Polish Review, 5 (Winter 1960), 86-89.

294. Navone, John. "The Myth and Dream of Paradise." Studies in Religion, 5 (1975), 152-161.

295. Nelson, Benjamin. "Avant-Garde Dramatists from Ibsen to Ionesco." *Psychoanalytic Review*, 55 (1968), 505-512.

296. ______. *The Plays of Tennessee Williams: Cat on a Hot Tin Roof; The Glass Menagerie; Orpheus Descending; A Streetcar Named Desire; and Others* (Monarch Notes). New York: Monarch, 1965. 96 p.

297. ______. *Tennessee Williams: The Man and His Work.* New York: Ivan Obolensky, 1961. 304 p. *Tennessee Williams: His Life and Work.* London: Peter Owens, 1961. 262 p.
Reviews: *Booklist*, 58 (1 April 1962), 516; *Catholic World*, 195 (May 1962), 121: Moira Walsh; *Kirkus*, 29 (15 October 1961), 962; *Library Journal*, 87 (15 January 1962), 227: J. C. Pine; *London Times Literary Supplement*, 8 June 1962, p. 428; *Manchester Guardian*, 13 October 1961, p. 7: W. J. Weatherby; *New York Herald Tribune Books*, 28 January 1962, p. 13; *New York Times Book Review*, 26 November 1961, p. 1: Brooks Atkinson; *Spectator*, 207 (22 December 1961), 933: Bamber Gascoigne.

298. Niesen, George. "The Artist against the Reality in the Plays of Tennessee Williams." Tharpe, pp. 463-493.

299. Nolan, Paul T. "Two Memory Plays: *The Glass Menagerie* and *After the Fall.*" *McNeese Review*, 17 (1966), 27-38.

300. Olley, Francis R. "Last Block on the *Camino Real.*" *Drama Critique*, 7 (Fall 1965), 103-107.

301. Oppel, Horst. "'Every Man Is a King!': Zur Funktion der lokalhistorischen Elements in *A Streetcar Named Desire.*" *Studien zur Englischen und amerikanischen Sprache und Literatur: Festschrift für Helmut Papjewski.* Edited by Paul G. Buchloh, et al. Neumünster: Wacholtz, 1974. Pp. 507-522.

302. ______. "Tennessee Williams: *A Streetcar Named Desire.*" *Das amerikanische Drama.* Edited by Paul Goetsch. Dusseldorf: Bagel, 1974. Pp. 183-207.

303. Ower, John. "Erotic Mythology in the Poetry of Tennessee Williams." Tharpe (P 375), pp. 609-623.

304. Packard, William. "Poetry in the Theatre--V." *Trace*, 16 (1967), 452-455.

305. Pavlov, Grigor. *Blood and Mustard: A Brief Look at Tennessee Williams' Major Theses and Techniques.* Sofia: 1971. 16 p.

306. Pease, Donald. "Reflections on Moon Lake: The Presences of the Playwright." Tharpe (P 375), pp. 829-847.

307. Pebworthy, Ted-Larry, with Jay Claude Summers. Williams' The Glass Menagerie (Bar Notes). New York: Barrister, 1966.

308. Peden, William H. "Mad Pilgrimage: The Short Stories of Tennessee Williams." Studies in Short Fiction, 1 (Summer 1964), 243-250.

309. Petersen, Carol. Tennessee Williams (Köpfe des XX Jahrhunderts). Berlin: Colloquium, 1975. 95 p.

310. Peterson, William. "Williams, Kazan, and the Two Cats." New Theater Magazine (Bristol, Eng.), 7 (Summer 1967), 14-20.

311. Phillips, Jerrold A. "Kingdom of Earth: Some Approaches." Tharpe (P 375), pp. 349-353.

312. Phillips, John, and Anne Hollander. "Lillian Hellman: An Interview." Paris Review, 9 (Winter-Spring 1965), 65-94.
Reprint: Writers at Work: The Paris Review Interviews, Third Series. New York: Viking Press, 1967. Pp. 115-140 (see especially p. 125).

313. Popkin, Henry. "The Plays of Tennessee Williams." Tulane Drama Review, 4 (March 1960), 45-64.

314. ______. "Realism in the U. S. A." World Theatre, 14 (March-April 1965), 119-126.

315. ______. "Tennessee Williams Reexamined." Arts in Virginia, 11 (Spring 1971), 2-5.

316. ______. "Williams, Osbourne, or Beckett?" New York Times Magazine, 13 November 1960, pp. 32-33, 119-121.
Reprint: Essays in the Modern Drama (Boston: D. C. Heath, 1964), pp. 235-242.

317. Porter, Thomas E. Myth and Modern American Drama [A Streetcar Named Desire]. Detroit: Wayne State University Press, 1969. Pp. 153-176.

318. Powers, Harvey M., Jr. "Theatrical Convention: The Conditions of Acceptability." Bucknell Review, 7 (May 1957), 20-26.

319. Prenshaw, Peggy W. "The Paradoxical Southern World of Tennessee Williams." Tharpe (P 375), pp. 5-29.

320. Presley, Delma Eugene. "Little Acts of Grace." Tharpe (P 375), pp. 571-580.

321. ______. "The Moral Function of Distortion in Southern Grotesque." South Atlantic Bulletin, 37 (Spring 1973), 37-46.

322. _______. "The Search for Hope in the Plays of Tennessee Williams." Mississippi Quarterly, 25 (Winter 1971-1972), 31-43.

323. _______, and Hari Singh. "Epigraphs to the Plays of Tennessee Williams." Notes on Mississippi Writers, 3 (Spring 1970), 2-12.

324. Quijano, Margarita. "El simbolismo del Tranvía llamado Deseo." Cuadernos Americanos, 159 (July 1968), 228-235.

325. Quirino, Leonard. "The Cards Indicate a Voyage on A Streetcar Named Desire." Tharpe (P 375), pp. 77-96.

326. _______. "Tennessee Williams' Persistent Battle of Angels." Modern Drama, 11 (May 1968), 27-39.

327. Rama Murthy, V. American Expressionistic Drama, Containing Analyses of Three Outstanding American Plays: O'Neill, The Hairy Ape; Tennessee Williams, The Glass Menagerie; Miller, Death of a Salesman. Delhi: Doaba House, 1970.

328. Ramaswamy, S. "The Short Stories of Tennessee Williams." Indian Studies in American Fiction. Edited by M. K. Naik, et al. Dharwar: Karnatak University, 1974; Delhi: Macmillan India, 1974. Pp. 263-285.

329. Rathbun, Gilbert L. Tennessee Williams' A Streetcar Named Desire (Monarch Notes). New York: Monarch, 1965. 72 p.

330. _______. Tennessee Williams' The Glass Menagerie: A Critical Commentary (Monarch Notes). New York: Monarch, 1967. 75 p.

331. Rebora, Roberto. "Estate fumo di Tennessee Williams: Ritagli crepuscolari decadenti." Fiera Letteratia, 29 October 1950, p. 8.

332. Reck, Tom S. "The First Cat on a Hot Tin Roof: Williams' 'Three Players.'" University Review (Kansas City, Mo.), 34 (1968), 187-192.

333. _______. "The Short Stories of Tennessee Williams: Nucleus for His Drama." Tennessee Studies in Literature, 16 (1971), 141-154.

334. Reid, Desmond. "Tennessee Williams." Studies (Dublin), 46 (Winter 1957), 431-446.
Reprint: Hurrell (P 194), pp. 100-110.

335. Ribey, Cora. "Chloroses--Pâles Roses and Pleurosis--Blue Roses." Romance Notes, 13 (1971), 250-251.

336. Richardson, Thomas J. "The City of Day and the City of Night: New Orleans and the Exotic Unreality of Tennessee Williams." Tharpe (P 375), pp. 631-646.

337. Riddel, Joseph N. "A Streetcar Named Desire--Nietzsche Descending." Modern Drama, 5 (February 1963), 421-430.
Reprint: J. Y. Miller (P 282), Interpretations, pp. 80-89.

338. Roberts, James L. The Glass Menagerie and A Streetcar Named Desire: Notes. Lincoln, Neb.: Cliff's Notes, 1965. 77 p.

339. Roberts, Preston T., Jr. "Bringing Pathos into Focus." University of Chicago Magazine, 47 (February 1954), 7-11, 18.

340. Roderick, John M. "From 'Tarantula Arms' to 'Della Robbia Blue': The Tennessee Williams Tragicomic Transit Authority." Tharpe (P 375), pp. 116-125.

341. Rogoff, Gordon. "The Restless Intelligence of Tennessee Williams." Tulane Drama Review, 10 (Summer 1966), 78-92.

342. Roth, Robert. "Tennessee Williams in Search of a Form." Chicago Review, 9 (Summer 1955), 86-94.

343. Roulet, W. M. "Sweet Bird of Youth: Williams' Redemptive Ethic." Cithara, 3 (1964), 31-36.

344. Rowland, James L. "Tennessee's Two Amandas." Research Studies (Washington State University), 35 (1968), 331-340.

345. Russell, Ray. The Little Lexicon of Love. Los Angeles: Sherbourne Press, 1966. Pp. 157-170 [parody].

346. Sacksteder, William. "The Three Cats: A Study in Dramatic Structure." Drama Survey, 5 (Winter 1966-1967), 242-266.

347. Sagar, K. M. "What Mr. Williams Has Made of D. H. Lawrence." Twentieth Century, 168 (August 1960), 143-153.

348. Samuels, Charles Thomas. "Sex, Dreams, and Tennessee Williams." Syracuse Review, 2 (January 1957), 12-19.

349. Sarotte, Georges-Michel. Comme un frère, comme un amant: L'homosexualité masculine dans le roman et le théâtre americains de Herman Melville à James Baldwin. Paris: Flammarion, 1976.
Translation: Like a Brother, Like a Lover: Male Homosexuality in the American Novel and Theatre from Herman Melville to James Baldwin. Trans. Richard Miller. Garden City, N.Y.: Anchor Press, 1978. Pp. 107-120.

350. Sasahara, Hiraku. "Tennessee Williams to Emily Dickinson--The Glass Menagerie wo Chushin ni." Eigo Seinen, 120 (1974), 270-272.

351. Satterfield, John. "Williams's Suddenly Last Summer: The Eye of the Needle." Markham Review, 6 (1977), 27-33.

352. Schaefer, Hans Joachim. "Zum Verstandius amerikanischer Dramatik." Begebnung, 18 (November 1963), 318-322.

353. Scheick, William J. "'An Intercourse Not Well Designed': Talk and Touch in the Plays of Tennessee Williams." Tharpe (P 375), pp. 763-773.

354. Scheller, Bernhard. "Die Gestalt der Farbigen bei Williams, Albee und Baldwin und ihre szenische Realisterung in DDR-Aufführungen." Zeitschrift für Anglistik und Amerikanistik, 20 (1972), 137-157.

355. Scheye, Thomas E. "The Glass Menagerie: 'It's no tragedy, Freckles.'" Tharpe (P 375), pp. 207-213.

356. Schubert, Karl. "Tennessee Williams: 'Desire and the Black Masseur' (1948)." Die amerikanische Short Story der Gegenwart: Interpretationen. Edited by Peter Freese. Berlin: Schmidt, 1976. Pp. 119-128.

357. Sharma, P. P. "The Predicament of the 'Outsiders' in Tennessee Williams' Plays." Indian Journal of American Studies, 5 (January-July 1975), 69-75.

358. Sharp, William. "An Unfashionable View of Tennessee Williams." Tulane Drama Review, 6 (March 1962), 160-171.

359. Sievers, W. David. Freud on Broadway: A History of Psychoanalysis and the American Drama. New York: Hermitage House, 1955; Toronto: George J. McLeod, 1955. Pp. 370-388.

Reprint: J. Y. Miller (P 282), Interpretations, pp. 90-93.

360. Simons, Piet. "De bonte geitebok of de verwelkte roos." Ons Erfdeel, 18, iii (1975), 443-444.

361. Sklepowich, Edward A. "In Pursuit of the Lyric Quarry: The Image of the Homosexual in Tennessee Williams' Prose Fiction." Tharpe (P 375), pp. 525-544.

362. Skloot, Robert. "Submitting Self to Flame: The Artist's Quest in Tennessee Williams 1935-1954." Educational Theatre Journal, 25 (May 1973), 199-206.

363. Sorell, Walter. "The Case of Tennessee Williams." Cresset, 36, viii (1973), 26-27.

364. Spevack, Marvin. "Tennessee Williams: The Ideal of the Theatre." Jahrbuch für Amerikastudien, 10 (1965), 221-231.

365. Stamper, Rexford. "The Two-Character Play: Psychic Individuation." Tharpe (P 375), pp. 354-361.

366. Stanton, Stephen S., ed. Tennessee Williams: A Collection of Critical Essays. Englewood Cliffs, N.J.: Prentice-Hall, 1977.

366a. Stanton, Stephen S., ed. Tennessee Williams Newsletter, subscription issue (January 1979).

367. Starnes, Leland. "The Grotesque Children of The Rose Tattoo." Modern Drama, 12 (February 1970), 357-369.

368. Stavrou, Constantine N. "The Neurotic Heroine in Tennessee Williams." Literature and Psychology, 5 (May 1955), 26-34.

369. Stein, Roger B. "The Glass Menagerie Revisited: Catastrophe without Violence." Western Humanities Review, 18 (Spring 1964), 141-153.
Revised abridgment: Stanton (P 366), pp. 36-44.

370. Steinbeck, John. John Steinbeck: A Life in Letters. Edited by Elaine Steinbeck & Robert Wallsten. New York: Viking Press, 1975. Pp. 441-442, 591.

371. Stutzman, Ralph W. "The Sting of Reality: The Theology of Tennessee Williams." Unitarian Universalist Register-Leader, April 1963, pp. 11-13.

372. Styan, John. The Dark Comedy. Cambridge: Cambridge University Press, 1968. Pp. 217-226.

373. Taylor, William E. "Tennessee Williams: Academia on Broadway." Essays in Modern American Literature # 31. Edited by Richard E. Langford et al. De Land, Fla.: Stetson University Press, 1963. Pp. 90-96.

374. ______. "Tennessee Williams: The Playwright as Poet." Tharpe (P 375), pp. 624-630.

375. Tharpe, Jac, ed. Tennessee Williams: A Tribute. Jackson: University Press of Mississippi, 1977.
Reviews: Choice, 14 (February 1978), 1649; Library Journal, 102 (1 November 1977), 2263: L. E. Bone.

376. Theim, Willy H. Tennessee Williams (Buchreihe des Dusseldorfer Schauspielhausen). Düsseldorf: W. Girardet, 1956. 152 p.

377. Thomas, E. A. "A Streetcar to Where?" Wingover, 1 (Fall-Winter 1958-1959), 30-31.

378. Thompson, Judith J. "Symbol, Myth, and Ritual in The Glass Menagerie, The Rose Tattoo, and Orpheus Descending." Tharpe (P 375), pp. 679-711.

379. Tillich, Paul. The Courage to Be. New York: Yale University Press, 1952. Pp. 145-146.

380. Tischler, Nancy M. "The Distorted Mirror: Tennessee Williams' Self-Portraits." Mississippi Quarterly, 25 (1972), 389-403.
Reprint: Stanton (P 366), pp. 158-170.

381. ______. "A Gallery of Witches." Tharpe (P 375), pp. 494-509.

382. ______. Tennessee Williams (Southern Writers Series). Austin, Tx.: Steck-Vaughn, 1969.

383. ______. "Tennessee Williams' Bohemian Revision of Christianity." Susquehanna University Studies, 7 (June 1963), 103-108.

384. ______. Tennessee Williams: Rebellious Puritan. New York: Citadel Press, 1961. 317 p.
Reviews: Booklist, 58 (1 June 1962), 681; Library Journal, 87 (15 January 1962), 227: J. C. Pine; New York Herald Tribune Books, 28 January 1962, p. 13; New York Times Book Review, 26 November 1961, p. 1: Brooks Atkinson; Theatre Arts, 46 (April 1962), 8: George Freedley.

385. Toohey, John L. A History of the Pulitzer Prize Plays. New York: Citadel Press, 1967. Pp. 212-219, 266-275.

386. Toschi, Gastone. "La morbida e diabolica magia de Tennessee Williams." Letture, 19 (1964), 563-582.

387. Traubitz, Nancy Baker. "Myth as a Basis of Dramatic Structure in Orpheus Descending." Modern Drama, 19 (March 1976), 57-66.

388. Turner, Diane E. "The Mythic Vision in Tennessee Williams' Camino Real." Tharpe (P 375), pp. 237-251.

389. Tynan, Kenneth. "American Blues: The Plays of Arthur Miller and Tennessee Williams." Encounter, 2 (May 1954), 13-19.
Reprints: Curtains. New York: Atheneum, 1961. Pp. 257-266; Hurrell (P 194), pp. 124-130. The Modern American Theatre: A Collection of Critical Essays. Englewood Cliffs, N.J.: Prentice-Hall, 1967. Pp. 34-44.

390. Ulanov, Barry. The Two Worlds of American Art: The Private and the Popular. New York: Macmillan, 1965. Pp. 348-354.

391. Usui, Yoshitaka. "Tennessee Williams, Rebel and Martyr." English Literature (Waseda), 20 (January 1962), 59-70; 21 (March 1962), 42-53.

392. Vahland, Barbara. Der Held als Opfer: Aspekte des Melodramatischen bei Tennessee Williams (Angelsächsische Sprache und Literatur). Bern: Herbert Lang, 1976.

393. Verkein, Lea. "Von Broadway naar Picadilly." Vlaamse Gide, 45 (July 1961), 492-495.

394. Vidal, Gore. "Love, Love, Love." Partisan Review, 26 (Fall 1959), 613-620.

395. Villard, Léonie. Panorama du théâtre américain du renouveau, 1915-1962 (Vent d'Ouest). Paris: Seghers, 1964. Pp. 251-259.

396. Von Szeliski, John L. "Tennessee Williams and the Tragedy of Sensitivity." Western Humanities Review, 20 (Summer 1966), 203-211.
Excerpts: J. Y. Miller (P 282), Interpretations, pp. 65-72.

397. Vowles, Richard B. "Tennessee Williams and Strindberg." Modern Drama, 1 (December 1958), 166-171.

398. ______. "Tennessee Williams: The World of His Imagery." Tulane Drama Review, 3 (December 1958), 51-56.

399. Wallach, Ira. "A Tattooed Streetcar Named Rose." Twentieth Century Parody, American and British. Edited by Burling Lowrey. New York: Harcourt, Brace, 1960. Pp. 204-212 [parody].

400. Watson, Charles S. "The Revision of The Glass Menagerie: The Passing of Good Manners." Southern Literary Journal, 8 (Spring 1976), 74-78.

401. Watts, Richard, Jr. "Orpheus Ascending." Theatre Arts, 42 (September 1958), 25-26.

402. Weales, Gerald C. American Drama Since World War II. New York: Harcourt, Brace & World, 1962. Pp. 18-39.

403. ______. "Drama." Literary History of the United States: History, Fourth Edition. Edited by Robert E. Spiller, et al. New York: Macmillan, 1974; London: Collier Macmillan, 1974. Pp. 1447-1449.

404. ______. The Jumping-Off Place: American Drama in the 1960's. New York: Macmillan, 1969; London: Collier Macmillan, 1969. Pp. 3-14.
Excerpts: Stanton (P 366), pp. 61-70.

405. ______. Tennessee Williams (University of Minnesota Pamphlets on American Writers). Minneapolis: University of Minnesota Press, 1965.
Revision: American Writers: A Collection of Literary Biographies, Volume 4. Edited by Leonard Ungar. New York: Charles Scribner's Sons, 1974. Pp. 378-401.

406. ______. "Tennessee Williams Borrows a Little Shaw." Shaw Review, 8 (May 1965), 63-64.

407. ______. "Tennessee Williams' 'Lost' Play" ["At Liberty"]. American Literature, 37 (November 1965), 321-323.

408. Weightman, J. G. "Varieties of Decomposition." Twentieth Century, 164 (November 1958), 461-463.

409. Weissman, Philip. "Psychopathological Characters in Current Drama: A Study of a Trio of Heroines." American Imago, 17 (Fall 1960), 271-278.
Reprint: Creativity in the Theater: A Psychoanalytic Study. New York: Basic Books, 1965.
Excerpts: J. Y. Miller (P 282), Interpretations, pp. 57-64.

410. Wells, Joel. Grim Fairy Tales for Adults. New York: Macmillan, 1967; London: Collier Macmillan, 1967. Pp. 21-30 [parody].

411. Willett, Ralph W. "The Ideas of Miller and Williams." Theatre Annual, 22 (1965-1966), 31-40.

412. Williams, Robert. Modern Tragedy. Stanford: Stanford University Press, 1966. Pp. 106-120.

413. Wilson, Albert Edward. Playwrights in Aspic. Denver: University of Denver Press, 1960. Pp. 118-124 [parody].

414. Wolf, Morris Philip. "Casanova's Portmanteau: Camino Real and Recurring Communication Patterns of Tennessee Williams." Tharpe (P 375), pp. 252-276.

415. Wooten, Carl. "The Country Wife and Contemporary Comedy: A World Apart." Drama Survey, 2 (Winter 1963), 333-343.

416. Yacowan, Maurice. Tennessee Williams and Film. New York: Frederick Ungar, 1977. 168 p.
Reviews: Booklist, 74 (15 December 1977), 654; Choice, 15 (March 1978), 82; Library Journal, 102 (July 1977), 1521: Marshall Deutelbaum; West Coast Review of Books, 4 (May 1970), 531.

417. Young, Vernon. "Social Drama and Big Daddy." Southwest Review, 41 (Spring 1956), 194-197.

418. Zlobin, G. "On the Stage and Behind the Scenes." Inostrannaja Literature, 7 (July 1960), 199-210.

Q. DISSERTATIONS

(DA= Dissertation Abstracts; DAI= Dissertation Abstracts International)

1. Asral, Ertem. "Tennessee Williams on Stage and Screen." University of Pennsylvania, 1960. DA, 22 (October 1961), 1169-1170.

2. Beasley, Henry R. "An Interpretative Study of the Religious Element in the Work of Tennessee Williams." Louisiana State University, 1973. DAI, 34 (March 1974), 5954-5955 A.

3. Beltzer, Lee. "The Plays of Eugene O'Neill, Thornton Wilder, Arthur Miller, and Tennessee Williams on the London Stage 1945-1960." University of Wisconsin, 1965.

4. Blades, Larry T. "Williams, Miller and Albee: A Comparative Study." St. Louis University, 1971. DAI, 32 (February 1972), 4600 A.

5. Britton, Joe S. "Extra-Literary Accents in the Drama of Tennessee Williams." Southern Illinois University, date not verified.

6. Calandra, Denis Michael. "Comic Elements in the Plays of Tennessee Williams." University of Nebraska, 1970. DAI, 31 (April 1971), 5390-5391 A.

7. Calvery, Catherine Ann. "Illusion in Modern American Drama: A Study of Selected Plays by Arthur Miller, Tennessee Williams, and Eugene O'Neill." Tulane University, 1964. DA, 25 (April 1965), 6111-6112.

8. Cherry, Grady. "Life and Art: A Classification of the Artist-Figure in Selected Fiction of Tennessee Williams." Texas A&M University, 1977. DAI, 38 (October 1977), 2121 A.

9. Chesler, Stanley A. "Tennessee Williams' Literary Reputation in the United States." Kent State University, 1971. DAI, 32 (May 1972), 6418 A.

10. Clayton, John S. "Themes of Tennessee Williams." Yale University, 1960. DA, 30 (August 1969), 718 A.

11. Corrigan, Mary Ann Romer. "Expressionism in the Early Plays of Tennessee Williams." University of Michigan, 1975. DAI, 36 (April 1976), 6681 A.

12. Dawson, William Meredith. "The Female Characters of August Strindberg, Eugene O'Neill, and Tennessee Williams." University of Wisconsin, 1964. DA, 25 (October 1964), 2663.

13. Dillard, Robert Lee. "The Tennessee Williams Hero: An Analytic Survey." University of Missouri, 1965. DA, 26 (March 1966), 5592-5593.

14. Dobson, Eugene, Jr. "The Reception of the Plays of Tennessee Williams in Germany." University of Arkansas, 1967. DA, 28 (July 1967), 226-227.

15. Drake, Constance M. "Six Plays by Tennessee Williams: Myth in the Modern World." Ohio State University, 1970. DAI, 32 (July 1971), 426 A.

16. Draya, Ren. "The Frightened Heart: A Study of Character and Theme in the Fiction, Poetry, Short Plays, and Recent Drama of Tennessee Williams." University of Colorado, 1977. DAI, 38 (November 1977), 2773 A.

17. Embry, Glenn Thomas. "Sexual Confusion in the Major Plays of Tennessee Williams." University of California at Los Angeles, 1975. DAI, 36 (July 1975), 309 A.

18. Fedder, Norman Joseph. "The Influence of D. H. Lawrence on Tennessee Williams." State University of New York, 1962. DA, 24 (August 1963), 742-743.

19. Fisher, William J. "Trends in Post-Depression American Drama: A Study of the Works of William Saroyan, Tennessee Williams, Irwin Shaw, Arthur Miller." State University of New York, 1952.

20. Fleit, Muriel. "The Application of Interaction Process Analysis to Selected Plays of Tennessee Williams." New York University, 1978. DAI, 39 (October 1978), 1931 A.

21. Fleming, William P., Jr. "Tragedy in American Drama: The Tragic Views of Eugene O'Neill, Tennessee Williams, Arthur Miller, and Edward Albee." University of Toledo, 1972. DAI, 33 (July 1972), 308 A.

22. Friedrich, Jutta. "Individuum and Gesellschaft in den Dramen von Tennessee Williams." Universität Jena, 1963. Zeitschrift für Anglistik und Amerikenistik, 13 (1965), 45-60.

23. Geier, Woodrow Augustus. "Images of Man in Five American Dramatists: A Theological Critique." Vanderbilt University, 1959. DA, 20 (October 1959), 1463-1464.

24. Glantz Shapiro, Margarita. Tennessee Williams y el teatro norteamericano. Mexico City: Universidad de Méxique, 1963.

25. Gobnecht, Eleanor Alberta. "A Descriptive Study of the Value Commitments of the Principal Characters in Four Recent American Plays: Picnic, Cat on a Hot Tin Roof, A Long Day's Journey into Night, and Look Homeward, Angel." University of Southern California, 1963. DA, 24 (July 1963), 433-434.

26. Hauptman, Robert. "The Pathological Vision--Three Studies: Jean Genet, Louis-Ferdinand Céline, Tennessee Williams." Ohio State University, 1971. DAI, 32 (March 1972), 5229 A.

26a. Henenberg, Rosemary Elaine. "The Psychomachian Dilemma in the Middle Ages and in the Twentieth-Century in 'Camino Real' by Tennessee Williams and in Paintings by Max Beckmann." Ohio University, 1973. DAI, 34 (March 1974), 5834 A.

27. Hurley, Paul J. "Tennessee Williams: Critic of American Society." Duke University, 1962. DA, 29 (November 1963), 2034-2035.

28. Inglis, William Heard III. "Strindberg and Williams: A Study in Affinities." University of Washington, 1975. DAI, 37 (August 1976), 698-699 A.

29. Jackson, Esther Merle. "The Emergence of a Characteristic Contemporary Form in the Drama of Tennessee Williams." Ohio State University, 1958. DA, 19 (May 1959), 3053-3054.

30. Langsam, Paula A. "A Study of the Major Characters in Selected Plays of Tennessee Williams." State University of New York, 1966. DA, 27 (May 1967), 3972 A.

31. Lasko, Joanne Zunzer. "'The Fiddle in the Wings': An Approach to Music in Drama." American University, 1977. DAI, 38 (September 1977), 1391 A.

32. Levy, Valerie B. "Violence as Drama: A Study of the Development of the Use of Violence on the American Stage." Claremont Graduate School, 1970. DAI, 31 (June 1971), 6618-6619 A.

33. McRae, Russell Williams. "Tennessee Williams: An Artifice of Mirrors." York University (Canada), 1975. DAI, 36 (July 1976), 311-312 A.

34. Matthew, David Charles Cameron. "The Ritual of Self-Assassination in the Drama of Tennessee Williams." Columbia University, 1974. DAI, 35 (March 1975), 6147 A.

35. Miller, Robert Royce. "Tragedy in Modern American Drama: The Psychological, Social and Absurdist Conditions in Historical Perspective." Middle Tennessee State University, 1975. DAI, 36 (December 1975), 3717 A.

36. Mishoe, Billy. "Time as Antagonist in the Dramas of Tennessee Williams." Florida State University, 1972. DAI, 33 (December 1972), 2944-2945 A.

37. Mraz, Doyne Joseph. "The Changing Image of the Female Characters in the Works of Tennessee Williams." University of Southern California, 1967. DA, 28 (April 1968), 4304.

38. Patterson, Nancy Marie. "Patterns of Imagery in the Major Plays of Tennessee Williams." University of Arkansas, 1957. DA, 17 (September 1957), 2014.

38a. Perrier, Ronald Gordon. "A Study of the Dramatic Works of Tennessee Williams from 1963 to 1971." University of Minnesota, 1972. DAI, 33 (October 1972), 1879 A.

39. Presley, Delma Eugene. "The Theological Dimensions of Tennessee Williams." Emory University, 1969. DA, 30 (November 1969), 2038.

40. Quirino, Leonard Salvator. "The Darkest Celebrations of Tennessee Williams: A Study of Battle of Angels, A Streetcar Named Desire, Orpheus Descending, Camino Real, Cat on a Hot Tin Roof and Suddenly Last Summer." Brown University, 1964. DA, 25 (February 1965), 4706.

40a. Rogers, Ingrid. Tennessee Williams: A Moralist's Answer to the Perils of Life. Frankfurt: Peter Lang/Bern: Herbert Lang, 1976. 267 p.

41. Scanlan, Thomas M. "The American Family and Family Dilemmas in American Drama." University of Minnesota, 1970. DAI, 32 (September 1971), 1529 A.

41a. Shaughnessy, Mary Ellen. "Incomplete Sentences: A Study of Tennessee Williams since 1960." State University of New York at Buffalo, 1977. DAI, 38 (March 1978), 5485 A.

42. Smith, Harry Willard Jr. "Mielziner and Williams: A Concept of Style." Tulane University, 1966. DA, 27 (August 1966), 552.

42a. Spero, Richard Henry. "The Jungian World of Tennessee Williams." University of Wisconsin, 1970. DAI, 31 (May 1971), 6205 A.

43. Starnes, R. Leland. "Comedy and Tennessee Williams." Yale University, 1965.

44. Steiner, Robert J. "Toward an Integrated Personality: A Study of the Dramas of Tennessee Williams." St. John's University, 1965.

45. Stephens, Suzanne Schaddelee. "The Dual Influence: A Dramatic Study of the Plays of Edward Albee and the Specific Dramatic Forms and Themes Which Influenced Them." University of Miami, 1972. DAI, 34 (July 1973), 342 A.

46. True, Warren Roberts. "Chekhovian Dramaturgy in the Plays of Tennessee Williams, Harold Pinter, and Ed Bullins." University of Tennessee, 1976. DAI, 37 (February 1977), 5131 A.

47. Von Dornum, John Howard. "The Major Plays of Tennessee Williams." University of Southern California, 1962. DA, 23 (October 1962), 1371-1372.

48. Warren, Clifton Lanier. "Tennessee Williams as Cinematic Writer." Indiana University, 1963. DA, 25 (July 1964), 489-490.

49. Watson, Ray A. "The Archetype of the Family in the Drama of Tennessee Williams." University of Tulsa, 1973. DAI, 34 (September 1973), 1299 A.

50. Wolf, Morris Philip. "Casanova's Portmanteau: A Study of Camino Real in Relation to the Other Plays of Tennessee Williams, 1945-1955." University of Georgia, 1959. DA, 20 (January 1960), 2817.

INDEX OF CRITICS, REVIEWERS, INTERVIEWERS, AND EDITORS

(Note: When there is more than one author or editor, only the name of the first is indexed. Translators are not listed here. Also, because Section K entries are subdivided, a parenthetical number has been added to some K numbers to indicate the number of sub-entries in which that name appears.)